Reader's Digest Paperbacks

Informative ..... Entertaining ..... Essential .....

Berkley, one of America's leading paperback publishers, is proud to present this special series of the best-loved articles, stories and features from America's most trusted magazine. Each is a one-volume library on a popular and important subject. And each is selected, edited and endorsed by the Editors of Reader's Digest themselves!

Berkley/Reader's Digest books

THE ART OF LIVING
THE GREAT ENTERTAINERS
"I AM JOE'S BODY"
LAUGHTER, THE BEST MEDICINE®
MORE TESTS AND TEASERS
ORGANIZE YOURSELF
SECRETS OF THE PAST
SUPER WORD POWER
TESTS AND TEASERS
THEY BEAT THE ODDS
WORD POWER

THE GREAT ENTERTAINERS

THE EDITORS OF *READER'S DIGEST*

A BERKLEY/READER'S DIGEST BOOK
published by
BERKLEY BOOKS, NEW YORK

THE GREAT ENTERTAINERS

A Berkley/Reader's Digest Book/published by arrangement with Reader's Digest Press

PRINTING HISTORY
Berkley/Reader's Digest edition/November 1983

All rights reserved.
Copyright © 1983 by The Reader's Digest Association, Inc.
Copyright © 1953, 1954, 1955, 1957, 1960, 1965, 1966, 1967, 1968, 1969, 1971, 1972, 1973, 1974, 1975, 1976, 1977, 1978, 1979, 1980, 1981, 1982 by The Reader's Digest Association, Inc.

This book may not be reproduced in whole or in part, by mimeograph or any other means, without permission.
For information address: The Berkley Publishing Group, 200 Madison Avenue, New York, New York 10016.

ISBN: 0-425-06073-X

A BERKLEY BOOK ® TM 757,375
The name "BERKLEY" and the stylized "B" with design are trademarks belonging to Berkley Publishing Corporation.
PRINTED IN THE UNITED STATES OF AMERICA

Grateful acknowledgment is made to the following organizations and individuals for permission to reprint material from the indicated sources:

"Talking With Olivier" by Curtis Bill Pepper, copyright © 1979 by The New York Times Co., reprinted by permission of The New York Times Company, Curtis Bill Pepper and Julian Bach Literary Agency. "The Manorial Air and Larcenous Eye of W. C. Fields" from the book THE TIME OF LAUGHTER by Corey Ford, copyright © 1967 by Corey Ford. By permission of Harold Ober Associates, Inc. "W. C. Handy: Father of the Blues" by Carl B. Wall, copyright © 1957 by Post Printing & Pub. Co. Denver, Colorado. William Morrow & Company, Inc. for "My Heart Belongs to Peter Pan" from the book MY HEART BELONGS TO PETER PAN by Mary Martin, copyright © 1976 by Mary Martin Halliday. "Presenting Liv Ullmann" from the book CHANGING by Liv Ullmann, copyright © 1976, 1977 by Liv Ullmann, reprinted by permission of Alfred A. Knopf, Inc. "Destiny's Child" reprinted from PRINCE OF PLAYERS: EDWIN BOOTH, by Eleanor Ruggles, by permission of W. W. Norton & Company, Inc., copyright © 1953 by W. W. Norton & Company Inc., copyright renewed © 1981 by Eleanor Ruggles O'Leary. "Charlie" from A GIFT OF JOY by Helen Hayes, copyright © 1965 by Helen Hayes and Lewis Funke, reprinted by permission of the publisher, M. Evans and Company Inc. New York N.Y. 10017. "Young At Heart" words and music by Carolyn Leigh and Johnny Richards, copyright © 1954 Cherio Corporation, copyright renewed © 1982 Cherio Corporation. International copyright secured. All rights reserved. Used by permission. "Katie and the Hard Hats" reprinted by permission of Viking Penguin Inc. from TRACY AND HEPBURN by Garson Kanin. Copyright © 1970, 1971 by T.F.T. Corporation.

Contents

SECRET WORLDS OF THE STARS
On the Road With Bob Hope   by Maurice Zolotow   **3**
The Last Days of a Barrymore   by Cameron Shipp   **9**
Pearl of Our Hearts   by Ponchitta Pierce   **16**
Charles Laughton: A Benevolent Captain Bligh   by Bentz Plagemann   **21**
The Finesse and Fury of Laurence Olivier   by Curtis Bill Pepper   **27**

THE WISDOM OF LAUGHTER
Groucho's Secret Word   by Earl Wilson   **35**
Bill Cosby: Humor With Lessons   by Ponchitta Pierce   **39**
Will Rogers: Cowboy Comedian of Common Sense   by Eddie Cantor   **43**
George Burns' Golden Age   by Maurice Zolotow   **48**
Danny Kaye: Pied Piper of Laughter   by John Reddy   **53**
Sam Levenson's Extended Family   by Earl Wilson   **58**

TRIUMPH AND TRAGEDY

"The Wire is My Life" by Joseph P. Blank **67**
Melancholy Clown by John Culhane **74**
Woody Guthrie's Hard Travels by John Reddy **80**
The Passionate Isadora Duncan by Sir Frederick Ashton **86**
The Man No Lock Could Hold by James Stewart-Gordon **91**

GRAND ECCENTRICS

Tumultuous Tallulah by Anita Loos **99**
Is That *Really* Walter Matthau? by Maurice Zolotow **105**
The Movies' Master of Suspense by John Culhane **110**
How the 2000-Year-Old Man Became a Movie Giant by Maurice Zolotow **115**
This Was Toscanini by Samuel Antek **121**
The Manorial Air and Larcenous Eye of W. C. Fields by Corey Ford **125**
Here's Steve Martin...Maybe by Maurice Zolotow **131**

THE SOUNDS OF AMERICA

The Queen of Country Music by George Vecsey **139**
The Man Who Put the Top Hat on Jazz by John Reddy **145**
W. C. Handy: Father of the Blues by Carl B. Wall **150**
Sousa Marches On! by Ann M. Lingg **155**

BEAUTIFUL FRIENDS

Bing Crosby: A Road Buddy's Memories by Bob Hope **161**
High Priestess of the Dance by S. Hurok **166**
The Round Table's Blithest Spirit by Marc Connelly **171**
Richard Tucker: Brooklyn's Caruso by Robert Merrill **177**
A Gift of Laughter by Allan Sherman **183**

THE PERSONAL TOUCH

Katie and the Hard Hats by Garson Kanin **191**
The Day I Met Caruso by Elizabeth B. Rodewald **194**

Donahue: Darling of the Daytime Dial   by William Brashler **199**
What It Was Like to Kiss Clark Gable   by Mary Astor   **204**
The Many Faces of Jack Lemmon   by Maurice Zolotow **210**

MUSIC MAKERS AND DREAMERS

The Heroic Conscience of Pablo Casals   by Isaac Stern   **217**
Leopold Stokowski: The Glamour Boy Conductor   by Andre Kostelanetz   **222**
The Three Lives of Ethel Waters   by Allen Rankin   **228**
Horowitz the Thunderer   by Hubert Saal   **234**
Itzhak Perlman: "The Polio Didn't Affect My Hands"   by Annalyn Swan   **239**

WEAVERS OF FANTASY

My Heart Belongs to Peter Pan   by Mary Martin   **247**
Walt Kelly's Furred and Feathered Friends   by Joseph P. Mastrangelo   **251**
Happily Ever After With the Brothers Grimm   by George Kent   **256**
Dr. Seuss: Fanciful Sage of Childhood   by James Stewart-Gordon   **261**
The Magical Muppets   by John Culhane   **266**
Walt Disney's Impractical Dreams   by Roy Disney   **271**

THE HEART OF AN ARTIST

Presenting Liv Ullmann   by Liv Ullmann   **279**
Destiny's Child   by Eleanor Ruggles   **285**
Alan Alda: Madcap Doctor from "M*A*S*H"   by George Vecsey   **290**
Ray Bolger: Leprechaun of the Light Fantastic   by Andrew Jones   **295**
"Charlie"   by Helen Hayes with Lewis Funke   **300**

NO BUSINESS LIKE SHOW BUSINESS

Ethel Merman Knocks 'em Dead   by Landt Dennis   **307**
The Great and Only P. T. Barnum   by W. Bruce Bell   **312**
Mickey Rooney Takes a New Bow   by James Stewart-Gordon   **318**
The Human Cyclone Called Carol   by James Stewart-Gordon   **324**
The Great Schnozzola   by Frank Capra   **329**

THE GREAT ENTERTAINERS

Secret Worlds of the Stars

On the Road With Bob Hope

by Maurice Zolotow

IT WAS ALMOST midnight that Saturday in November 1980, and I was walking very fast along a dark and deserted street in Lexington, Ky. I had set out on a four-mile hike with a famous star of stage, screen, radio, television and golf courses—Bob Hope, age 77. He was risking his life and worse, my life, to take his regular nocturnal constitutional. I was Hope's traveling companion for one of his "college tours" and shared his hectic and unbelievable life for almost four days.

We all know what is out there in the night—muggers, killers, rapists, carriers of knives and Saturday-night specials (and I don't mean Hope's kind of NBC special). I suggested we go back to our hotel as we had to get up early and fly to Houston, and on Sunday it was Orlando, Fla., and Monday to Las Vegas.

Suddenly my worst fears were confirmed. Out of the night, a white Mustang pulled up sharply. From it stepped a lissome young female in a tight cashmere sweater, crying, "Oh, Mr. Hope! Oh, Mr. Hope!" She said she had seen his wonderful show that evening after the University of Kentucky homecoming football game. Could she please hug and kiss him? Pleeeeze?

To my horror, he agreed. It was the old badger-game ploy! While she distracted him, her young confederate would club me on the head, mug Hope and rob both of us. But her friend only wanted to shake Bob's hand and say how much he admired him and his work for the armed forces. Then other cars started pulling over. It was the middle of the night, but Hope amiably signed scraps of paper, cracked jokes, allowed himself to be kissed by beautiful Kentucky girls, shook hands like a Presidential aspirant, smiled and listened. A few blocks later there was a police car. The officer wanted an autograph and he mentioned a place in Korea.

At one point, we found ourselves on a really evil-looking street with suspicious-looking creatures of the night—hollow-cheeked women and larcenous men. But all they wanted was to hug Bob Hope or get his autograph. Then up ahead were *two* police cars. After Hope signed autographs and joked around with the officers, one of them said we were in a high-crime area and they would escort us back to our hotel. I thought this was a splendid idea, but Hope declined. He found another deserted hill to climb, quipping all the way. And the fans found him again.

Almost every week of the year, Leslie Townes Hope leaves his abode and flies on similar jaunts. (Actually, he has two abodes—one a pastoral English-style house on six acres in Toluca Lake, North Hollywood, and the other a sumptuous castle on a hill in Palm Springs, Calif.) Since 1941, Hope has flown almost ten *million* miles. In 1980, he starred in five 90-minute NBC specials and went to 24 college campuses to play one-man shows. He is as popular with the razzle-dazzle collegians as with the older groupies who remember him from his 1940s radio program for Pepsodent.

"My Pepsodent fans," Hope likes to say, "are now using Polident." But not Hope. He has all his own teeth. And he does not wear a "rug" like the late Bing Crosby, though Hope's hair is thinning on top. He not only seethes with high energy but possesses the skin, the muscularity, the energy, the effervescent gleam in his dark-brown eyes, of a man in the prime of life.

In 1980, Hope was either the master of ceremonies or the main speaker at 35 testimonial banquets and "roasts." And you can hardly put on a charity golf tournament without asking Hope to tee off. He also did 23 guest shots on television talk shows and appeared on six telethons.

Last summer there were 12 weeks of touring in country fairs, auditoriums, theaters—places that would book Hope for a night at his fee of $35,000. But many if not most of the soirees and matinees are charity appearances; Hope receives no fee and pays his own travel expenses.

Why does the man keep up this pace? Certainly not for the money. He is one of the richest men in the world; he modestly

On the Road With Bob Hope

says that he is worth about $75 million—"give or take a few digits."

Is it then possible that Hope is suffering from an obscure form of insanity known as dromomania—an exaggerated desire to wander? Maybe, though he also likes to fly home and be with his wife, Dolores, to whom he has been happily wedded since 1935. So what drives him to pack up (he does his own) and sleep in a different hotel room every night? I think there is a deep impulse in Hope to give and receive love. It is not enough for him to receive the mass adulation of a theater or television audience. He craves direct contact with people.

This makes Hope a rare bird among superstars, many of whom shun direct contact with their fans and find the loss of privacy a terrible price to pay for fame. Comic Woody Allen is the best example. He is a recluse. Yet Woody's favorite comedian is—who else? Bob Hope!

Hope's first evening performance on our trip together was a benefit ball for the Chicago USO. A quintet of strolling violinists played "Thanks for the Memory"—the first of about 148 renditions I was to hear in the next few days. No sooner were we seated than people began seeking autographs, interrupting him as he tried to put a forkful of meat in his mouth, asking him to pose for pictures.

I was sitting alongside Jim Barrett, a Washington, D.C., businessman who heads the USO. "Bob knows the best bootblack in every city—and the best millionaires—and he treats them all the same way," Barrett said. Barrett told me that in the morning Hope had gone out to the Great Lakes Naval Training Station to give the graduating class a pep talk. Then Hope had attended a charity luncheon. That afternoon he had talked to a few hundred people. Now it was almost 9:30, and he was still going strong. I soon realized that Hope drew energy from people.

After the banquet and the handshaking and the posing with the fans, it was time for Hope to do his monologue. A jazz band played a swinging arrangement of "Thanks for the Memory." Hope stood there, tall and smiling, and jaunty in his dinner jacket, flashing the famous ski-proboscis profile, belting out those one-liners.

He said many people had asked him whether his old friend Ronald Reagan would offer him a post in the Administration. "I hear I'll be made ambassador to the Bermuda Triangle. Frank

Sinatra may be named ambassador to Italy—but do they really need *two* popes? Jimmy Carter called Reagan after the votes were in, congratulated him and asked, 'Ronnie, is there anything I can do for you?' And Reagan said, 'Yes, run against me in 1984.'"

It was past 11:30 when the show was over, and Hope asked if I was ready to take a walk with him. I thought he was just testing my sense of humor because it was cold, windy and raining; so I laughed and said I was tired. He said he would meet me in the lobby precisely at 10 a.m.

The next morning I learned he had actually walked *two miles* the night before. Yet he was out of the hotel at 9:55. He is never late, and does not wear a wristwatch.

The first time I realized I was in real trouble was when we drove to the airport and parked alongside a small plane, about the size of a toy. I couldn't believe Hope would fly in such a fragile craft. We crawled into the plane, and he reached into a drawer for a box of ice cubes. I sat frozen in my seat for our three-hour flight to Lexington. Bob just sat there sucking ice cubes, talking about how he first met Bing Crosby on Broadway in the 1930s and how they would amuse themselves and their friends by ad-libbing routines at the Friars Club.

As we touched down at the small Lexington airport, he told me that he had been out here a few months previously and had done a show for Tom Gentry, a famous horse breeder who was paid $1.6 million for a yearling.

"What was the horse like?"

"I didn't get to meet the horse, but if I had, I would have asked him who his agent was," Hope said, grinning.

There was a crowd of reporters and fans to greet us as we deplaned. Hope was unfailingly polite and witty. We were due at the homecoming football game but took a minute for lunch in the hotel coffee shop. Again people began coming at him. *May I kiss you? May I have your autograph? I have been waiting 20 years to shake your hand, Mr. Hope. I saw you in Berlin during the airlift. I saw you in a Da Nang hospital. I love you, Bob.* Old men, young men, old ladies, young ones, little children five years old—they didn't leave him alone. But he didn't rush a single person.

Hope eats quickly. I was still nibbling, and he had already cleaned his plate—totally. I asked him about his high energy. "Do you think it's because you eat so fast?" I asked.

On the Road With Bob Hope 7

"Yeah, I do eat fast, don't I? Guess I'm in a hurry to get to the next place."

At the stadium, Hope and I were driven onto the field for the half-time ceremonies. Again boys and girls started asking for autographs. Then a 290-piece marching band, with marimbas, came out blaring, yes, "Thanks for the Memory!" If I were Hope I'd be sick of this number. But he told me he just dotes on it. He can't get enough of it.

Hope received the young homecoming queen as she walked through a crossed-swords line. He placed a crown on her head and said, "It's lovely to be here. I knew I was in Kentucky when I got off the plane, because they threw a saddle on me."

Back in the limousine later, we tore across campus to the Memorial Coliseum, where Hope was giving a concert and show that night. The undergraduate orchestra was playing "Thanks for the Memory" as if the musicians were rendering Mozart's "Sinfonia Concertante."

The next morning at 9:30, there was a knock on my bedroom door. It was Hope, smiling and debonair in his blue pajamas and gold bathrobe, ready for breakfast. He always has stewed fruit first, then Nescafé. He took a powerful multivitamin pill. He also takes megadoses of vitamin C and niacin.

And that, members of the President's Commission on Problems of Aging, is about all I can offer in the way of evidence on how to grow old—not gracefully, really—buoyantly? ecstatically? Stewed fruit, Nescafé, niacin and, oh yes, long hikes in dark streets, playing three, four shows a week and, don't forget this, Commissioner, flying in tiny planes.

While we were flying in the plane from Lexington to Houston, Bob began reminiscing about his happy days as a young actor—going out on the road to play vaudeville. He talked about his love for the small towns and the big towns. He remembered dates in Terre Haute, Ind,; Madison, Wis.; towns so small they weren't on maps—and split weeks and one-nighters and packing up after a show and going to the railroad station to wait for the early-morning train.

That's when he got into the habit of walking the streets of America. He would send his trunk down to the depot and walk through the "clean little towns, with the white picket fences and the neat lawns, and that smell of the good earth in the air. I'd meet lots of folks just walking along, and it always made me feel glad I was a comedian and could bring these folks a little laughter. But I found out what they brought me was more than I brought them."

In Houston it was like Lexington and Chicago and as it would be the next day in Orlando, and the day after that in Las Vegas, and the day after that. He would go on, but I was dropping off here. We said good-by, and I boarded an enormous 747 for Los Angeles. By the time I got home, I was already missing the toy plane and the wonderful song-and-dance man with his happy-go-lucky attitude. I even missed the thrills of a dangerous walk along a dark street.

The Last Days of a Barrymore

by Cameron Shipp

HE WAS AN OLD MAN when I knew him, with only a few years to live. He was crippled, unable to walk, but he loved to drive his battered car—"in eight directions at once" as someone said. He used to show up two or three times a week, park by my driveway and blast his horn. I would hurry out, grabbing beer and sandwiches on my way through the kitchen. Mr. Barrymore had arrived!

It took me a long time to work up the nerve to call him "Lionel." He was hard to know because there were so many of him, and I was never sure which of his numerous and astonishing characters he'd choose to be. He might appear wagging his head and snorting—as the grampus-voiced Gillespie of the *Doctor Kildare* series, he might be the grimacing pirate Billy Bones of *Treasure Island*, or the fierce mad monk of *Rasputin and the Empress*. From time to time he would decide to be Dicken's skinflint Scrooge, whom he brought to grumbling life on the radio every Christmas Eve for some 20 years.

To confuse things further, Lionel had facets and talents which few people knew about. He composed symphonies for great orchestras. He wrote a first novel at 74. He painted beautifully in oils and was a skillful etcher. He was an authority on the Civil War, superbly informed in philosophy and literature, fluent in French and German. Such interests he considered his private business, and he resented intrusion. For the most part he revealed only his irascible acting character, with all the marvelous Barrymore theatrical tricks thrown in.

But behind this gruff eccentricity there was another Lionel— a warm, lively, courageous old fellow, my friend. He had guts and he taught me a lesson.

This Lionel I didn't get acquainted with for some time. I met the other Lionel because I'd been assigned to help him write his family's biography, which we wrote, literally, in the front seat of his car, parked under an orange tree by my driveway in Glendale. The job took about a year, but when it was over Lionel kept coming for conversation and beer. He was lonely and needed someone to talk to.

As for the biography, that got done, begrudgingly, between snatches about Ludwig van Beethoven, James McNeill Whistler, a confusion of baseball players and prize-fighters (he knew them all) and a number of current enthusiasms, including Lucille Ball and the dog Lassie.

He bemused me so thoroughly in the beginning that I suspected he was concealing some vast wickedness in his past that he didn't want in the book. For a long time I couldn't make him account for 18 whole years of his life!

One afternoon over the beer cans when I pried for some information he didn't want to remember, he suddenly decided that we had to write an opera. "I have a lot of old barrelhouse tunes lying around," he said, "and parts of some symphonies. You do me some opening words, see, and then the chorus, composed entirely of white horses, comes in..."

We spent weeks on that opera, humming and singing together in the front seat, then dropped it.

Lionel was not a great composer. "I studied music for fun and not with the idea of putting Bach and Beethoven out of business," he said. But he was talented, with a phenomenal love and a fabulous memory for music. In his last years when suffering was constant his music was, literally, a lifesaver. He would avoid pain-killing drugs by turning to his piano and his scores, working as long as six hours at a stretch. Sometimes, when he hit a great chord that sounded right to him, he would laugh out loud.

Lionel's professionally performed music included "In Memoriam," in honor of his brother John, which was played by Eugene Ormandy and the Philadelphia Orchestra; "Partita,"

The Last Days of a Barrymore

performed by Arthur Rodzinski and the New York Philharmonic; and a number of compositions recorded by MGM, such as his "Music for Halloween," "Rip Van Winkle," and "Ali Baba and the Forty Thieves."

Once, in a moment of rare seriousness, Lionel told me of his feelings for music. "Listening to 'Partita' with the great New York Philharmonic was, I confess with no modesty and no shame, a tremendous experience. I took care to be alone by my radio that Sunday—I didn't want anybody to see me weep." There was a pause. Then like a boxer, which he had been—he boasted proudly of having once sparred with Bob Fitzsimmons—Lionel threw up his guard and started telling stories about Illinois and Abraham Lincoln and a wrestling match.

Barrymore's descriptions of Civil War times were colorful and precise. He told me he became interested in the period when he was preparing to play his famous role as Milt Shanks in *The Copperhead*. He had haunted secondhand bookstores and studied every scrap he could lay hands on about people of those days. After that, Civil War history became his lifelong hobby. Yet none of the historical figures Lionel talked about seemed to exist in the past; he spoke as if he'd had breakfast with Lincoln and lived next door to U.S. Grant.

When Lionel was 74 he completed his odd and exciting Civil War novel, *Mr. Cantonwine*. He wrote it in long, looping thoughts, seldom in sentences, bringing it over for me to read. He would howl when I insisted on grammar, then he would go home, make corrections while sitting up in bed and phone me at midnight to read the results. The published novel was no great literary success, but it was lively and full of color, like its author.

Novel writing, composing and acting weren't enough to keep Lionel busy. He kept up his painting and etching. He won a One Hundred Best Prints of the Year award, but he never talked about it. How he managed to hold a delicate engraver's tool to work on his small, precise etchings was a miracle; his hands were gnarled and stiff and he was in constant pain.

One day I mentioned arthritis. Lionel roared a denial, said he did *not* have arthritis, or rheumatism, or any other blankety-blank ailment, then sulked for an hour. I never knew him to have a headache, a cold, or to be fatigued. At least he never admitted any such weakness.

Gradually, as we talked under the orange tree, Lionel's past emerged. He was born into the theater's "Royal Family," stemming from his grandmother, Louisa Lane Drew, who starred with Joseph Jefferson. His younger brother John was one of the handsomest, most talented actors who ever lived. His sister Ethel was a beauty who became the "first lady" of both stage and screen. Lionel's first notable stage role was in 1902, a small part as an organgrinder in a Broadway hit with his uncle, John Drew. Lionel learned to play the part by haunting Italian restaurants and watching organgrinders. "I always have several people in consultation when I play a role," he said, "but more often than not they don't know it. If you are going to act the part of a plumber, study a plumber—if you are socially fortunate enough to know one."

Although Lionel always considered both his brother's and sister's acting as great, he thought that his own talents were mediocre. By 1906 he grew so discouraged that he quit the stage and went to Paris for three years to study art. He returned with a collection of paintings, intending to become a professional artist. He lasted one day—the day he called at *Collier's* with his samples, and saw on the reception room walls the work that other artists contributed regularly to the magazine. He fled at once, dumped his paintings in a trash can and never again tried to sell a picture. He returned to the "family trade" because he was hungry.

To his surprise, he became a star. His best plays were *Peter Ibbetson* and *The Jest* in 1917 and 1919, in which he worked with brother John, and *The Copperhead* in 1918. His worst was *Macbeth*, in 1921. It was a failure largely because he was so full of good will that he never, then or later, managed to play a villain so that the audience didn't wind up fonder of the villain than of the hero. All told, he did 31 plays before he settled in Hollywood, where he performed in some 100 movies.

Slowly, as I began to understand Lionel, I learned something revealing. But that, too, was a long time coming.

In 1904 he had married a 16-year-old girl named Doris Rankin. They drifted apart and were divorced in 1922. They had two daughters who died in infancy. Those 18 years he was married to her were the ones he tried to omit from the biog-

The Last Days of a Barrymore

raphy. Afterward, Lionel married a talented actress named Irene Fenwick. It was a happy marriage. Irene retired from the stage, devoted herself to Lionel, amused him, looked after him. From the moment he married Irene, Lionel never again mentioned Doris.

When Lionel and Irene came to Hollywood they lived in Beverly Hills. Then after a long, painful illness, Irene died on Christmas Eve, 1936. That night Lionel locked the doors of their luxurious home and never set foot in it again. And he never again mentioned Irene Fenwick.

Close friends of Irene's, Mrs. Mary Ellen Wheeler and her two daughters, took him in. Later, Lionel bought a house in a Los Angeles suburb, and the four of them lived in it the rest of his life. He was there during the years I knew him, painting, writing, etching—and conducting vendettas with the Wheelers. These perhaps sounded like quarrels to outsiders, but those who knew Lionel recognized them as expressions of affection.

In 1936, while painting at a heavy easel, Lionel tripped, fell and broke his hip. The fracture never healed. From that moment on he was in pain, and as an actor who was getting on in years he was considered washed-up. But the idea of his quitting never occurred to Lionel, or to his good friend, Louis B. Mayer, head of MGM.

"If Lionel goes, I go, too," Mr. Mayer told his board of directors. Mr. Mayer thereupon invented the *Dr. Kildare* series specifically for Lionel, creating the cantankerous but lovable old doctor whom Lionel could play in his wheel chair. The series pleased millions on both screen and radio, but it meant only one thing to Lionel: evidence of Louis B. Mayer's kindness. He said that often—but he could never bring himself to thank Mr. Mayer. Overt gratitude, Lionel felt, was fawning and ungentlemanly.

As our friendship grew I learned that Lionel was not only ill and in pain most of the time, he was dead broke and in debt to the government for more than $100,000 in back taxes. No one knows where all the money went. It is a fact that Lionel had lived extravagantly, and that financially he was as casual as a child with a handful of sunlight. Now in his old age, he was sick, in debt and frightened. But I had to learn of these troubles from other sources. Though in his last years I was one of his closest friends, he never complained to me.

Then one day he disappeared for three days. Later I learned he had flown to Washington and made his way to the Treasury Department. I would give a prize to know what he said. I imagine it was a dramatic performance, with Lionel shedding a few theatrical tears. But when I asked, he merely grunted, slapped my thigh and said, "Why, old man, they're not going to put me in the calaboose after all! Why, those are *splendid* fellows in Washington! They're just doing their wretched jobs."

Lionel confessed then that he had actually been terrified that the government would imprison him. But in Washington he had made a deal and arranged to forfeit all his earnings, including his $1500-a-week MGM salary, to pay his taxes. He retained a mere pittance.

Being a Barrymore, Lionel did everything dramatically. He reported to MGM every Thursday afternoon, payday, drove as close as he could to the window of the accounting department and honked. A fishing pole would emerge with a small basket dangling at the end. The basket contained his check. Lionel would scrawl his name, and the basket would be drawn back. Then the pole would be thrust out again and the basket would contain a small sum in cash which Lionel would take home and turn over to Mary Ellen Wheeler.

I doubt that Lionel ever consciously taught me anything. He did give me a fresh appreciation of art, music and literature. And he gave me a lesson in courage and humility. But most of all, he taught me, by example, to live one day at a time, forgetting the mistakes and tragedies of yesterday. That is why he avoided mentioning his first wife and why, when Irene died, he closed their house and never returned. When he broke his hip, he accepted it and refused to talk about it. To the end of his life he lived only for today—and tomorrow—eschewing regrets.

And so I finally understood why he insisted on driving many miles to my house when I should have gone to his. His old car was a symbol to him, a symbol of not giving up. He was, in that old car, as much a man as any man, able to go where and when he pleased—no helpless and dependent cripple. He dismissed all complaints, was annoyed if you inquired about his health, always "felt wonderful" if he had to reply to such an infantile query. He knew what most of us never learn: that our troubles and our pains seldom concern anybody else.

One of the last things he said to me before he died in November, 1954, was this: "These are the important things: youth and health, and someone to love you."

He was old and he had no health, but he made himself young—and there were many who loved him.

Pearl of Our Hearts

by Ponchitta Pierce

SHE STOPS in the middle of a song, and her black, sparkling eyes search the audience for a man. "Darling," she says with a knowing wink, "you're gonna *love* this!" The band starts up again and Pearl Bailey rips into a tap dance. As the spotlight follows the intricate steps, her eyes dart back to the man. "Baby, you'd better love it," she says, "'cause my feet are *killing* me!"

There's an explosion of laughter, and then, as Pearl continues the song, suddenly her hands are dancing—waving, fluttering through the air, punctuating the lyrics. The audience roars for more. Pearl blows a big kiss. "I love you," she says. "Each and every one of you."

The love Pearl Bailey has for people is the hallmark of an extraordinary woman who is entertainer, wife, mother, author, diplomat and student. In 1967, she starred on Broadway in *Hello, Dolly!*, giving what is generally regarded as one of the greatest performances in the history of the musical theater. In December, 1982, she appeared in the role of Berenice Sadie Brown in the highly acclaimed *NBC Live Theatre* production of Carson McCullers' *The Member of the Wedding*. She has frequently entertained at the White House, and served as a special adviser to the United States Mission to the U.N. General Assembly. Her humanitarian work so impressed Jordan's King Hussein that he presented her with one of his country's highest awards.

Blessed with natural intelligence, humor and wit, Pearl Bailey has written five books, including an autobiography entitled *The Raw Pearl* (1968). She also lectures, mainly at colleges. Although she never finished high school, she enrolled at Georgetown University in Washington, D.C., to study theology. Pearl was already well-known on the campus. In 1977

Pearl of Our Hearts

she had given the university's commencement address and received an honorary Doctor of Humane Letters.

A determined and disciplined woman, Pearl has persevered despite serious heart problems, which have plagued her since 1965. A near-fatal attack occurred in 1972. Her husband, drummer Louis Bellson, summoned an ambulance. On the way to the hospital the attendant told Louis, "I don't think your wife is breathing. She's gone." But the hospital staff revived her, and the indomitable Pearl was soon back at work.

Pearlie Mae Bailey was born on March 29, 1918, in Newport News, Va. After her parents separated when she was eight, she lived for a while with her father, a preacher, in Washington, D.C. Then she moved to Philadelphia to stay with her mother. Much of her character and winning personality come from the maternal side. "I'm my Mama up and down," she says. "She could charm a snake and she was a natural actress." But it was Pearl's often stern father who instilled a deep sense of religion in her. She still reads the Bible regularly and has studied the Islamic, Hindu and Jewish religions.

As a youngster singing in her father's church, Pearl displayed unusual musical talent. At 15, she entered an amateur-night contest at the Pearl Theater, a vaudeville house in Philadelphia, where she won the $5 first prize by singing "Poor Butterfly" and "It's the Talk of the Town." Pearl dropped out of school to sing on the vaudeville circuit for $18 a week, plus tips, in Pennsylvania coal-mining towns. Then, her talents honed, she graduated to nightclubs and theaters.

After a while she thought she should see her name out front, along with other performers. "You talk about a heartbreaker," she recalls. "I was at the Royal Theater in Baltimore, where they threw whiskey bottles if they didn't like you. I stopped the show, and yet I couldn't find my name on the billboard." Finally, her name did go up. "It was on a little piece of cardboard," she remembers, "but it was there."

In 1944, Pearl's career really took off. She appeared in New York at the Village Vanguard and then at the Blue Angel, an exclusive East Side nightclub. It was during this period that Pearl developed her inimitable, languid style of entertaining, and particularly her habit of talking—something she loves to do—during her songs. "I still don't call myself a singer," Pearl says. "I see myself more as an entertainer."

Success in nightclubs led her to Broadway where, in 1946, she appeared in the production of *St. Louis Woman*. Other stage shows and films followed, including *Carmen Jones, That Certain Feeling, Porgy and Bess* and *Bless You All*. But few opportunities were open to blacks in Hollywood, and Pearl found herself in all-black films or playing traditional black roles in white productions.

In 1952, Pearl met Louis Bellson, a drummer with the Duke Ellington Orchestra. Four days later he asked her to marry him. Pearl said yes, but asked if he understood what their marriage would involve. In those days interracial marriage—Bellson is Italian—was still highly controversial.

Bellson wasn't worried. He knew that Pearl was strong and mature. "I felt a real profoundness about her," he says. On November 19, 1982, they celebrated their 30th wedding anniversary.

"Louie" Bellson became Pearl's musical director and frequently appeared in concert with her. When they were first married, people asked him, "Don't you feel funny that your wife is the star of the show?" He says he never thinks of Pearl as being the star. "She's just—Pearl." Both of them have a healthy attitude toward fame. "I don't use the word 'star' at all," Pearl says. "Stars are in the sky. Human beings are on earth. And God is above us all."

Marriage didn't slow Pearl's busy schedule. She continued performing in top nightclubs and in concerts; then, in 1967, producer David Merrick chose her to star in an all-black Broadway production of *Hello, Dolly!* Critics and fans loved her saucy, humorous portrayal of the notorious matchmaker Dolly Gallagher Levi. "People would pop out of their seats," Pearl says, "like bread out of a toaster."

Pearl's success in *Dolly* increased her popularity on and off the stage. She was invited several times to entertain at the White House, and in 1975 stayed there as a guest of President and Mrs. Gerald Ford. Pearl, normally one to take things in stride, was impressed. "Hot dog, Louie! Look at us!" she told her husband as they rested in the Lincoln Bedroom. "Boy, if Mama could see me now."

Her friendship with the Fords led to her appointment in November 1975 as a special adviser to the U.S. Mission to the U.N. General Assembly. Pearl took the honorary position very

Pearl of Our Hearts

seriously, actively participating in meetings at the Mission and attending dinner parties for foreign delegates.

In 1976, she was re-appointed as a special adviser under Ambassador William Scranton. While at the United Nations she traveled to Africa on a personal trip, visiting hospitals, orphanages and institutions for the mentally retarded and the handicapped. Later she journeyed again to Africa as a member of the U.N.'s Economic and Social Council, to study the economic conditions of several countries and their potential for development.

When Pearl enrolled at Georgetown University, she said, "I always wanted to be a teacher. It's just that this wonderful thing called show business interfered." She likes to say that entertainers are teachers, and that teachers, to reach students, have to be able to entertain as well. But a teacher also has to have a degree.

Initially, Pearl had some difficulty with her studies, especially writing papers. "I knew the answers, but not how to describe them. But I've got the secret now." Wilfrid Desan, who taught Pearl philosophy at Georgetown, praised her devotion and fervor. "She is an intelligent, intuitive and dynamic person," he said.

If Pearl eventually decides to teach, she can draw on years of experience with her own children. Her son Tony and her daughter Dee Dee are both adopted. A disciplinarian as a mother, Pearl is tired of hearing parents say, "I'm going to give my children what I didn't have." "Instead," she says, "they ought to say, 'I'm going to give my children what I *did* have. Things like good manners, how to treat people, compassion.'"

It is her rapport with people that is the secret to her vitality and enthusiasm. After singing a medley at a 1979 concert, Pearl said to the audience, "I want to tell you what you really do." She started singing "You Light Up My Life," then stopped. "People talk about this song like it's a boy and girl thing. But this is how *I* feel about *you*." She then continued singing:

You light up my life. You give me hope, to carry on.
You light up my days and fill my nights with song.*

She walked across the stage and pointed her finger at various individuals in the audience. "You and you and you and you—

---

*From "You Light Up My Life" by Joseph Brooks.

you all light up my life, and I thank you for it."

From the near-deafening applause, it was clear the audience felt exactly the same way about Pearl Bailey.

Charles Laughton:
A Benevolent Captain Bligh

by Bentz Plagemann

CHARLES LAUGHTON the actor was Charles Laughton's greatest role. But he sometimes spoke disparagingly of other actors. He avoided their company, he said, because they had no conversation. To him, most of them were empty shells waiting to be filled; they had nothing to say until a playwright furnished them with lines.

This could not be said of Laughton himself, who had a great deal to say about every subject under the sun—about art (he had one of the finest collections of paintings in America), about beekeeping, about music, about cooking.

Nearly always, predictably, what he had to say bore some reference to himself. For he had the actor's ego. The benign, benevolent figure which he turned to his public was not false, but it was not the whole man. Under the gentle manner, there was something imperious, something of Captain Bligh in him, a carry-over, perhaps, from his having played the role in *Mutiny on the Bounty*.

I worked closely with him for about seven months on the dramatization of a novel of mine for a play which he planned to direct and co-produce. I did not tell him that I was also taking notes about him, but I am certain he would have liked the idea of having a Boswell to play to his Dr. Johnson.

He had a complete and exhausting devotion to his craft—and he brought the same passionate intensity to everything he did. One day Charles came to see my wife and me at our house in La Jolla. He had promised to show her the spring flowers in bloom in the desert. He had a deep love of flowers and, among his many honors, he was a member of the Royal Horticultural Society.

We started out early in the morning. My wife and Charles sat in the back seat. I was merely the chauffeur, spoken to only to receive directions, the most frequent being a peremptory "Stop!" when Charles wanted to point out something—once, in a landscape that seemed at first glance to be as barren as a crater on the moon, a floor of tiny, brilliant blossoms, fragile as a breath of air.

We climbed the winding road to the top of Mount Palomar and descended on the other side. At one "Stop!" Charles leaped from the car, with that agility which always seemed so amazing in one of his bulk, and disappeared over a deep embankment. Twenty minutes passed before he came back and climbed, puffing, into the car.

"I hope you're satisfied," he said with mock gruffness to my wife, placing in her hand a rare blue wildflower which he knew grew there.

It was for my wife a most memorable day, but for me, after weeks of working with Charles, it was not relaxing. Laughton's energy and expression flowed like a great stream which, having reached its delta, spreads out and covers all the lowlands at its base. One could only submit, or run.

Soon we began looking for a place to have lunch. A great many of my memories of Laughton are concerned with eating or with restaurants, and this is not coincidental. He was, as his appearance would suggest, a rather self-indulgent man in his appetites. The actor who had delighted his audiences as Henry the Eighth by eating chicken with his hands enjoyed food every bit as much in real life. Once, while I was dining with him in Hollywood, he was halfway through an enormous meal when he looked up to find Cary Grant seated opposite us, elegant, fit and sun-bronzed, eating a salad. "Imagine," he said gloomily, taking up his fork again and glancing at Grant, "we're exactly the same age."

We finally had lunch the day of our outing in an inn near the old mission east of La Jolla. There was no one else in the dining room, and over brandy Charles began to tell us, in a version perhaps embroidered by his creative gift, the story of his early life.

He had been brought to acting, he said, by Edith and Sacheverell Sitwell, members of the famous English literary family.

Charles Laughton: A Benevolent Captain Bligh

Highly aristocratic, the Sitwells were lords of the manor in the Yorkshire town where Laughton was born, and they sometimes came for dinner to the hotel his father owned there. When he was about 17, Charles was assigned to serve the Sitwells at table.

His innate sense of mimicry and considerable composure were not lost on Edith and Sacheverell. After several dinners Edith delivered the verdict.

"We have made up our minds about you," Charles reported her as saying. "You are not a waiter; you are acting the part of a waiter. You are an actor."

This was the turning point of his life. It had been presumed that he would go into the family business. Instead, with the encouragement of the Sitwells, he went to acting classes in London. More than that, they took him in hand and molded him into the sort of man they thought he could be. His education in literature, music, painting began with the Sitwells. They introduced him to excellence and helped to create his taste.

With his enormous energy and his natural talent, he accomplished the rest for himself. On the London stage, he put his personal stamp on a multitude of roles, from Shakespeare's Prospero to Agatha Christie's Hercule Poirot. He was also the first English actor to appear with the Comédie Française—speaking flawless French. Meanwhile, he had launched his movie career. Not long after his success in *The Private Life of Henry the Eighth*, for which he won an Academy Award, he came to America. He never returned to England for any long period, and eventually he became an American citizen.

Although he firmly believed in the aristocratic principle of keeping a proper distance between himself and his admirers, Laughton was warm with an audience, especially during his famous public readings from the Bible, Shakespeare and poetry, which became so popular in theaters and later on television. He began the readings during World War II, by entertaining bedridden veterans with excerpts from Thurber or Dickens or Aesop. He often concluded with a simple rendition of the Gettysburg Address which left his listeners with a new sense of the beauty and rhythm that words can evoke.

Laughton's readings from the Bible became especially popular, partly because he could bring half-forgotten characters and passages vibrantly alive. The smallest movement—the flick of his eye, a twitch of his mouth—gave life and reality to his readings. At one performance Laughton noticed that he was being watched closely by an old lady. Appreciative of her attention, Laughton approached her afterward and discovered that she was deaf. "I couldn't hear a word you said," she confessed. "But you make the most interesting faces." Eventually, Laughton toured the country, bringing the Bible and other great literature to capacity audiences wherever he went.

He attacked his work with relentless drive. Late one afternoon he telephoned me in La Jolla from Hollywood. He had gone over some of the playscript which I had sent him, and he wanted to talk about it. It was a subtle point, but an important one, and he couldn't make himself clear over the telephone. He would come down in the morning.

He stepped off the plane looking disheveled. He had had very little sleep, and his manner was a combination of exhilaration and exhaustion. In the car he launched at once into what he had stayed up half the night rehearsing to tell me: that at the heart of a romantic relationship between a man and a woman there was something raw and primitive, something that smelled of the flesh, and unless that was present, even in a domestic comedy such as we were working on, the production would not be convincing.

I thought, why couldn't he have told me this over the telephone? But then I was struck with the truth of the old adage that genius is an infinite capacity for taking pains. Just as in any role played by Charles the slightest gesture, intonation or movement of body was the result of long analysis, so he could not convey an important idea for the script over the telephone; it was necessary for him to come and act it out for me.

He began when we reached the house. Some people, when trying to explain a difficult idea, use their hands in speaking; Charles used his whole body. For me it was rather like sitting alone in the first row of a play, having directed at me the creative force designed to fill an entire theater. He was the man and then he was the woman. He paced about the room; his voice rose, it fell. He wooed and challenged. In the middle of this performance, he stopped to ask if I had Thomas Wolfe's *The Web and the Rock*. There was a passage in it which would show what he meant. I didn't have a copy. Off we went on a hunt through bookstores. In the fourth one we found a copy; he declaimed the passage, and then went back to more acting out of his point about the relationship of man and woman.

Charles Laughton: A Benevolent Captain Bligh 25

It was an astonishing performance, interrupted by a gargantuan lunch, after which we went back to our house for more work and more acting, until he was sure that I had understood his point.

Charles was in an exuberant mood when he left late in the afternoon. I was so exhausted that I fell asleep at dinner.

It was with no small apprehension that my wife and I finally went back to Hollywood for the last revisions on the script. We stayed in a small villa near Laughton's house, and were quickly caught up in the orbit. I soon discovered that there existed a kind of pecking order of intimidation. While I was in awe of Charles, Charles was in awe of his household help.

The Laughtons—Charles had been married since his London days to actress Elsa Lanchester—were cared for by a butler and an excellent cook. A cocktail tray was brought in one day, and Charles made martinis for us. We had just raised our glasses when the butler appeared in the doorway.

"Dinner is served," he said.

Charles was on his feet instantly. "Please drink quickly," he said, his hands outstretched for our glasses.

I gulped my martini, and Charles apologized as he took the glass from my hand.

"We have to go in when we're called," he whispered. "The last time we didn't, the cook threw the dinner in the garbage pail."

Our script was finally finished, but the problems of casting and production were never resolved. With his enormous energy, Laughton, at any given time, was involved in perhaps half a dozen projects. Some succeeded, some did not. Now an opportunity suddenly came that he could not resist—to direct and play a leading role in a Broadway production of Shaw's *Major Barbara*.

It was an intelligent, meticulous production. Laughton's way of adding animation to the long, talky third act was particularly imaginative: he arranged the people in groups, like figures on a frieze—an idea that had come to him while studying the paintings of Puvis de Chavannes at the Metropolitan Museum.

This was typical of Laughton, for whom all the arts formed one whole, the spectrum from which he could draw for his own creative work. He was fortunate; few men are so fulfilled.

To be exposed to the ruthlessness of his professional commitment was no small privilege, and I am indebted to him for the many things he taught me. For Charles Laughton believed, as only an artist can believe, in the value of work. His life was a magnificent testimony to his conviction that for each of us, in success or even in failure, only the work in which we are involved is of ultimate importance.

The Finesse and Fury of Laurence Olivier

by Curtis Bill Pepper

LAURENCE OLIVIER was in his dressing room in London, applying the elaborate makeup required for Richard III, when the gift arrived. It was a sword inscribed: "This sword is given to Laurence Olivier by his friend John Gielgud in appreciation of his performance of *Richard III* at the New Theater, 1944."

Olivier was stunned. The sword was one of the most famous in England. It had belonged to the actor Edmund Kean who had used it when playing the role of Richard III, and had then been passed on to the great Henry Irving the first night he played Richard. Finally, Gielgud had been given it. In relinquishing the weapon, Gielgud paid homage to Olivier's brilliant performance which, for many critics, had dethroned Gielgud from a 15-year rule of England's stage.

It is an immortal symbol, created by a successive line of immortal names. In 1979 Olivier was asked to whom he planned to pass the noble sword. "No one," he said. "It's mine."

No performer of Shakespeare's plays ever achieved the global fame of Laurence Olivier. On stage, he has been the most ambition-haunted Macbeth, the most perfidious, yet painfully human Shylock and the most primordial Othello. In films, he brought *Henry V*, *Hamlet* and *Richard III* to millions—millions who also remember Olivier as the brooding Heathcliff of *Wuthering Heights*, and the handsomely haughty Mr. Darcy in *Pride and Prejudice*, as well as the man who married Vivien Leigh, the unforgettable Scarlett O'Hara.

Olivier began acting in 1925 at the age of 18 and is the first actor in English history to reach the House of Lords (although he prefers his lesser knighthood title of Sir Laurence to that of Lord Olivier). At the Academy Awards presentation in Hollywood in April, 1979, he received an honorary Oscar for his "lifelong achievement in films"—to place alongside a 1946 Oscar for his film *Henry V* and best-actor and best-picture awards two years later for *Hamlet*.

Olivier continued to grow as an artist while fighting off cancer, thrombosis, myositis (a muscle-inflammation disease), an obstructed kidney and several attacks of pneumonia. As each of these ills struck, he fought back with rage and fury.

Seeking some clue as to how he has managed life at the top of his profession for so long, I went to see him in Venice in 1978 during the filming of *A Little Romance*, a George Roy Hill film in which he stars. Inside a portal of St. Mark's Cathedral, the cameramen were filming a young boy and girl running out of a door and down a short flight of steps. Olivier rushed out after them—but halted before taking the steps.

"Cut!" cried director Hill.

Moving slowly, Olivier descended the steps and sat in a chair. The scene was then continued, with Olivier's double leaping down the steps and running after the children. It did not please Olivier, however, for he called his double aside and, rising, laboriously went through the slow-motion movements of running.

"You can't just run," he said. "You have to *look* as if you're running."

As Hamlet, Olivier had leaped 12 feet through the air to kill a king. As a dying Coriolanus, he had fallen in a backward somersault down a flight of stairs. Now, he could run only in his head.

"Larry's still weak from his past illnesses," explained Hill. "We have a key scene with a bike, but he may not be able to ride one. We had a special machine built for him."

Olivier, whose still-dark hair had been tinted gray for the film, came up for a polite "How do you do?" His eyes, a strange gray-green, did not match the tone of his words; they stared without blinking, like a shark's, primitive and threatening. One sensed deep and violent emotions held in precarious balance: anger and love, sensuality and asceticism, and a driving need to create—or destroy.

Olivier had once said of himself: "I'm not sure what I'm

The Finesse and Fury of Laurence Olivier   29

like and I'm not sure I want to know."

Moss Hart, the Broadway director and playwright, claimed he had almost never known an actor without an unhappy childhood. Was that true of Laurence Olivier?

"Oh, yes!" he told me. "There was no cruelty or unkindness, but I couldn't wait to get out. Ours was a genteel poverty, in some ways worse than real slum poverty. The idea of going onstage was heaven."

The decision came when Olivier was 16, on the day his brother, Richard, went to India to be a tea planter. "After he left I felt miserable—my mother had been dead for three years. That evening, as usual, to save water, I got into my father's bath after he'd finished. 'When can I follow Dickie out to India?' I asked. My father said, 'Don't be a fool—you're going to be an actor.'"

Young Olivier was astonished, never suspecting that his father, a strict Anglican clergyman, could read his heart, even though his inclination had been plain from the age of seven. He had converted an overturned wooden packing box into his first theater and began presenting plays, created by himself. "To pretend you're somebody else, I suppose, is where the first impulse for acting starts."

At ten, Olivier played Brutus in a school play, attracting the attention of the celebrated actress Ellen Terry, who wrote in her diary: "The small boy who played Brutus is already a great actor." When 17, he won a one-year scholarship with the famous actress Elsie Fogerty at the Central School of Speech and Drama. Then came a three-year apprenticeship (1926–28) with the Birmingham Repertory Theater, learning many of the great roles.

After a brief, initial Hollywood stint in 1929, he returned to England and six flop plays in a year. Then Noel Coward picked him for *Private Lives*, and later John Gielgud took him on for *Romeo and Juliet*, in which Gielgud and Olivier alternately played Romeo and Mercutio. Overnight, he became a name.

Following two years' war service as a lieutenant in the Fleet Air Arm, Olivier joined the Old Vic Theatre Company. There, in 1944, he played the cruel and ambitious Richard III. He was not impressed by the first-night cheers. At the following matinee, however, he sensed the audience's tremendous excitement. "For the first time in 19 years onstage, I felt it. I felt them saying"—here his voice sank to a whisper—"'He's coming on!'"

Olivier sees the great Shakespearean roles as "cannibals." While playing Othello, he once described their consuming effect: "You give them all you've got and the author says to you: 'You've given all you've got? Good. Now, more. Good. Now, more, damn you. *More! More!*' Until your heart and guts and brain are pulp and the part feeds on you. Acting great parts devours you. It's a dangerous game."

Olivier constructs a character by using selected traits, techniques, ideas, images. Then he moves inward into unknown territory and finds the part inside himself. In the process, he has often interrelated the comic and the tragic, drawing laughter while portraying such monsters as Titus Andronicus and Richard III. "It's frightfully important for the tragedian to be a comedian," he told me. "Otherwise, he will be inhuman. I love comedy every bit as much as tragedy."

"Can playing a role be an escape from life?" I asked. "My God, yes!" replied Olivier. "There've been times when I've been 'most deject and wretched,' as Ophelia puts it . . . so absolutely miserable because my life has been an equal meting out of horror of what I'm going through and guilt for what I plan to go through. And then to say, 'For the next three hours I'll be Coriolanus, nothing like me, not one of my problems.' It can be a blessing to be an actor, really."

I thought of Vivien Leigh, whom Olivier had married in 1940, and of her drive to be her husband's equal onstage—until she fell into manic depression. She was his greatest love; he was, until the end of her life, her "beautiful, shining, brilliant, darling Larry." Yet he had left her, after 20 years when she was 47, bewildered by her mental illness. And she had died seven years later.

"You can reach a point," Olivier said, "where it's like a life raft that can hold only so many. You cast away the hand grasping it because otherwise it's both of you. Two instead of one. Then you go on living and there you are, with it, knowing what has happened, remembering its details. Yet what else is there to do?"

In 1961, Olivier married actress Joan Plowright, and with her he has had three children. He also has a son by his first wife, actress Jill Esmond. "When I make films now, people criticize me in the papers. 'Why's he doing such muck?' I'll tell you why: to pay for three children in school, for a family, and their future. I can no longer be a stage actor because I don't feel I've got the power or the physical attributes."

Olivier's illnesses began with cancer of the prostate. "I literally said, 'Oh, bug off. You're not gonna get me that way, boyo.'" Then thrombosis developed in his right leg, until it weighed 20 pounds more than the other. Next came the muscular inflammation, myositis. "Leaves you so weak you can't stand. I tried to get up and bashed my eyes on the corner of the bed. Joanie was terrified. Thought I was done for, and I almost was."

He licked the disease, emerging from the hospital in 16 weeks, instead of an anticipated six to nine months. After that, however, he was hit again when a fibrous tissue blocked his kidney flow and required surgery.

"I haven't recovered yet," he said. "I'm hanging together by wires, rattling a bit as I go. But I can sure as hell ride a bicycle."

I discovered later what he meant when the silver-gray Citroën, with a bicycle visible in the trunk, halted at the top of a hill near Verona. "Can you see him, Orestes?" Olivier asked the driver, referring to film director George Roy Hill, the one man he did not want to see. "I don't want him hovering over me like some bloody hen."

Orestes had heard it before, ever since Olivier had taken one look at another and special bicycle, produced to ensure against his falling. Built to look as if he were pedaling, it was actually propelled by a hidden mechanism. Clever, but odious to Olivier.

Now, atop the hill, Orestes took a regular bicycle out of the car and watched as Olivier perched himself unsteadily on the seat. A young man supported each handle bar. "Fear not, noble Greek," Olivier said to Orestes. "Let's go."

With that, the two helpers ran alongside, holding him as he teetered to left and right. "Let go!... By God, let goo-OOOHH!" cried Olivier, his voice rising to the pitch of his Henry V Agincourt battle cry.

He flew down the hill, black suit jacket flapping, his legs seeming to pick up strength as he raced around the bottom curve, finally halting beside a fountain bearing water from an ancient Roman aqueduct.

The following day he did it again, whizzing into camera range, then halting before Hill—and the fake bicycle Hill had caused to be built. Olivier's eyes turned a cold, opaque gray as he glanced at the expensive machine, a fallen enemy, the battle won.

"Don't worry, dear boy," he said to Hill. "I'll reimburse them for their silly toy."

The Wisdom of Laughter

Groucho's Secret Word

by Earl Wilson

THE CROUCHING, lecherous lope was a trifle slower, and the fake mustache of black shoe polish was now real and white, but at 82 Groucho Marx's mind had lost none of its dyspeptic zing. It was 1972 at New York's Carnegie Hall. A capacity audience, many of them young men and women togged out in familiar Groucho regalia—painted mustache, frock coat, glasses and outsize cigar—had turned out to pay homage to the man who had made Americans laugh for over half a century. Puffing on his cigar, his eyebrows yo-yoing expressively, Groucho sang in his crow's-caw voice, regaled the crowd with memories of vaudeville and movie days, and told stories of his unlikely assortment of friends, including Harry Truman and poet T.S. Eliot. When he finally sauntered offstage, the audience stood and begged for more.

As I watched the laughing faces of the people around me, I was taken back to my days as a college student in Ohio when I first became enchanted with Groucho's outrageous antics in Marx Brothers' movies. My friends and I could rattle off their jokes from memory. (Chico: "I'd like to say good-bye to your wife." Groucho: "Who wouldn't?") Now I was seeing people young enough to be Groucho's grandchildren howling in glee at his evergreen irreverence. Groucho had hurdled the generation gap, saying the things most of us would like to say if we had the nerve, not to mention the wit. Once my wife told him, "We had a wonderful stew for dinner last night." "Anyone I know?" inquired Groucho. When a woman told him she was "approaching 40," Groucho asked, "From which direction?" On a plane he was told he could smoke if he didn't annoy the lady passengers. "If there's a choice," he exclaimed, "I'll annoy the ladies!"

I first met Groucho in Hollywood in 1945 when I interviewed him for my newspaper column. We were lunching at one of Beverly Hills' poshest restaurants, but Groucho was not impressed. "We have some nice rolled pancakes," the waiter suggested solicitously. "If I'm going to roll anything," Groucho said, "it won't be a pancake." He spotted an imposing dowager dripping with jewelry. "The last time she counted her rings she was the oldest living thing in California," he declared. At the conclusion of the lunch, after he had bantered with passing patrons, playfully stuffed the silverware up his sleeves and otherwise disrupted proceedings, the maitre d' asked him how he liked the food. "I'll let you know in a couple of hours," he said. Then he surprised me by saying he would like to give a party for me.

"I'll invite a lot of top movie stars," he promised. "How would Thursday night be?"

"Fine," I said eagerly. "What's your address?"

"Wouldn't you like to know?" said Groucho, turning on his heel and walking off.

He did give a dinner, though, and it was a big success— at least from my point of view. For I got my first insight into the real Groucho in his own home, and found him a serious and thoughtful man as well as a very funny one.

At that time Groucho and his brothers were about to start shooting a picture called *A Night in Casablanca*. However, Warner Brothers Studio threatened suit over the title as they had made a picture a few years before called *Casablanca*. "I had no idea that the city of Casablanca belonged to Warner Brothers," Groucho replied to their protest. "What about 'Warner Brothers?' Do you own that, too? You probably have the right to use the name Warner, but what about Brothers? Professionally we were brothers long before you. And before that there had been other brothers—the Smith Brothers, the Brothers Karamazov and Dan Brothers, an outfielder with Detroit." After a lengthy exchange, in the same wacky vein, the studio ceded the name Casablanca to the Marx Brothers.

Groucho was born in New York, one of five sons of a tailor so inept he was known as "Misfit Sam." His mother, a redoubtable woman named Minnie, formed her five young sons, plus an aunt, into an act called "The Six Musical Mascots."

Groucho's Secret Word

After considerable shuffling, the "Six Mascots" became the "Four Marx Brothers": Groucho was the glib, lugubrious charlatan; Chico, who looked like a gangster, spoke Italian dialect and played the piano; Harpo, wearing a curly blond wig and never uttering a word, played the harp; Zeppo, the most respectable looking of the quartet, provided what scant romantic interest might be required.

For years the brothers pursued a desultory career playing tank towns across America. "We played in towns," Groucho recalls, "I would refuse to be buried in."

Eventually, however, they worked their way up to playing New York's Palace Theater, the mecca of vaudeville. Looking for new worlds to conquer, they produced a Broadway show of their own called, for no apparent reason, *I'll Say She Is!* Overnight they became the toast of Broadway. They followed up with two more smash hits—*Cocoanuts* and *Animal Crackers*. Theatergoers had never seen anything quite as wild, funny and unpredictable as the antics of the four brothers. In *Animal Crackers* Groucho played perhaps his most memorable character, Captain Spaulding, the African explorer. "One morning I shot an elephant in my pajamas," he bragged. "How he got into my pajamas, I'll never know."

With the success of their shows, the brothers were summoned to Hollywood. They made equally successful films of their shows, as well as good original comedies such as *A Night at the Opera* and *A Day at the Races*. Their films, like their shows, were a melange of wild antics, non sequiturs and improbable situations. In one, Groucho took the pulse of an inert girl and muttered, "Either she is dead or my watch has stopped."

The brothers proved to be as unpredictable off screen as on. Once Groucho was in an elevator when Greta Garbo got on. Then the greatest female star, Garbo looked distinctly mannish in slacks and a broad-brimmed hat that almost hid her classic features. Impulsively, Groucho reached out and tipped Garbo's hat over her eyes. She turned on him in a cold fury and flared, "How *dare* you!"

"I beg your pardon," Groucho apologized. "I thought you were a fellow I knew from Kansas City."

Groucho generally shunned the Hollywood social swim and remained mostly a homebody. "Home is where you hang your head," he said. His idea of a good time was reading, playing Gilbert and Sullivan on the guitar and puttering in his garden.

Despite being a top star, Groucho always maintained a fine irreverence toward the movies. Once a studio invited him to a screening of *Samson and Delilah* starring Victor Mature and Hedy Lamarr. When asked how he liked the movie, he declared, "No picture can hold my interest where the leading man's bust is larger than the leading lady's."

After having conquered vaudeville, Broadway, movies and radio, Groucho made one of his most resounding hits of all in his long-running TV quiz show called "You Bet Your Life." The prizes were small, but the show gave Groucho a chance to do what he does best: ad-lib with contestants, undistracted by script, gaudy sets or dancing girls. On one show a contestant was a tree surgeon. "Tell me, Doctor," Groucho said. "Did you ever fall out of one of your patients?" On another show he asked a model about her most exciting experience. The girl couldn't remember any. "A model with no exciting memories," mused Groucho. "What were you modeling—clay?"

The program ran more than ten years and when it finally went off the air, Groucho was philosophical. "I have no complaint," he said cheerfully. "I've gone through two wives and four or five NBC presidents during the show."

A talented writer, Groucho wrote several books and a play, in collaboration with Norman Krasna. His amusing letters are now reposing in the Library of Congress and were published as a book, *The Groucho Letters*. After cataloguing these letters, John C. Broderick of the Library said: "Mr. Marx is a much deeper and more complex man than I ever would have guessed."

Perhaps this is why Groucho had many friends among the literati, going back to Carl Sandburg, with whom he used to sleep through movies in Chicago when the poet was toiling as a movie critic. James Joyce included a reference to the Marx Brothers in *Finnegan's Wake*, and a dozen books have been written about the brothers. During World War II, word was brought to Winston Churchill that Nazi leader Rudolf Hess had parachuted from a plane over Scotland and been captured. "Would you mind seeing me later?" Sir Winston asked. "We're running a Marx Brothers picture now."

Groucho's television program featured a "Secret Word" which was changed for each show. If a contestant happened to mention the word during his appearance, he received an extra prize. Speaking of Groucho's Carnegie Hall performance a critic said, "The secret word was 'love.'"

Bill Cosby:
Humor With Lessons

by Ponchitta Pierce

THE DAY BILL COSBY told his mother that he wanted to quit college and become a comedian, she took sick from the shock and stayed in bed for seven weeks. In the 21 years since then, Cosby has recorded 21 comedy albums which have sold 9.5 million records and won eight Grammy Awards. As an actor, he has starred in movies, and four television series which have netted him four Emmy Awards. Last year, he made over 100 appearances throughout the country, earning as much as $50,000 a night.

Bill Cosby's original and imaginative humor is often compared to Mark Twain's. While Twain told childhood stories of river life on the Mississippi, Cosby paints the side of America he experienced growing up in a North Philadelphia ghetto. A classic Cosby routine describes a game of street football:

"We had the greatest quarterback in the world," he says. "He had to control 23 men on his side. He called a play like this: 'Okay, listen to this now. Arty, you go down ten steps and cut left behind the black Chevy. Cosby, you go down to Third Street, catch the J bus, have him open the doors at 19th Street, and I'll fake her to ya.'"

Until he was 12, William Henry Cosby, Jr., lived in an all-black housing project. Some people in the neighborhood worked hard. Others, winos and unemployed fathers, hung out on the street corners. Youth gangs, some harmless, others more menacing, roamed the streets. Cosby and his friends often played in a junkyard.

Cosby's father, a ship's steward, was rarely home. His mother worked as a domestic, and at times she and her three sons were on welfare. Young Bill contributed to the family income by delivering groceries and working as a shoeshine boy. Cosby's brush strokes were often matched by jokes which left his customers in stitches. Even then, he was the undisputed neighborhood cutup. His teacher once wrote to his mother: "Bill is an alert boy who would rather clown than study."

Cosby's favorite people were comedians, especially television's Sid Caesar. "I used to dream of being Caesar's second banana," he recalls. Bill and his friends would spend hours watching television, making jokes about what they saw, especially the commercials. But as soon as a comedian came on the screen, Cosby became serious, studying how funny material was delivered.

Besides imitating other comedians, Cosby learned to joke about everything—even things like poverty, or alcoholics. A favorite story concerns the time he and his friends were walking home late at night after seeing a monster movie and were scared out of their wits by an old wino coming out of an alley. "Bill could turn painful situations around and make them funny," his brother Robert says. "You laughed to keep from crying."

While Cosby grew up in a neighborhood which offered many opportunities for getting into trouble, he steered clear. The Police Athletic League and Salvation Army offered the youngster alternatives, especially sports activities. And his fifth- and sixth-grade teacher, Mary Forchic Nagle, instilled in him feelings of pride and self-confidence.

Perhaps the greatest influence was his mother, Anna Cosby. Young Bill knew that if he did anything seriously wrong it would embarrass her. When asked what she felt she contributed toward her son's success, however, she modestly replied, "The only thing I had to give him was plenty of love, and oh, dear God, I gave him all I had. But success comes from within, and Bill was determined to be something."

That determination did not include being a dedicated scholar. Cosby was placed in classes for gifted students at Germantown High, but he was more interested in goofing off. After repeating the tenth grade, he dropped out and joined the Navy. Always a good athlete, he became a basketball and track star. He also finished high school through a Navy-sponsored extension course. His athletic skills won him a scholarship to Temple University, where he made the dean's list, ran track and played varsity football. Eventually, some of his best comedy routines would

Bill Cosby: Humor With Lessons

portray him as a player afraid of being hurt in scrimmage.

In his sophomore year, Cosby started bartending in a Philadelphia café to help meet his college expenses. He served jokes with the drinks, and his customers encouraged him to set his sights on a show-business career. His first nightclub appearance was in a room so small that Cosby, six feet tall, had to sit while performing—making him perhaps the world's first sit-down comedian. One night the owner of the Gaslight Café, a club in New York's Greenwich Village, caught his act and hired him for $60 to appear there on weekends. Cosby remained briefly at Temple in his junior year, then quit, at age 25, to concentrate on being a nightclub comic.

Although his parents disapproved of Cosby's new career, his grandfather Samuel, then 81, recognized Bill's flair for telling stories. One day when Cosby explained the jokes he was trying to tell, his grandfather said, "Why don't you tell the story about when you and your brothers..." Cosby has been doing that ever since, tapping a tremendous reservoir of boyhood experiences and magnifying them for comic effect.

He became a hit on the nightclub circuit and television variety shows, and in 1965 was selected by TV producer Sheldon Leonard to co-star with Robert Culp on "I Spy," a series in which he and Culp played a pair of hip U.S. undercover agents masquerading as traveling tennis players. From 1969 to 1971, he played a physical-education teacher on "The Bill Cosby Show."

But it was always humor and his childhood experiences that Cosby kept coming back to, and in 1972, in association with Filmation Studios, he created the TV show, "The New Fat Albert Show." Fat Albert, Weird Harold, Dumb Donald and Rudy the Rich are animated-cartoon re-creations of childhood buddies, and the fact that they live in a black ghetto has made no difference to the six million children who tune in to laugh at the gang's antics. Unlike most children's shows, however, lessons are served up with the laughs. As Cosby warns on camera in each episode: "Here's Bill Cosby coming at you with music and fun, and if you're not careful, you may learn something."

The emphasis is on education aimed at influencing feelings, behavior and value judgments. Produced with an advisory committee of educators, psychologists and sociologists, the show has proved so effective that it won The Children's Theater

Association Seal of Excellence (1973) and the Ohio State University Award for meritorious achievement in education broadcasting (1975). McGraw-Hill Films recently made shortened versions available to schools.

Since the show went on the air, Cosby has attracted an army of little fans, who send him thousands of letters a month. Children trust him. He understands their world. "I can be silly, I can be grown-up, I can be an older brother, I can be just a funny man that they know," Cosby says of his popularity.

In 1971, Cosby surprised many of his friends by going back to college to work toward a Ph.D., which he completed in 1976. Extensive tests showed that Cosby, even though he lacked a bachelor's degree, was self-educated enough to enter graduate school at the University of Massachusetts with a program of flexible class attendance. His field was the media as a tool for teaching. As part of his studies, Cosby developed a group of films, along with booklets, to be used in teaching children from lower- and middle-class economic areas.

The Cosby's now live in a small town outside Amherst, Mass., where they have restored a 15-room, 140-year-old clapboard farmhouse and furnished it with colonial antiques collected by Bill's wife, Camille. They were married in 1964, much to the distress of her parents, who thought he would never amount to much. The Cosbys have five children, ages 7 to 17.

Unlike many stars, Bill Cosby does not travel with an entourage and does not like hero worship, except perhaps from his little fans. He is a secure man who says, "I'm not struggling anymore. All the things I've ever wanted, I have."

As often as possible Cosby returns to his old neighborhood in Philadelphia. "Part of me will always be there," he explains. "Man, that's my home." Not long ago, during one of these visits, he saw a group of kids playing stickball. To the children's delight, he stopped to play with them. The back street was so small that for a home run you had to hit the ball straight up in the air. That's exactly what Cosby did—and by the look on his face, he was a child once again, playing with Fat Albert and the gang.

Will Rogers: Cowboy Comedian of Common Sense

by Eddie Cantor

EVER SINCE that tragic day in 1935 when Will Rogers crashed to his death in Alaska on a round-the-world flight, America has been searching for someone to take his place. So sorely missed is Will's way of making us laugh at ourselves that anyone with the slightest hint of his sharp, dry humor is quickly dubbed "the new Will Rogers."

Impossible! Will was irreplaceable.

I first met Will Rogers in 1912 when we were on the same vaudeville bill at the Orpheum Theater in Winnipeg, Canada. Right away I knew this Oklahoma cowboy was like no other actor I'd ever met. He actually enjoyed listening as much as talking. Before I knew it, I had told him how I'd grown up in a New York tenement, how I'd gotten into show business, and on and on. I think I realized then that the day was to come when I would love him more than any other man I'd ever known, with the kind of deep and admiring love I might have had for a father or older brother.

Once, trying to muster nerve to make a radical change in my act, I asked his advice. He gave me that wonderful squinty smile of his and said in his casual way, "Why not go out on a limb? That's where the fruit is." His own success as a performer, and as a man, was the result of a lifetime "out on a limb"—never hesitating when instinct impelled action, always saying what he thought.

Born William Penn Adair Rogers in Oologah, Indian Territory, near Claremore, Okla., he was proud of his 5/16 Indian blood. In the early days he billed himself "The Cherokee Kid," and he later originated the classic comment, "My ancestors didn't come over on the *Mayflower*—they met the boat."

By the time I met Will he had already made a name for himself. He was the ridin'est, ropin'est, bronco-bustin'est cowboy anywhere. Will was punching cattle in Ladysmith, South Africa, back in 1902, when he first turned his hand (literally his rope) to performing in Texas Jack's Wild West Circus.

It was at the old Hammerstein Theater in New York that Will began talking in his trick-roping act. One night when he found himself snared by the lariat he drawled, "A rope ain't bad to get tangled up in if it ain't around your neck." His casual humor made a hit. Soon he was ad-libbing about what he'd read in the papers, and his fame as a homespun philosopher began to grow.

There was an enduring quality about what Rogers said or wrote:

"Our foreign dealings are an open book—a checkbook."

"I reckon some folks figure it's a compliment to be called 'broadminded.' Back home, 'broadminded' is just another way of sayin' a feller's too lazy to form an opinion.

"Too many people spend money they haven't earned to buy things they don't want to impress people they don't like."

A while ago, watching television, I was startled to hear a joke Rogers had ad-libbed to me back in 1917. While we were standing together in the wings, looking at the Ziegfeld Follies girls, Will whispered, "Eddie, it's too bad that those gorgeous gals—20 years from now—will all be five years older."

Perhaps his best-known quip was made at a dinner in New York. I sat on the dais next to Will, who was toastmaster. All of us who were to speak had agreed that each would "get on and off" in eight minutes. But one man kept rolling along for 45 minutes before he wound up with, "Mr. Toastmaster, I'm sorry if I overstayed my time, but I left my watch at home."

Rogers hunched forward, furrowed his brow and said, friendly-like, "There was a calendar right behind you."

Will poked fun at people only if they were riding the crest of the wave and could take it. He was prompt to come to the defense of someone he felt was getting a bad break. When the young Prince of Wales (later The Duke of Windsor) came to the United States, humorists made much of the fact that he seemed to be forever falling off a horse. Will's only comment was, "I see pictures showing that every time the horse falls, the Prince falls, too. What should he do—stay up in the air?"

Will Rogers: Cowboy Comedian of Common Sense 45

This uncommon man with his laugh-wrapped common sense did much to steady the nation in time of trouble. After the crash in 1929, when things were going from bad to worse, President Hoover was blamed for everything from athlete's foot to the entire Depression. Rogers came to his rescue by throwing him a line: "You'd think Hoover got up one morning and said, 'This is a nice day for ruining the country—I think I'll do it today.'"

With his daily column in hundreds of newspapers, his stage and radio appearances and his motion pictures, Will had enough success to swell any man's head. But he continued to wear a wrinkled "store" suit and a ready-made shirt. He used his time and money for more important things. During World War I, a good part of his salary went to the Red Cross. He always had indigent actors on his payroll—and paid them so well that some refused small parts in pictures and plays because it would mean less than they were getting from Rogers. As a speaker he received hefty fees, which he turned over to various charities. And he was the only person I ever knew who didn't use these contributions as tax deductions!

He never had a written contract with Florenz Ziegfeld. In 1915 they just shook hands and that was it. Until Rogers, Ziegfeld looked upon all comedians as mere parsley around his main dish—the girls. Will didn't hesitate to kid him about this. The first words he uttered on a Ziegfeld stage were: "Y'know, folks, I'm just out here while the girls make a change. Imagine, changin' from nothin' to nothin'!"

On one of Will's radio broadcasts he announced a surprise guest, "the President of the United States, Calvin Coolidge." Then, imitating Coolidge's voice, he began: "It gives me great pleasure to report on the state of the nation. The nation is prosperous on the whole, but how much prosperity is there in a hole?" Many listeners thought it really was the President and were incensed later when they learned it had been Rogers. Will felt bad about the misunderstanding but President and Mrs. Coolidge enjoyed the gag and invited him to the White House for dinner.

Just before Will was to meet Coolidge, one of Will's friends bet him that he couldn't make dour Cal laugh in two minutes.

"I'll bet he laughs in 20 seconds," answered Will.

Then came the introduction: "Mr. Coolidge, I want to introduce Mr. Will Rogers."

Will held out his hand, looked confused and said, "Excuse me, I didn't quite get the name."

He won his bet.

During the White House dinner, Mrs. Coolidge said there was only one person who could do a better impersonation of Calvin Coolidge than Will—and that was herself. She went into a monologue that won Will's applause. "Yes, that's mighty fine, Mrs. Coolidge," he conceded. "But think what you had to go through to learn it."

Will liked making motion pictures because it gave him a chance to spend more time with his family. By 1934, he was the top favorite on the screen. One of his great hits was *State Fair*, in which a prize boar called "Blue Boy" was used. The last day of shooting, the studio suggested that Rogers buy the boar for the family larder. Rogers declined. "I wouldn't feel right eatin' a fellow actor," he said.

Blessed with rugged health, Will never thought of consulting a doctor, much less an eye doctor. One day his fellow star, Thomas Meighan, saw him holding a paper at arm's length. "For heaven's sake, Will, take my glasses," he said. Will put them on, finished his paper and walked away with the glasses in his pocket. He used them from then on.

Rogers got into his famous gumchewing routine quite by chance. One matinee, by mistake he walked on stage, chewing gum. The audience burst into laughter as Will parked the gum on the proscenium arch. When he'd taken his last bow and was about to walk off, he got another laugh as he retrieved the wad and said, "It ain't that I'm stingy, but there's a lot of mileage left in this."

In my 50 years of show business I never met a man with a quicker mind than Will's. One noon he was walking through the dining room of the Hotel Astor when a critic who had often taken Will to task about his bad grammar invited him to join a group for lunch. "No thanks," Will said. "I already et." In good fun the critic corrected, "You mean you've 'already eaten.'" Will grinned. "I know a lot of fellers who say 'have eaten' who ain't et."

When Eugene O'Neill's play *Ah, Wilderness!* opened in San Francisco, Will played the lead. His performance had the audience throwing their hats in the air and the critics their adjectives even higher. But during the play's run something happened which, I feel sure, indirectly led to his death. Will

Will Rogers: Cowboy Comedian of Common Sense 47

received a letter from a clergyman: "Relying on you to give the public nothing that could bring the blush of shame to the cheeks of a Christian, I attended your performance with my 14-year-old daughter. But when you did the scene in which the father lectures the son on the subject of his relations with an immoral woman, I took my daughter by the hand and we left the theater. I have not been able to look her in the eye since."

This so disturbed Rogers that he finally withdrew from the play. He also asked to be released from his commitment to do the screen version for Metro-Goldwyn-Mayer, promising to do another film in its place as soon as a suitable script was found. While waiting, Will accepted an invitation from the famous pilot, Wiley Post, to fly around the world—the trip which ended in the death of both men.

Not long after Will was killed I went to Claremore, where a Will Rogers Memorial Museum had been established. Walking through the museum, I noticed the church-like silence. People were speaking in whispers. It was a moving tribute to a man whose goodness had been as eloquent as his wit.

In glass cases were mementos which Will had given some of his friends and which we, in turn, had sent to the museum. I lingered in front of one containing a heavy silver filigree belt and gun. I remembered how happy I was the day he gave them to me and how sad I was when I shipped them off.

Set apart from the rest of the treasures was the most poignant object of all: his typewriter, with a page still in the roller. The smashed keys told the story of the crash more graphically than if they had pecked out the words. Will had been typing his daily column when the end came. It's small comfort, but at least he died doing what he liked best—writing and flying.

As I left the building, I looked back, and there was Will—a likeness so real you could hardly believe it was bronze. Jo Davidson, the sculptor, had captured everything—even to the twinkle in Will's eyes. He almost seemed to be speaking. And in a way he was, for carved at the base of the statue were the words that are the key to his personality: "I never met a man I didn't like."

George Burns' Golden Age

by Maurice Zolotow

IN HIS 84TH YEAR in 1980, George Burns was one of the hottest stars in Hollywood. His book of humorous recollections, *The Third Time Around*, had hit the bookstores. He had also recorded his first country-western album, and one of the songs, "I Wish I Was Eighteen Again," had been on the charts.

I asked him if he really wanted to be 18 again.

"When I was 18 I went out with young girls," he said. "Now I'm 84, and I go out with young girls."

George Burns is lovable and charming and witty, and he seems to defy the rules about growing old gracefully. He eats and drinks and smokes in a way that would give the Surgeon General a heart attack. His stomach is cast iron. At lunch in the deli he sat studying the menu.

"I'll have the corned-beef hash, and burn it," George muttered. "And tomatoes with the skin on. Don't peel the tomatoes. People ask me how I stay young. I say 'Eat tomatoes with the skin on.' In fact, I like anything that makes a noise when I put it in my mouth."

"Oh, really?" I asked.

"No, O'Reilly," he chortled.

I had been watching Burns' film *Oh God!* Part Two, which is a sequel to *Oh God!*, one of the most engaging movies of 1977, in which Burns played Jehovah as a benevolent if rather raffish character who sometimes wore safari suits and other times a golf cap. In an era when so many films portray tragic degradation, Burns has made a success of sweetness and light and virtue, of truth and goodness. It is true that in *Going in Style*, in which he costarred with two kids named Lee Strasberg

George Burns' Golden Age

(78) and Art Carney (61), Burns masterminded a bank robbery. But somehow it was all sweet and nice.

The real Burns is as kindly and as gentle and as good a human being as the characters he has been playing since he broke into the movies as a star at the age of 79. "It takes just as much energy to be rotten as to be nice," he explains. "I'd rather put my energy into being nice. And I'll tell you something else—when you give energy into being nice, you usually get more back than you give out."

George Burns had been around for a long time as a vaudeville actor, a radio star, a television star, as half of the team of Burns & Allen. But he was strictly a comedian. If he had ever had any acting talent, in the sense of putting himself into an imaginary role, he had never shown it—until he fell into his co-starring role in Neil Simon's *The Sunshine Boys*. Filming of the hit comedy was about to start in 1975, with Jack Benny, George's oldest and closest friend, slated to play Al Lewis, one-half of a retired vaudeville team, opposite Walter Matthau's Willie Clark. Then Benny died. Burns was persuaded to step into the breach, although he protested that he did not know how to act.

It was in the course of making this film that Burns learned how to get into a character. At one point he was to knock on a hotel-room door; when Richard Benjamin (Matthau's, or Clark's, nephew who was summoning him out of retirement) opened it, he was to go in. He could not get this seemingly simple piece of business right. It was wrong and artifical. He knew, without theorizing about it, that he was trying to "act" when what he had to do was live—and feel. That's why, when you ask him about acting, he pretends it's easy.

"What is acting after all?" he asks. "Somebody says hello to me, I say hello back. Richard Benjamin says come in and I come in. If I stay out in the hall, I'm a bad actor. If I walk in, I'm a good actor."

He says these things in a gravel-voiced baritone with a cigar between his lips and a glint of gentle mockery in his eyes. Because, as anybody knows who ever tried to act, delivering a simple line, like "Please pass the salt," is much harder to do convincingly than a big hysteria scene. While making one film, Burns mastered a simple, naturalistic, honest way of letting his own emotions and feelings enter into the words and actions of *The Sunshine Boys*. When he won his first Oscar for Best

Supporting Actor in the movie, he was 80 years old.

George Burns was born Nathan Birnbaum on January 20, 1896, in a slum tenement on the Lower East Side of Manhattan. His close friends still call him "Natty." He had seven sisters and four brothers. His father died when George was seven, and the family, which had always been poor, was now poorer. By the time he was 15, George knew he wanted to be a vaudeville star. He did a skating act, worked with a seal and performing dogs, was a hoofer and a comic; but most of all he wanted to be a suave, sophisticated song stylist.

He did not think he had a comedy flair. Gracie Allen did. She was an Irish Catholic girl from San Francisco and she wanted to be in show business. They met in 1923 on a blind date. For George, it was love at first sight. By 1925 they were playing the big-time. By 1926 they were married, and their sketch, known as "Lamb Chops," had taken form.

The curtain rose and showed them standing on a street. They talked in nonsequiturs for about 15 minutes, George making intelligent remarks or asking searching questions and receiving baffling replies from a wide-eyed, smiling, naïve Gracie. The skit got its name from this part of the act:

BURNS: Do you like loving?
ALLEN: No.
BURNS: Do you like kissing?
ALLEN: No.
BURNS: What do you like?
ALLEN: Lamb Chops.
BURNS: A girl like you, a little girl like you, can you eat two lamb chops alone?
ALLEN: Alone I can't eat them. With potatoes I can eat them. . . .

Theirs was a loving and blissful marriage. They adopted two children, Sandra and Ronnie, and the mansion on Maple Drive in Beverly Hills became filled with toys and laughter and wonderful family life. "Burns & Allen" had become one of the leading radio programs. Over the years, he and Gracie played their vaudeville selves in about 20 musical movies. She retired in 1958. George tried to do a single in television and struck out, so he worked up a new act and began to play nightclubs. Then, in 1964, Gracie Allen died.

For almost a year, George could not come to terms with her death. Life without Gracie was meaningless and empty.

George Burns' Golden Age

She was buried in Forest Lawn, and he went there every day, sat by her marker and carried on conversations with her. Perhaps he was replaying fragments of their old scripts: *Do you love kissing?... What do you love?... Lamb chops....*

And then one night, in his pit of loneliness and despair, he could not sleep. He got out of his bed and crossed the room and decided to stay in Gracie's bed. That night, for the first time since Gracie's death, he slept soundly and peacefully, as if her spirit reassured him that she was with him.

He slowly came back to work, with television specials and nightclub shows and his television-production company. Then, out of the blue, he became a movie star at 79, and won an Oscar at 80. At 84, he was filming his seventh picture as an actor.

Asked by strangers and reporters for the secret of longevity and health, he is likely to reply, "Drink three martinis a day, get very little sleep, eat fried foods, make love at least four times a week and smoke cigars."

"How many cigars a day do you smoke?" I once asked him.

"About 15," he replied. "Three doctors told me to stop the cigars years ago. Of these three, two are already dead—and the third one has been coughing a lot lately."

Since he had enacted the divine spirit so warmly in the first *Oh God!*, I asked him about his religion. He said he had not practiced a formal religion since he was a young man, but "I believe in God. I believe that God is in every person and therefore I don't get angry with people and I don't hate people. If something bad happens—I forget it right away." He paused to relight one of his 33-cent cigars. "Or at least ten minutes later."

"What is the most important piece of advice you have to give older men and women?"

"Get out of bed," he told me. "Get out of bed as soon as possible after you wake up." Burns gets up at 6:30 a.m., does exercises for 20 minutes, swims for another 20 minutes. After breakfast, he drives to his office.

"Most people," he says, "are in rehearsal for old age from the time they're 25, or 30, like that. They are already planning their retirement at 40. It's hard to learn to be old. So folks start learning to walk slow and forget things and get absent-minded and foggy. Well, by the time they're 60, 65, they're getting real good at being old, so when they're 70, hallelujah, they're a big smash hit—now they're old. I don't want that. And I'm not studying to be young either. Young. Old. Just words. You just don't aggravate yourself, and try to get along and do what you have to do today."

Danny Kaye:
Pied Piper of Laughter

by John Reddy

WHITE pigeons rose by the hundreds into the skies above Istanbul, Turkey, while, laughing and clapping, comedian Danny Kaye led 150 children from many nations across a towering new bridge over the Bosporus, the first permanent highway link between Europe and Asia. For this dedication ceremony on October 30, 1973, there could not have been a happier choice of a leader than Danny, a modern Pied Piper who had spent more than 20 years entertaining and helping children for the United Nations. After years of Broadway, movies, radio and television, Danny began utilizing his talents and boundless energy as a goodwill ambassador to the world, bringing cheer and comfort in the wake of catastrophe.

"Children are always the innocent victims," Danny says. To which Henry Labouisse, former executive director of the United Nations Children's Fund (UNICEF), adds: "Over the years Danny has been an invaluable friend to UNICEF and, through it, to the world's children. On countless occasions, he has helped raise money for our work on their behalf. We can never thank him enough."

This serious funnyman has toured combat areas and hospitals not only in wars involving the United States, from World War II to Vietnam, but in foreign conflicts including the India-Pakistan fighting and the Arab-Israeli wars. In one hospital in 1973 he greeted an Israeli soldier who had just been blinded. "Why, Danny Kaye, how nice to see you!" the sightless man said. "That just knocked me out," Danny remembers, "saying it was nice to *see* me when he would never see anything again." For badly burned soldiers who wanted to read but couldn't because they were unable to use their burned hands, Danny sent to the United States for a supply of gadgets which hold books and turn pages automatically. In Jerusalem he conducted a concert for Arab and Israeli children. "If they mix together as little ones, maybe they can form some basis for understanding as adults," he said.

During the Vietnam War, he put on shows in jungle clearings and often surprised GIs by worming his way into foxholes to offer them a cigarette or just chat. Visiting hospitals, he found out that wounded boys liked having their picture taken with him. "So he took along a camera, and wrote messages on the snapshots for the boys to keep," his wife, Sylvia, says. "And when he got home he spent weeks calling the boys' families to tell them how their sons were."

At the height of the fighting in Vietnam, he and singer Vikki Carr, who accompanied him, were marooned for a night in a forward area surrounded by the ominous sound of mortar fire. "I began crying," Vikki recalls. "In the middle of those mortars going off around us, Danny talked to me of everything under the sun. My terror subsided. I know he's played to some great audiences, but he never gave a finer performance than just talking softly to one frightened girl singer in that Vietnam jungle."

Danny first became involved with the U.N. Children's Fund in the early 1950s. "I was about to leave on a tour of the Orient, and Maurice Pate, UNICEF'S executive director, asked me if I'd look in on some of the organization's outposts," he recalls. "I did—and I haven't stopped looking yet." Danny has covered the world for the U.N. organization and lent a hand wherever he went. For instance, children are apprehensive when a UNICEF team of doctors and nurses shows up at an outpost with medicines and needles. Then Danny appears, wins their confidence by making them laugh. "Kids will laugh at anyone willing to act like an idiot," Danny says. "And I *am* a good idiot." He has romped with Greek kids in a polio bath in an Athens rehabilitation center and played ball with Italian boys who had to balance on one leg or catch with stumps of arms.

In Thailand he met a little boy who was suffering from yaws—big, running sores. "His name was Boonting Choeykholai," Danny remembers. "But that was too much for me, so I called him Sam. We treated him with two shots of penicillin

Danny Kaye: Pied Piper of Laughter 55

which cost about five cents." In two weeks he was completely cured. Seven years later at an Asian reunion of UNICEF in Japan, attended by young people from each UNICEF-aided country, Sam came from Thailand. "He was then about 14," Danny remembers, "and tall, straight, dignified. He didn't remember our first meeting, but when we showed him pictures of himself covered with sores he realized what had been done for him. He put his hand on my shoulder in a quiet, eloquent gesture of love."

Kaye refers to his ceaseless work as "limited to the little world of laughter," yet that world is also universal. "I just try to make people laugh," he says. "I play to kids who have never heard of America, much less Danny Kaye. What's more, they can't understand what I say. But to these kids I am a funny man with red hair. I walk funny, and make faces. Somehow they have fun, and that is all that matters."

As a youngster, David Daniel Kaminski, the son of an immigrant Ukrainian tailor in Brooklyn, dreamed of becoming a doctor (even today his idea of a good time is watching famed Dr. Michael DeBakey perform open-heart surgery). However, with his carrot-hued hair, skinny, loose-limbed frame and wistful features, he seemed born for comedy. In his teens he joined a dancing and singing trio which toured the Orient. Encounter with the Far East began Danny's lifelong love affair with Oriental cooking, and it taught him to communicate by gestures and expressions with people who do not speak English—a talent that has proved invaluable.

Back in this country, he met Sylvia Fine, a pretty pianist whose flair for writing witty lyrics blended perfectly with his own knack for verbal acrobatics. They were married, and have a daughter, Dena, whom they call "our best collaboration." When Dena was a child they placed some food in front of her, and, without tasting it, she announced, "I don't want any." Danny then gave her his life philosophy: "You can dislike anything, but *try it first*. Be curious. It may get you in trouble, but you'll have a fuller life."

Danny, with Sylvia writing his material, graduated to nightclubs. His first big break came in the Broadway musical *Lady in the Dark*, with Gertrude Lawrence, in which he rattled off the names of some 50 tongue-twisting Russian composers in less than a minute with such dizzying éclat that he stopped the show. Hollywood beckoned, and Danny starred in such movies as *Up in Arms*, *The Secret Life of Walter Mitty* and *Hans Christian Andersen*.

The movies made him an international star. "Gad, they treat him as if he were a nation!" exclaimed Sir Anthony Eden, observing a royal welcome in England. King George VI said Danny had done more than most diplomats to cement Anglo-American relations.

Kaye's informality with audiences, which early became his trademark, started by chance during a show in London. Winded from a dance routine on top of a morning of golf, he plopped down on the apron of the stage and announced, "I think I'll just rest here a minute." He bummed a cigarette from someone in the first row and told the audience about his exhausting round of golf. Then he bounced up refreshed and finished his performance. The intimate approach worked so well that he has kept it a part of whatever he does.

Danny stayed away from television until 1956, when a Columbia Broadcasting System film of one of his 35,000-mile tours for UNICEF was shown in 25 countries, including Soviet Russia. The movie depicted him as Pied Piper to the kids of 14 countries—he impersonated a flamenco dancer in Spain, sang a Neapolitan folk song at a school for handicapped children in Rome and did a wild lindy hop with a leper girl in Nigeria. The film brought such warm response from viewers that it led to Danny's own weekly, hour-long television show, which ran four years and won a mantelful of awards.

Every fall, Danny spearheads UNICEF's annual "Trick or Treat" campaign to raise money for the organization. The 1981 Trick or Treat campaign brought in $2,223,000.

An interview with Danny at his Beverly Hills home in 1974 was like one of his nine-course Chinese dinners: it contained a little of everything. He cooked lunch for us, featuring an omelet à la Kaye, spoke Chinese, sang an old Scottish song and brooded over the state of the world. He was depressed about the killing of 21 schoolchildren at Maalot in Israel. His sensitive clown's face looked sad, and he ran his fingers through his luxuriant hair. "You've seen much misery," I observed. He answered, "Yes. But I've seen a lot of joy, too."

Danny is not sorry he went into show business instead of medicine. "When I was young, I wanted to be a doctor because the idea of making people happy appealed to me," he mused.

Danny Kaye: Pied Piper of Laughter

"Well, I'm not a doctor—but I think I make people happy anyway. When you make someone laugh, you're giving him medicine."

Two of his enthusiasms are conducting orchestras and teaching opera to children. Danny has acted as guest conductor for the New York, Philadelphia, London, Boston, Chicago and Los Angeles symphony orchestras. The money raised from his performances—so far, over $6 million—goes to the musicians' pension funds. "My conducting started as a lark," he says. "I can't read music, but I have a good ear. Of course, the orchestra has a terrible time of it!" Conducting the Los Angeles Philharmonic on one occasion, Danny led the "Flight of the Bumblebee" with a fly swatter.

For all his other numerous activities, Danny's heart remains closest to his work with children. "It's the most wonderful thing I have ever done," he says. "The health and welfare of all countries depend on their children. If we can better understand the problems of the world's children, the world might be well on its way to understanding itself."

Sam Levenson's Extended Family

by Earl Wilson

"WHO EVER HEARD of a professional comedian who laughs at his own jokes?" The words came from a critic sitting next to me in a New York cabaret. It was a Sunday in 1946 and a group of young comedians were trying out for the show, including a 34-year-old Brooklyn high-school teacher named Sam Levenson. I'd known some rather prim and pedantic teachers as a child, but this one was so round and jolly that I likened him immediately to a Jewish Santa Claus. "That teacher ought to stay in his classroom," the critic continued. "He doesn't know where to put his hands. And look at how he fidgets with his eyeglasses."

But the teacher's stories were sidesplitting. I sensed they were an extension of his own life and the people he knew and loved. I was confident he would have broad appeal—and I was impressed that he didn't stoop to dirty jokes or dialect, as some of the other fledgling comics did, to get cheap laughs.

After the show I introduced myself to Levenson, explaining that I was a Broadway columnist for the New York *Post* and intended to write a column about him. "Good, I'll go over it with my students, have them criticize it, then send in your grade," he quipped.

We soon became good friends. Sam told me he was thinking of giving up teaching to perform full-time. But he had doubts. Several people had told him that his anecdotes had only local, "ethnic" appeal. He asked my opinion. "I'm a Methodist from Ohio," I said, "but I see myself and people I grew up with in the stories you tell. Your critics are wrong."

So he took the plunge and soon had bookings all over the

Sam Levenson's Extended Family 59

country. Ed Sullivan put him on TV, he became a panelist on another program, and eventually starred on his own TV show. He went on to author best-selling books that blended bittersweet childhood memories with his effervescent humor. Once, when he performed in Washington, D.C., a guest from Abilene, Kan., collapsed in laughter. "You know, Sam, when you talked about the tribulations of the Levensons, I thought you were talking about the Eisenhowers," the President later told him.

In private life, many comedians are petty egomaniacs. But the Sam Levenson you saw on television was the same person away from show business—warm, funny, unpretentious, a lover of mankind and of his own neighborhood. When Sam first started to earn a six-figure income, I told him he should be living on Park Avenue. But he insisted he was comfortable in Brooklyn. When he finally moved, it was only over the border to a larger house in Queens. He kept his office in his home, and his "working hours" consisted of making the rounds in his old neighborhood, chatting with the postman, the candy-store lady, children going to school, the cop on the beat, the deli man. He would pick up nuggets from their conversations and note them on 3-x-5 index cards, then file the cards in shoeboxes. For many years these shoeboxes were his only "gag files."

Once a neighborhood man approached him and said, "Now that you're on TV, will I be able to talk to you anymore?" "You'd *better* talk to me or I won't have a show for next week!" Sam answered. His modest demeanor extended into his home. When his daughter Emily began kindergarten she came home one day shrieking, "Mommy, Mommy, I just found out daddy is Sam Levenson!"

Sam was not just family-oriented; he was family-obsessed. His wife of 43 years, the former Esther Levine, was a cousin. Harry Levine, his brother-in-law and cousin, was his business manager. His brother Albert helped produce his shows. When Sam made out-of-town appearances, he would take along a list of phone numbers of relatives living nearby, call them all and ask if they had any problems. When he returned home, he would call their families and report: "I talked to your Henry (or your Susie). All is well."

Good friends, by informal adoption, became part of Sam's extended family. When a show-business friend told me his son was talking of running away from home, I got Sam to see him. He told the boy about a time *he* decided to run away. "I rushed to the front door. 'Where are you going?' Mama asked. 'I'm running away,' I answered. Mama said, 'Wait! I'll call you a taxi.'" The boy laughed and then Sam went to his school and helped straighten out the problem there; later he acted as mediator between the parents and the son.

Sam was one of eight children (two others died at birth) born to immigrants from Russia and raised in a New York slum. "When my parents were in the old country," Sam would say, "somebody mailed them a postcard that showed a lady holding up a torch and bearing an inscription by Emma Lazarus reading, 'Give me your tired, your poor. . . .' Papa figured that Emma must be an aunt and since nobody was more tired or poor than he was, he felt Emma was inviting him over. He had heard that in America the streets were paved with gold. When he got to New York, he found the streets were not paved at all, and that *he* was expected to pave them.

"Ours was a life of plenty—plenty of relatives, boarders, landlords, politicians, cockroaches and junk. Our neighborhood had open-air pushcarts with genuine bargains: over-ripe onions, frostbitten tomatoes, 'surprise lunches.' Transactions often went like this: 'How much?' 'A penny.' 'Too much.' 'So make me an offer!'"

In Sam's family, there was cleanliness even in tatters, and respect for parents and authority. Mama would provide a meal menu with two choices: "Take it or leave it." Papa worked first in a sweatshop, then opened a little tailor shop. He never earned more than $20 a week, yet there was no question of who was the head of the household. "Papa raised us on *Parents' Magazine*," Sam would say. "He never read it, just rolled it up and whacked us on the behind."

The Levensons insisted their children capitalize on America's free education. In the evenings, they did their homework around the dining room table, under Mama's eagle eye. They turned out well: a doctor, a dentist, a prominent artist, two business executives, a housewife and a show-business assistant. And, of course, Sam, the teacher.

When the older brothers began to earn their livings, they arranged for a cleaning woman to help their mother. But on the first morning the woman was due, Mama got up at 5:30, scrubbed every room and put clean linen on the beds. "You think I would let a stranger come in to a dirty house?" she asked.

Sam Levenson's Extended Family   61

When Sam was only 13, Mama died suddenly. Sam's rabbi and good friend, Dr. Joseph Weiss of West End Temple, Neponsit, Queens, told me that Sam's many "Mama" stories in his monologues manifested his desire to always keep her memory alive with him.

Sam graduated from Brooklyn College with a BA in Spanish and became a Spanish teacher. His teaching methods were unorthodox. He used the lyrics of a popular rhumba to teach vocabulary. Instead of textbook sentences like "The umbrella is on the table," he taught: "I will meet my boyfriend in the balcony of the Palace Theater." Fellow teachers vied to sit with him in the cafeteria to hear his stories.

Later, he became a guidance counselor at Samuel J. Tilden High School. "As a counselor I learned compassion," he said. He also picked up nuggets for his shoebox files. Once a student came up to him and said, "I'd like some advice, Levenson." "It's MISTER Levenson," Sam told him. "Oh," the boy shot back, "did you get married?"

In fact, Sam did get married about that time. On his Depression salary of $2140 a year, the only honeymoon he and Esther could afford was a subway trip to Manhattan. They found a hotel room for $3.75 a night and in the morning had room service, Levenson-style—Sam went out for bagels, lox, cream cheese, and milk.

One summer, when the couple rented a small bungalow in the Catskills, a teacher named Phil Foner came to Sam with a request. He and three brothers had formed a jazz band which played at the Arrowhead Lodge. They had promised the owner they would provide a professional comic for the season-ending show. When the pro backed out they asked Sam to fill in. "We've heard you telling your stories and we know you'll be great," they insisted. Sam "laid them in the aisles" at Arrowhead and the owner then proposed: "Come up next summer and perform regularly and you can have free room and board." "How about my wife?" Sam asked. The owner looked dubious so Sam added, "I can play dinner music for you, too. I'm good with the violin." He was hired.

During the school year he found small organizations willing to pay him $5 for an appearance, and later circulated flyers reading: "Sam Levenson, Folk Humorist, $15 An Evening." His success along this local circuit brought him to the Broadway cabaret where we first met.

After he became a headliner, 70 percent of his personal appearances were for benefits. He also made free appearances at hospitals and nursing homes, and before local PTA groups. Giving was part of his family tradition. Even in stark poverty, Papa and Mama had kept a little "pushke" to save pennies for charity.

During his later years, Sam aimed much of his spoofing at parental permissiveness. "Permissiveness is like saying to a kid, 'No, you're not going to do it and that's *semi*-final,'" he said. "It's letting your child do whatever he likes on the premise that if he gets killed doing it, he won't do it again. These days you can give your teen-ager a car. You can give him an allowance. You can give him your brand new sportjacket. But you cannot tell him to 'have a good time.' He will glare at you and say, 'Don't tell me what to do.'"

Sam believed that children brought up in a climate blending parental love with a standard of morals and discipline would enjoy happier, fuller lives. "Give your children a couple of *dis*advantages," he would say. "The reason you have things now is because your lack of them as a child spurred you to strive for them."

Sam's death from a heart attack in the fall of 1980, at the age of 68, came as a shock to the people who loved him. Yet he must have had a premonition, because a few months before death he had showed me an "Ethical Will and Testament" written for his grandchildren. It read, in part:

"*I leave you my unpaid debts. They are my greatest assets. Everything I own, I owe.*

"*To America I owe a debt for the opportunity it gave me to be free and to be me.*

"*To my parents I owe America. They gave it to me and I leave it to you. Take good care of it.*

"*To the Biblical tradition I owe the belief that man does not live by bread alone nor does he live alone at all. This is also the democratic tradition. Preserve it.*

"*I leave you everything I had in my lifetime: a good family, respect for learning, compassion for my fellow men, and some four-letter words for all occasions. Words like help, give, care, feel, and love.*

"*I leave you the years I should like to have lived so that I might possibly see whether your generation will bring more love and peace to the world than ours did. I not only hope you will, I pray that you will."*

Sam brought more than his share of love and peace to the world—*much* more.

Triumph and Tragedy

"The Wire is My Life"

by Joseph P. Blank

HELEN WALLENDA began urging her husband Karl to retire from the high wire in 1970 when he was 65 years old. She was afraid for his safety. "There are other things you can do," she implored.

"Look, honey, let me do it as long as the good Lord lets me," he answered in his German accent. "He's up there with me." Before stepping out on the wire, the greatest high-wire performer in circus history always popped a piece of hard candy into his mouth ("It keeps me from getting nauseous") and said silently, "God, please..."

"How will you know when the good Lord tells you to stop?"

"When He leaves me, I'll know," Karl said.

Karl Wallenda was born in 1905 into a Magdeburg, Germany, family that had been acrobats and trapeze artists for three generations. At six, Karl was performing in the family show. Five years later he was doing stunts in beer halls. His best act was stacking three chairs and doing a handstand on the top chairback.

In the early 1920s Karl met a high-wire walker named Louis Weitzmann who taught him to walk the wire. Weitzmann designed an audience heart-stopper that would use Karl's handstand prowess. With a balancing pole, Weitzmann would walk to the center of the wire, Karl would follow, with a hand on Weitzmann's shoulder for balance. Weitzmann would bend low at the knees. Karl would climb his back to a handstand position on his shoulders, and Weitzmann would then stand erect.

The innovative stunt and its variations were quickly booked throughout central Europe.

Two years or so later Karl formed his own troupe with his older brother, Herman, and a young woman. She was the highmounter who balanced on Karl's shoulders or on a bar yoked between Herman and Karl as they walked across the wire. When she left the act, Karl placed an ad for a replacement. The only reply was from Helen Kreis, a teen-ager who turned out to be a natural on the wire—graceful, confident, gritty.

In 1927 The Great Wallendas were invited to perform in Havana. The highlight of their show was a three-tier act: Herman and a young man named Joe Geiger were the understanders. Karl stood in a chair on the pole yoked between them, with Helen mounted on his shoulders. John Ringling caught the performance and offered Karl a contract with "The Greatest Show on Earth." Karl signed.

One audience-thrilling feature of The Great Wallendas' act was the absence of a net under the 40-foot-high wire. While a flying trapeze act *must* use a net because missed catches are not unusual, Karl believed that a net was dangerous for The Great Wallendas.

Flyers practice falling and know how to land on their backs to help avoid injury. But it was impossible for a four-person act to practice falling. Bodies would strike bodies on the net, and the cascade of balancing bars, bicycles and a chair could kill or injure. The net offered no security. It was better to rely on skill and quick-thinking in an emergency.

Karl was 23 when his troupe opened in New York's Madison Square Garden in 1928. As the Wallendas stepped out on the ¾-inch wire in their deerskin slippers, the band music muted and salesmen stopped hawking their wares. After the 15-minute performance, the audience broke into loud applause, feet-stamping and whistling. The troupe was dismayed. In Europe such a display is the same as being booed. They took a quick bow and fled. The noise continued until the ringmaster told Karl, "We can't go on with the next act until you take your bows." "But the whistling?" Karl asked. "That's appreciation," the ringmaster explained.

* * *

"The Wire is My Life"

Karl always tried to give the audiences a new feat. In one, Helen perched without a bar on Karl's shoulders as he stood on a chair balanced on a bar across the shoulders of two men on bicycles. In another, Herman stood on a bar yoked between two under-standers and Karl did a handstand on his shoulders. But the act that established the Wallendas as truly special was the seven-person pyramid. Conceived by Karl in 1947, it was to bring the family triumph and tragedy.

The pyramid consisted of four under-standers, the first and second pairs yoked together by shoulder bars. Karl and Herman, also yoked, were the second level of the pyramid, balanced on the two first-tier bars. Then a top-mounter, either Helen or her younger sister, sat and stood in a chair balanced on the second-tier bar.

The troupe started practicing on a wire three feet high, then 12 feet and finally at about 40 feet. Karl harped continually on precautions. "Never drop the pole. Make it a part of your body. It is your security. If you drop the pole you endanger your life and the lives of everybody else on the wire."

"On the wire you concentrate," Karl repeated. Concentration enabled the seven-person pyramid to stave off the unexpected. Once, the wire suddenly slackened about six inches. All the balancing poles see-sawed precariously, but every person kept his erect position and the pyramid held firm. In outdoor performances the pyramid survived cloudbursts and unpredictable gusts of wind.

Helen, who married Karl in 1935, retired from the circus in 1959, but agreed to tour with him during the summer months. But being a spectator was different from being a part of the act: she couldn't take the anxiety and suspense, and would remain fearfully in her quarters praying during a performance. After two summers she told Karl she would stay home.

He telephoned her every day. Then, on returning home, he tried to help with household chores. Helen wished he wouldn't. "As graceful as he was in air, so was he clumsy on the ground," she recalled. "He couldn't put up a picture hook without banging his thumb. Once he was painting a wall and he fell off the ladder and broke two fingers."

In January 1962, The Great Wallendas took their famous pyramid to the Shrine Circus in Detroit. During the second night's performance, the pyramid moved out smoothly at the command of Gunther, the last under-stander. At mid-wire, it paused dramatically as Jana, the top-mounter, rose to her feet on the chair, balanced between Karl and Herman. Then the 1300-pound pyramid continued its slow, even pace to the terminal platform. About 15 feet from the end of the wire, Dieter Schepp, the front under-stander, suddenly stopped and his pole inexplicably wavered. Karl called out in German, "What's the matter?"

Schepp cried, "I can't hold any longer." The pole slipped from his grasp and he toppled 35 feet to the arena floor (he would die later that night). Karl, who had been standing on the bar yoked between Schepp and Dick Faughnan, fell, striking and grabbing the wire as his leg got twisted between the wire and a guy line. Faughnan, Karl's son-in-law, fell to the dirt-packed concrete (he died 35 minutes later), followed by Karl's adopted son Mario, the third under-stander (he suffered a spinal injury that would paralyze him for life from the waist down). Gunther, the last under-stander, kept both his pole and his balance. His father, Herman, crashed into the wire, gashing his head but managing to clutch the wire with both hands. Jana fell, striking Karl in the back with an impact that he thought would split him in two. She grabbed his leg as he caught her arm.

Gunther took a step to Herman, "Are you all right, Dad?"

"Yes, I can make it to the platform. Help Karl."

Gunther stepped over his father's hands, and managed to reach Jana's other arm. The two men tried to pull her to the wire, but they had little strength left and even her 100-pound weight was too much for them. "Don't drop me," Jana pleaded. Gunther yelled for a net, but circus hands could find only a tumbling mat.

"They'll catch you," Gunther told her.

"No!" Jana screamed as she plummeted, feet first. She landed on one side of the mat, tearing it from the hands that grasped it. Her head struck the arena floor, causing a mild concussion.

Karl was hospitalized with a hairline crack in his pelvis, a double hernia and bruised ribs. Herman required only a patch on his gash. Of the seven in the pyramid, only Gunther escaped injury.

The day after the accident Herman, Gunther and a backup performer climbed the ladder for the evening performance. Karl wept as he watched them on television in his hospital room. On the following morning he was running a fever of 102° and hurt all over, but he asked his doctor to discharge him. "I feel like a dead man on the ground," he told Helen. "The wire is my life."

Grief was more bearable for him on the wire than on the ground. Karl gave a performance that day and concluded his act with a chair-stand on the shoulder bar between his brother and nephew, deliberately making the chair wobble to bring gasps from the spectators. He took his bows, then walked out of the arena, crying.

As Karl moved through middle-age he became increasingly popular as a "skywalker," a solo act in which he walked long cables between buildings and across sports stadiums. In 1970, at the age of 65, he contracted to do a 1000-foot walk, more than 700 feet above Tallulah Gorge in Georgia. About 30,000 people paid admission.

Climbing to the wire was a strength-sapping effort in itself. Then Karl hefted the 35-pound pole, looked across the gorge and stepped out. He trembled during the first few steps, then committed himself. Midway he stopped, slowly bent his knees, lowered the pole to the cable and did a headstand. A thunderous ovation echoed through the gorge.

Since the cable had about a 60-foot slack, the second half of the walk was uphill, and the pole grew heavier by the second. But Karl was grinning when he completed the 20-minute walk. Helen embraced him and silently vowed never again to watch him perform. His manager, Stephanie Shaw, also embraced him—and poured him a martini.

In early March, 1978, Karl and three protégés—his 17-year-old granddaughter Rietta, Farrell Hettig, 22, and Phillip Gikas, 25—went to Puerto Rico to join the Pan American Circus.

The three young performers adored their 73-year-old mentor. Rietta had fallen in love with the wire at age three and asked her grandfather—whom she affectionately called *Vati*—to teach her. Ten years later she was performing professionally. Farrell had trained and performed with Karl for seven years. Phillip had joined the troupe a year earlier and San Juan was to be his debut.

During the second week of the booking, the circus management asked Karl to do a skywalk between two resort hotels as a promotional stunt. Karl readily agreed.

But Stephanie Shaw was concerned. This walk seemed particularly hazardous. The wire would be strung between the 10th floors, 120 feet above the street, and there was no way to measure the updraft—or the gusts of wind from the sea. When Stephanie couldn't talk him out of it, she asked Helen to intervene.

Helen flew to San Juan and asked Karl to cancel the publicity walk. "Why do it, Karl?"

"I gave my word to a man I've known a long time."

"But it's windy out there. I'd rather you break your word than your neck."

"Helen, it's just a breeze. I've made longer walks in worse winds."

Helen sighed and gave up. On Tuesday she and Karl roamed around Old San Juan, hand-in-hand. "They were like young lovers," Phillip remembers.

About 10:30 the following morning a crowd began gathering in the street. Helen accompanied Karl to the hotel room where he would begin his walk. She sat stiffly on a couch, away from the window. Rietta and Phillip watched from the street. Farrell went to the room where the walk would terminate. Karl checked the wind. It was about 12 m.p.h. on the ground, with much higher gusts.

Shortly after 11, Karl, carrying a 33-pound, 24-foot pole, stepped out on the wire. The crowd quieted. He took five steps forward, then hesitated. The gusts were picking up. He took one step backward, paused, then decisively moved forward.

About midway the wind ballooned his shirt and whipped his trousers. After another some 15 steps Karl bent his knees as if to reduce his profile to the wind. Rietta saw the balancing pole waver and knew that Karl's situation was perilous. She shrieked. "Sit down, *Vati*, sit!"

Karl bent his knees as if to take the sitting position, then grimaced as his feet slipped from the wire. He grabbed for the wire with his right hand and momentarily caught it. But he held on to the pole with his left hand. *Never drop the pole.* Then the wind turned the pole, pulling him from the wire. As he plummeted to the street he grasped the pole in both hands in the professional elbows-crooked wire-walking position.

Helen heard a commotion from the street and froze as she

recognized cries of anguish and horror. Then there was a pounding on her door and she heard Rietta cry, "Let me in, let me in!"

Helen slowly opened the door. She looked at her granddaughter, and said, "He fell."

"Yes."

"He's dead."

"Yes." Rietta clutched Helen in her arms. "Say something, *Mutti* [grandmother]," Rietta cried. "Cry." But Helen couldn't. The time for tears and loneliness would be later. Now, there was only paralyzing shock.

The three protégés decided to do the matinee that day. Each knew that it was what Karl would have wanted. He strongly believed that "the show must go on."

"Doing the matinee was our way of saying that we loved him," Phillip said. After the performance Rietta, Farrell and Phillip took bows to a standing ovation. When they straightened up, their cheeks were glistening.

Karl's death did not surprise Herman and Gunther. It was a piece of sad news that they expected to hear some day. "It was the way he wanted to go," Herman said.

When Gunther told his six-year-old daughter, Lisa, she said, "But Uncle Karl had a long and good life, didn't he?"

Until his very last minute.

Melancholy Clown

by John Culhane

THE MELANCHOLY CLOWN was playing solitaire on top of the circus wagon. He wasn't getting good cards, so he looked even sadder than usual. Then, at last, he got a good card—and that never-quite-quenched look of hope lighted up his face. He was about to slap the card down when a gust of wind blew the game away.

The good ones always seemed to get away from Weary Willie. Sometimes, it was because he didn't try hard enough. He would hang around the seal act with a frying pan in his hand, hoping one of the fish thrown to the seals would come to him by mistake. (But a mistake in one's favor is as rare under the Big Top as it is at your bank.) Other times, it was because he tried too hard. He would crack open a peanut with a sledgehammer. I can see him now, poking at the pulverized shell, looking for pieces of nutmeat.

Emmett Kelly is an unforgettable man because, in Willie, he created an unforgettable character. Kelly once described to me the character he played for 45 years: "Weary Willie is a melancholy little hobo who always gets the short end of the stick and never has any good luck—but he never loses hope and keeps on trying." Millions of us recognized ourselves in that clown who never stopped believing his dreams would come true.

Emmett Kelly was born in Sedan, Kan., on December 9, 1898. His Irish-immigrant father was a section foreman for the Missouri-Pacific railroad, and his mother was a Bohemian girl whose family ran a boardinghouse. Circus colleagues came to see Kelly as a lonely, unhappy man with a terrific desire for

Melancholy Clown 75

acceptance and approval—and Kelly himself realized this was true. He grew up on a farm in southern Missouri and never forgot his anger when kids at school called him "The Irish Potater," and, finally, just "Tater," because his parents were immigrants.

Like Walt Disney, who was also a Missouri farm boy in the early years of this century, Kelly started out to be a cartoonist. One day in 1920, sitting at his drawing board at the Adagram Film Co. in Kansas City, Kelly drew a clown character who was a hobo, the kind of clown he would eventually become. He enjoyed drawing and animating little cartoon advertisements because some of them made people laugh; he later admitted that he spent a lot of his pay going to movie houses to hear people laugh at his cartoons.

But Kelly had another ambition: he wanted to be a star, a trapeze artist with the circus. He flabbergasted his boss at Adagram by turning down a raise when he got a chance to go with Howe's Great London Circus as a trapeze performer—who had to work extra as a clown.

Kelly's trapeze work proved so inept that he was told to stick with clowning. But like Weary Willie—who hadn't even been born yet except as a drawing—he just kept on trying. And he actually got better.

During his 1923 season with John Robinson's Circus, Kelly fell in love with Eva Moore, who did a sister act in double trapeze with the same show. Emmett and Eva eloped. Soon the newlyweds were featured in their own double-trapeze act.

When Eva became pregnant, Emmett tried to increase their income by coming up with a new clown character. He remembered the sad-faced hobo he had created in Kansas City, and based his costume and makeup on that. The boss clown was not impressed. He said that Kelly's tramp impersonation was "too dirty, too scruffy for the circus." Kelly finished out the season as a traditional whiteface clown.

For several years after Emmett Kelly, Jr., was born, Emmett Sr. and Eva did their trouble-trapeze act. But his dream of co-starring with his wife was smashed by the Great Depression. The Sells-Floto Circus, which had hired "The Aerial Kellys," closed down. Neither Kelly had a contract for the circus season of 1932 when Emmett received an offer to work as a full-time clown with the Hagenbeck-Wallace Circus. He accepted and decided that, win or lose, he would bring his sad little cartoon tramp to life under the Big Top. What he did in the next three years was to create a character clown who was a caricature of a type becoming all too familiar in Depression America—the sad hobo.

In 1935, Kelly joined the new Cole Brothers and Clyde Beatty Combined Circus. The trapeze act was not booked; Eva Kelly stayed behind with their two sons, and the marriage gradually fell apart.

After his divorce, circus folk noticed that Kelly was becoming increasingly melancholy, and this melancholy seemed to be affecting his "Weary Willie" character—for the better. It was the old story of the performer turning into a workaholic to keep his mind off personal problems.

After appearing in London for three years and in a Broadway musical, Kelly joined Ringling Bros. and Barnum & Bailey when they opened in Madison Square Garden in 1942. He was to stay with "The Greatest Show on Earth" for 14 years—the years of his greatest fame.

There, Kelly invented an intimate style of pantomime that is in the circus yet almost independent of it. Willie's cabbage was typical of this style. All during the show, he would wander among the audience and performers, carrying a wilted head of raw cabbage. Kelly figured that was as much as a hobo could count on for regular meals and he nibbled delicately on a leaf from time to time.

Ringling Bros. had never before permitted a clown to "freelance" like this, but they were wise enough to recognize the importance of what Kelly called his "continuity of character." He would participate in other performers' acts—but always in character. Riding comedian Lucio Cristiani, for instance, would purposely miss a somersault from the back of one galloping horse to another. Weary Willie would run up with a ladder and solicitously sweep the second horse's back so that Lucio wouldn't slip again.

"He made *me* laugh," says "Prince Paul" Alpert, who has been a clown with Ringling Bros. for 34 years. In an arena full of raucous clowns, explains Prince Paul, Willie would draw attention to himself by being very quiet and gentle. Right there in the middle of the performance, he would "hoe" a garden and start to "plant" it. Then he'd imagine the crops he'd have, get hungry and eat all his seeds. Critics called Kelly the greatest pantomime clown of the modern circus.

Melancholy Clown

If he was becoming an ever greater clown, Kelly was no luckier in love. In 1944, at age 45, he married 18-year-old Mildred Ritchie, also a circus performer. But he was still married to his work, and a few months later his bride told him that she was in love with a boy back home. Kelly gave her a divorce.

Typically, Kelly turned his unluckiness and pain into a pantomime comedy. Willie would find an attractive woman in the audience and focus on her one of his most famous expressions; he would look captivated, enraptured, enchanted, infatuated, and heartsmitten. He would offer his heart's desire a leaf of his cabbage. Some women would get uncontrollable giggles. Willie would pretend to see their laughter as rejection and walk sadly away.

One of Kelly's saddest real-life experiences took place on July 6, 1944. He was sitting outside the Big Top in Hartford, Conn., waiting for waltz music that would announce Karl Wallenda's human pyramid bicycling across the tightwire. Then hopefully-helpful Weary Willie would walk into the center ring directly underneath the Wallendas and spread out a tiny handkerchief in which to catch the family if they fell.

Just as the music began, somebody ran by, shouting, "Fire!" Kelly's first impulse was to try to put it out. Beside his trunk was a bucket of water for washing off his makeup after the show. He grabbed the bucket and ran toward the blazing Big Top, making poor headway in his flapping clown shoes. But the flames were already eating great stretches of canvas. The crowd was in panic. Many who had pushed through the exits now realized that they had lost loved ones—and were fighting to get back inside.

Emmett Kelly, the clown who never spoke in public, kept screaming: "You can't get back in there! Keep moving! Keep moving!"

He would always remember the little girl who came out of the burning tent crying for her mother. He pulled her from the stampeding crowd and said, "Listen, honey—you go over there and wait for your mommy. She'll come along soon." Kelly never learned whether or not that girl found her mother.

Within ten minutes on that terrible day, 168 people had been burned or trampled to death. And for millions of Americans the central pathetic image of that tragedy was an amateur photographer's snapshot of Weary Willie trying to put out the greatest circus fire in history with a bucket of wash water.

Many thought they saw a new depth to Kelly's clowning after all his private and public misfortunes. With simple gags that he had been doing for years, he suddenly seemed able to achieve Chaplin's ideal of making audiences laugh through their tears. And he found happiness at last in his third marriage, in 1955, to Elvira Gebhardt, one of the Four Whirlwinds, an acrobatic act Ringling found in Germany. He would have two daughters from that marriage.

Kelly left the circus in 1957 to join the old Brooklyn Dodgers, acting as a sort of hobo-clown mascot for the team known as "Dem Bums." Then, for the next 20 years, he found other non-circus roles for Weary Willie on television shows, in commercials, at nightclubs.

But Kelly was at his best with the circus: he provided the counterpoint to those glittering success stories in the wild animal cage and on the flying trapeze. His ragged hobo costume, putty nose, mournful eyes and battered derby said, "There is failure in life, too"—while the little gags he repeated from one end of the Big Top to the other said, "And there is starting over."

I'll always remember the time he made me cry. It was in 1953 in Rockford, Ill. I had seen Kelly several times before, but never walking so slow, never looking so sad. He was dragging a limp broom, and I guessed he was going to do his famous spotlight gag. Yes, there was the spotlight, shining into the ring, and now he had seen it, and was trying to sweep it up.

At first, he seemed to be succeeding. As Weary Willie swept, the circle of light grew smaller and smaller. Finally, only a flicker was left. From somewhere in his oversized, tattered black coat, he produced a dustpan, and swept up even this tiny residue of light.

Successful at last, he slung the broom over his shoulder and started to leave the ring—only to see, in front of him, another circle of light, just as large as the last. Patiently, he started sweeping all over again.

And then Willie added the little extra that touched the audiences to the heart. He blew up a balloon too big, and it burst. His expression made me think of all the children who lose something beautiful. With the broken balloon, he did exactly what a child would do: he gave it a little funeral and buried it, right there in the dirt under the Big Top.

Melancholy Clown

Much later in the show, during an act involving high-flying trapeze artists such as Kelly had once dreamed of being, I thought of that balloon, buried like so many of our dreams, and my eyes filled with tears. I laughed at myself for being so sentimental—and realized suddenly that Emmett Kelly's Weary Willie was the sentimental dreamer in us all.

On March 28, 1979, the very day "The Greatest Show on Earth" opened at Madison Square Garden in New York for its 109th circus season, 80-year-old Emmett Kelly suffered a heart attack and died in the front yard of his home in Sarasota, Fla. When comedian Red Skelton was told, he said, "I guess the angels needed a laugh."

Woody Guthrie's Hard Travels

by John Reddy

WOODY GUTHRIE was nothing much to look at—a wiry, weather-beaten bantam of a man, with a thin, intense face topped by a mop of frizzy black hair. He spent most of his life drifting around the country, playing his guitar and singing his folk songs. His flat Southwestern twang of a voice was like an old shoe: worn and cracked from long use, but comfortable.

Yet a capacity crowd of 3000 jammed New York's Carnegie Hall on a bitter night in January, 1968, to pay tribute to the footloose balladeer who had died tragically not long before. In the emotion-charged concert, eight of America's top folk singers sang Guthrie's best-loved songs, now part of America's heritage. It was their bow of gratitude to the wispy little man whose life and songs have made him a legend. For although folk songs have been part of the American scene since the arrival of the first settlers, it was Guthrie who touched off the folk singing boom of the '60s. So striking was his impact that he inspired most of the era's top singers, including Bob Dylan, and created a new kind of folk music popular around the world.

Woody's life was haunted by tragedy; from beginning to end it was a succession of calamities. Yet he never surrendered to the fate which treated him so cruelly, continuing even into his last pain-racked years to write hopefully of the joy of living. "I hate a song that makes you think you were born to lose," he once said. "I am out to sing songs that will prove to you that this is your world and that if it has hit you pretty hard and knocked you for a dozen loops, no matter what color, what size you are, you can take pride in yourself and in your work." He roamed the country recording what he saw in more than

Woody Guthrie's Hard Travels 81

1000 songs. Many, like "This Land Is Your Land" and "So Long," are folk classics that will probably endure as long as there are people to sing them. He sang of the grandeur and beauty of the country. He was almost drunk with the wonder of America.

Woodrow Wilson Guthrie was born in 1912 in the little town of Okemah, in the sand hills of Oklahoma—"one of the singingest, square-dancingest, yellingest, preachingest, talkingest, laughingest, cryingest of our ranch towns," Woody recalled. He soaked up the music around him. From his mother he learned the old sad country ballads; from his father, a prosperous land dealer, square-dance music and the blues. A black shoeshine boy taught him the harmonica, and he taught himself how to pick out tunes on a guitar borrowed from a bootlegger.

Then, almost overnight, Woody's carefree childhood turned into a nightmare: One of the family's homes burned down; another was torn away in a cyclone. A sister was burned to death. His mother died of Huntington's disease—a mysterious degeneration of the nerves—and his father lost every cent when the Depression hit.

As a teen-ager, Woody was taken in by a family of 13. He dropped out of high school and sold papers, picked cotton, drilled wells, painted signs and told fortunes. "I done might near everything," he said. When he was 17, he joined the swelling ranks of "Okies" fleeing the Dust Bowl.

Thus began Woody's lifetime of wandering. With guitar slung over his shoulder, he roamed the country, riding freights, working when he could find work, putting to music what he saw and heard and felt, in such songs as "Hard Traveling," "Goin' Down This Old Dusty Road," "Union Maid" and "Pastures of Plenty." "Everywhere I went, I throwed my hat down and sang for tips," he said. He sang in the migrant camps and shantytowns of almost every state in the Union.

Along the way, Woody acquired a wife and three children. They settled in Los Angeles for a while, and Woody got a job on a small radio station singing his songs for a dollar a day. Back east in New York, Woody met Alan Lomax, who was collecting folk songs for the Library of Congress. Lomax remembers him with "his guitar slung behind his right shoulder. As he sang his Okie ballads, we seemed filled with the presence of all Woody's southwestern kin." Woody went on Lomax's

CBS radio show, and the broadcast won a national award as the best music performance of the year.

Woody might be called the originator of the protest song. While Cole Porter, Noel Coward and Lorenz Hart were writing sophisticated lyrics about high society, Woody was writing simple, rough-hewn songs about the dispossessed and migrant workers. "I would rather," he said, "sound like the ashcans of the early morning, like the longshoremen yelling, like the cowhands whooping, and like the lone wolf barking." Yet even these songs ended on what folk singer Pete Seeger called "a note of shining affirmation." Describing a group of drifters riding a freight train, he sang:

> This train don't carry no gamblers,
> Liars, thieves and big-shot ramblers;
> This train is bound for glory,
> This train!

Woody's salty, homespun uncurried appeal was such that he might have become a major performing star if he had been willing to compromise his talents. But he was too ornery for that. Once he and his singing group auditioned at the posh Rainbow Room in New York. The manager agreed to hire them if they would "dress up the act" by having the men wear overalls and the women sunbonnets. By way of reply, Woody began sardonically improvising verses: "The Rainbow Room is 60 stories high, they say—It's a long way back to the U.S.A." Then he walked out. "When people start talkin' about goin' somewhere," he once said, "I'm the kind of a guy who has already got up and went."

"Woody was the best ballad maker to come down the American pike," Alan Lomax says. "In many ways he was the most truthful and talented man of his generation." He lived with the Lomaxes while Lomax recorded three hours of songs and conversations with Woody for the Library of Congress. "He slept on the floor, wrapped in his lumber jacket, and had his dinner standing by the sink," Lomax remembers. "I don't want to get softened up," Woody told his host. "I'm a road man."

The period at the beginning of World War II was the most productive of Woody's life. After his wife Mary, despairing of his improvident ways, divorced him, Woody settled in a shabby old unheated house in Greenwich Village, where he composed dozens of songs, wrote a newspaper column, sang with a group called the Almanac Singers. He also wrote his autobiography, *Bound for Glory*, which, according to the *New York Times*, had "more triple-distilled essence of pure personality than any book in years." Pete Seeger remembers the night when Woody went to see the movie *Grapes of Wrath*, based on John Steinbeck's book about Dust Bowl refugees. Woody came home, sat down and began typing furiously. In the morning, he was asleep on the floor, the completed ballad of "Tom Joad" scattered around the typewriter. Steinbeck later said that the 26 verses of Guthrie's song said as much about the plight of the Okies as his Pulitzer Prize-winning book.

In 1943, Woody joined the Merchant Marine. In on three invasions, he was twice on ships torpedoed by German submarines. Both times he emerged without so much as getting his guitar (with its printed slogan "This machine kills Fascists") wet. "I fed 50 gunboys, washed their dirty dishes, scrubbed their greasy mess room and never graduated up or down in the whole time," he declared. He married Marjorie Mazia, a Martha Graham dancer, and after the war they settled on Coney Island. Here they had four children, whom they tried to support on what Marjorie made giving dancing lessons and the pittance Woody earned writing and singing. Woody cut stencils and cranked the mimeograph machine to put out a little book of his songs for 25 cents each.

This interval on Coney Island was one of the few tranquil times of Woody's restless life. They were chronically broke, but the house was always full of children and music. The whole family would pile into their old jalopy and drive around while Woody made up rhymes and songs about whatever they saw. "That was our social life," Marjorie Guthrie says. She recalls their son Arlo, who was to become a popular folk singer himself, running home breathless when he was in the sixth grade and blurting out, "Mom! Did you know they sing Woody's songs at school—even know the words?"

Yet, incredibly, there was more tragedy in store for Woody. One day he went to New Jersey to sing for a labor union. When he arrived home, carrying balloons for the kids, he found a note saying, "Come to the Coney Island Hospital at once." When he got there he found his four-year-old daughter Cathy dying from burns suffered in a flash fire at their home. With her loss and news of a son killed by a train, the children's songs that Woody had dashed off so joyously dried up.

Moreover, he began suffering from mysterious dizzy spells, acting moodily and irrationally—once even attempting suicide. Hospitalized, he was found to have the same malady that had claimed his mother's life. Typically, Woody treated the news lightheartedly: "It makes me feel drunk without paying my bartender one blue cent." Yet the disease gradually drained his strength and creativity. There came a day when the man who had almost exploded in song with the sheer exuberance of being alive could not even speak. Finally, as he lay near death, he began receiving the recognition his talent and unquenchable spirit merited.

The folk-singing boom, which Woody's songs had kindled, burst into a multimillion-dollar worldwide industry. Famous singers such as Peter, Paul and Mary, Judy Collins and Pete Seeger recorded his songs in best-selling albums. "This Land Is Your Land" was sung in schools along with "America the Beautiful." Critic Clifton Fadiman declared: "Guthrie's talent is a national possession—like Yellowstone or Yosemite." In April 1966, Interior Secretary Stewart Udall honored Guthrie for his "lifetime efforts to make the American people aware of their heritage and their land." The citation read: "You have articulated in your songs the struggles and deeply held convictions of those who love our land and fight to protect it." In presenting the citation to Marjorie Guthrie, Udall said that the Interior Department was proud that in its history it had had on its payroll two great poets: Woody Guthrie and Walt Whitman.

Woody's ordeal of illness lasted 15 years. In October, 1967, at the age of 55, he died. Then came the Carnegie Hall concert where the top folk singers of the day played his songs and actors Will Geer and Robert Ryan read from his writings. The audience joined them at the end in singing "This Land."* Many were in tears as the buoyant words of Woody's folk anthem stirred them:

> This land is your land, this land is
> my land

---

*© 1956 and 1958, Ludlow Music, Inc., N.Y. Used by permission.

From California to the New York
island.
From the redwood forests to the
Gulfstream waters.
This land was made for you and
me.

The Passionate Isadora Duncan

by Sir Frederick Ashton

SHE WAS banned in Boston, hissed in St. Louis, toasted in Paris, idolized in Munich. She was an American without a country, the first of the hippies, a flower child whose flaming red hair and violet eyes seared a path across four continents. She was Isadora Duncan, star-crossed in her personal life, yet a great artist who pioneered modern dance and strongly influenced the ballet and theater of today.

I first saw her dance in 1921 when I was a schoolboy in London. Dressed in a Greek-type chiffon tunic, she did Brahms waltzes, Isolde's death and the Chopin funeral march. With melancholy grace and irresistible intensity, she moved through her new dance form—so fluid, so different from rigid ballet. She felt that the ballet of those days distorted the human form, and she influenced it to accommodate her principles of natural, expressive movement. I was quite carried away, and went back to see her time and again. The way she used her hands and her arms, the way she ran across the stage—these I have adapted in my own ballets.

The public remembers her for the headlines she made; but to me her spiritual vitality and trail-blazing work as an artist transcend everything else. She was utterly sensational and outrageous, of course, but she was always deadly serious about her work.

The youngest of four children, born in San Francisco in 1878, Dora Angela Duncan recalled her childhood in terms of landlords clamoring for overdue rent, and hasty moves from one dingy place to another. Her father, a banker of sorts and

The Passionate Isadora Duncan

a fugitive from the police, deserted the family shortly before her birth. Her mother kept the brood together by giving piano lessons and knitting mittens and scarves, which the children peddled from door to door.

Dorita, as she was then called, started improvising little dances to classical romantic compositions when she was barely able to toddle. By the time she was ten, she had left school and started giving dancing lessons. In her mid-teens, she was slim, long-legged and lushly beautiful. She was dancing at a Chicago roof garden when she met impresario Augustin Daly, who offered her a job with his repertory company in New York. Not much of a success as an actress, she soon embarked on a series of dance recitals.

The scandals were not long in coming. This was an era when the word "leg" was never uttered in polite society. Yet here was Isadora scampering about the stage with bare arms, bare neck, bare legs, and just a few bits of chiffon here and there. Forty ladies exited in a huff in the middle of one appearance.

Few performers ever received such barbed reviews. One concluded with the announcement that she was going to London, "which is sad, considering that we are at peace with England at present."

London, however, was fascinated by Isadora from the beginning. Her vibrant beauty and lusty American directness captivated society. She danced in private homes, and three of her performances were under the patronage of none other than Princess Helena, daughter of Queen Victoria. In Paris, the reception was equally enthusiastic. Sculptor Auguste Rodin sketched her and said, "She has borrowed from nature that force which cannot be called talent, but which is genius."

Isadora's chaotic private life contrasted starkly with her artistic success. Her tragedy was that she could never reconcile love and art, nor could she live without both. In Budapest, in 1902, a Hungarian actor wanted to marry her. After a tempestuous love affair, she decided that domesticity was not for her. She met Prince Ferdinand of Bulgaria, who promptly offered her his Italian villa. She accepted, and court circles were scandalized.

Even more of a scandal was the bathing suit she wore there. Ladies in those days went swimming primly garbed in black with midi-skirts, and black shoes and stockings. Isadora appeared in a pale-blue tunic reaching just above the knee, low-necked, with little shoulder straps, minus stockings and shoes. The Prince used to walk past the bathing area, his opera glasses trained on Isadora, muttering, "Ah, Duncan! Wonderful, marvelous!"

She was commanding huge fees now as the toast of Europe. Berlin acclaimed her as "holy, godlike Isadora." (There she met stage designer Gordon Craig, who was to be the father of her first child, Deirdre, born in 1906.) In Munich, students pulled her carriage through the streets and cheered her performance with uproarious enthusiasm. Instead of spending her money on clothes, jewelry and furs, she decided to adopt 20 poor children and to establish a school in Germany to teach them her theories of art and movement. Her idea was to "give them a finer life, so that later they can spread joy and beauty like a glow over this sad earth."

However fanciful the school idea was, it obsessed her all her days. No matter where she went or what she did, it was her primary interest, and she tried to raise money for it. (The girls, when they were sufficiently trained to perform in public, became a troupe known as "The Isadorables." They danced in England, on the Continent, and in America.)

Isadora now stormed Russia, cradle of the classical ballet that she detested. There, in her simple costumes, against simple draperies, she danced the music of Gluck, Beethoven and Chopin. Russia's best-known ballerinas, including Anna Pavlova, came to see her. No less an expert than Sergei Diaghilev said that she gave "an irreparable jolt to the classic ballet of Imperial Russia." Prince Peter Lieven, patron of the ballet, said that she was "the first to bring out in her dancing the meaning of music, the first to *dance* the music and not dance *to* the music."

Dizzy with success, Isadora met Paris Singer, an heir to the sewing-machine fortune. Though he was married and the father of five, she had a son by him named Patrick. When Singer took her and all her pupils to the Riviera, it seemed as if she had everything she wanted: a successful career, money for her school, two children, acclaim. For three years, her happiness was complete. And then came April 19, 1913.

Isadora's two children, ages seven and two, and their nurse were being driven to Versailles. On a curve near the Seine, the car's engine stalled. Without putting on the emergency brake, the chauffeur got out to crank. Driverless, the car lurched forward and plunged into the Seine, 40 feet deep at that point. An hour and a half passed before the car could be located.

That night, after the bodies of Deirdre and Patrick were brought to Isadora's studio, hundreds of art students covered the shrubbery outside with white flowers. At the funeral, Isadora kept saying, "No tears, no tears. I want to be brave enough to make death beautiful, to help all the other mothers of the world who have lost their babies."

Frantically now, she plunged into the nomad's life, moving from Paris to New York to Naples to Montevideo, Buenos Aires, San Francisco, Athens. When World War I broke out, the "Marseillaise" became her greatest dance triumph. She danced it for the first time in April 1916, at the Trocadéro in Paris, as the German guns were battering Verdun.

For her performance Isadora was dressed completely in red. Her deep feelings showed in her intense and superbly evocative movements. As she reached *"Aux armes, citoyens!"* the audience, weeping, rose and burst into the refrain. Finally, in one swift motion, she tore off part of her costume, leaving one breast bare. She looked the personification of Dame Liberty.

Yet the recognition Isadora wanted most was in America, and this she never had. Indianapolis, Louisville, Milwaukee were shocked by her. In her open, naïve way, Isadora would ask, "Why should one part of my body be more immoral than another?" In a Boston press interview, she maintained that she would rather dance nude than "strut in the half-clothed suggestiveness" of chorus girls. She told a Boston audience, "You once were wild here. Don't let them tame you. You don't know what beauty is!" Whereupon she tore down her tunic and pointed to her body, saying, "This—this is beauty!"

She caused a further furor when, in 1922, she married the Russian poet Sergei Esenin, 17 years her junior. In addition to being one of the finer poets of his time, Esenin was a supreme egoist and a constant drinker. He had been lionized at home in the Soviet Union, but it was Isadora who stole the show every time they were together. This he could not stand. His jealousy of her bordered on paranoia. He beat her, robbed her, betrayed her, tried to kill her.

One night, in Berlin, Isadora was weeping over an album of pictures of her dead children. It was her most treasured possession, and she never let it out of her keeping. Esenin arrived in a drunken rage, snatched the album, flung it into the fire, and stalked out.

Ultimately, at the Hotel Angleterre in Leningrad, in the very room where he and Isadora had honeymooned, Esenin hanged himself. But first he slashed a wrist and wrote his last poem in blood: "Good-by, my friend, good-by! You are still in my breast, beloved."

Although Isadora was not his only widow, the Soviet courts discovered that she was still his legal heir. From his five volumes of poetry they awarded her 300,000 rubles in royalties. She was virtually destitute, but she gave the money to his mother and sisters.

The twilight shadows were upon her now. The once-flaming hair was streaked with purple dye. She was racked with superstition and obsessed with the idea that blackbirds were the harbingers of death. Shortly before her children had drowned, she insisted that she had seen three blackbirds circling the ceiling of their room.

But even in those autumnal days of 1927 in Nice, Isadora never lost her zest for life. One evening she had a date for an after-dinner drive in a Bugatti sports car. As she waited, she turned on the gramophone. The record she played was the hit "Bye Bye Blackbird." She was dancing to it when her escort arrived. She picked up a long red shawl and, in a characteristic gesture, flung it around her neck and let it trail over one shoulder to the ground. As she stepped into the car, she waved to friends. "So long!" she called, laughing. "I'm off to glory."

The words were her last. The low two-seater lurched forward, the end of her shawl caught in the spokes of a rear wheel, and in an instant her neck was broken. As the shawl was cut away and her body lifted from the car, the tinny gramophone echoed across the cobbled street:

> "Pack up all my care and woe,
>   Here I go singing low...
>   Blackbird Bye Bye"

The Man No Lock Could Hold

by James Stewart-Gordon

IN MAY 1903, Harry Houdini was appearing at a Moscow cabaret. To publicize his act, he called on Lebedev, the gigantic bearded chief of Moscow's secret police. Houdini asked to be put in jail to demonstrate how easily he could escape. Lebedev, who knew of Houdini's reputation, smilingly refused. "How about the Carette then?" Houdini suggested.

Lebedev laughed. The Carette—a six-foot-square, steel-sheathed cube—was used to transport dangerous criminals to Siberia. It had only two openings—a tiny barred window, just eight inches square, and a solid-steel door. The key which locked the Carette's door in Moscow activated a device which could be opened only by a second key, kept by the prison governor in Siberia 2000 miles away. "No one has ever escaped from the Carette," Lebedev told Houdini. "I accept your challenge. But once we lock you up, you will have to be sent to Siberia to be released."

"I'll get out," Houdini insisted.

Stripped naked, searched for concealed picklocks, handcuffed and chained, Houdini was shoved into the tiny cell. The cell was then locked and moved so that it's door was hidden against a wall in the prison yard. Twenty-eight minutes later, dripping with sweat, Houdini staggered out from behind the cell. Amazed, the police rushed to examine the Carette. The seal on its door was intact, the handcuffs and chains which had bound the prisoner were still locked. But Houdini was free. How he did it remains a mystery.

Harry Houdini—escape artist, magician, author of more

than 40 books, inventor, film star, aviator, showman and psychologist—swept through the world like a hurricane between 1895 and 1926, leaving behind him a trail of vanquished prison cells, vacated handcuffs and gasping audiences. Sir Arthur Conan Doyle, creator of Sherlock Holmes, accused him of having "supernatural powers." A reporter in Germany, stunned by the ease with which Houdini was able to free himself from a sealed packing case without disturbing a single nail, declared, "Houdini has the ability to de-materialize his body and pass it through walls." In Washington, D.C., a handcuffed Houdini jauntily escaped from a maximum-security cell in the federal penitentiary. He then playfully moved 18 other locked-up prisoners to different cells before escaping to the outside—all in about 27 minutes.

Behind every exercise of Houdini's art was a painstaking attention to detail. To prepare for his demolition of claims that Indian fakirs possessed supernatural powers enabling them to be buried alive, he spent endless hours nailed inside a box while assistants timed his ability to remain conscious with a limited supply of oxygen. Finally satisfied that he could match the fakirs' performance, he climbed into a coffin, crossed hands on his breast and allowed himself to be sealed inside. An hour and a half later he was released, pale but very much alive. Snorting at suggestions of supernatural powers, he told reporters, "It's just a trick. I don't eat or drink for 24 hours beforehand and I remain absolutely still; that way I don't use up much oxygen."

In his pursuit and exposure of fake spirit mediums, Houdini was relentless. His most famous case revolved around the blond, beautiful Boston medium, Margery. So convincing was her performance—which featured a bell box under the séance table by which the spirits supposedly answered questions—that the staid and lofty *Scientific American* was prepared to pay her its prize of $2500 for genuine contact with the world of spooks. In July, 1924, Houdini—who himself made an open offer of $10,000 to any medium who produced psychic phenomena he could not duplicate by natural means—canceled a stage engagement and journeyed to Boston to challenge Margery. Stipulating that he was to be seated next to the medium, Houdini sensitized his right leg—which was to be pressed against Margery's left during the séance—by binding it below the knee with a tight elastic bandage on the morning of the séance. By séance time, the leg was so tender it could detect a butterfly's sneeze at ten paces. After the lights went out and Margery had gone into her trance, Houdini edged up his trouser leg, exposing his bare skin to Margery's silken calf. When Margery made an all-but-imperceptible move of her foot to press a hidden button—a maneuver Houdini had long suspected—the master's leg vibrated like a well-struck gong. Jumping to his feet, Houdini proclaimed Margery a fake, denounced the entire affair and went back to his stage work with his $10,000, and *Scientific Amercian's* $2500, still intact.

Offstage, Houdini was a shy, diminutive man (just five feet five inches), who wore rumpled suits and spoke in a mess of mangled verbs and tenses. Onstage, however, everything changed. Houdini seemed to swell to giant's stature; his gray-blue eyes glowed, his diction became impeccable, his clothing was immaculate and his mastery of his craft so outstanding that, as the late Fulton Oursler said, "That man could escape from anything—except your memory."

The Great Houdini was born Ehrich Weiss in Budapest, Hungary, in 1874, the fifth of eight children of a poor rabbi who immigrated to Wisconsin when Ehrich was still an infant. As a small boy, Ehrich sold newspapers, shined shoes and worked in a Milwaukee luggage shop where, during his free time, he liked to tinker with the locks on trunks and valises. At 16, after reading the autobiography of Robert-Houdin, the great 19th-century French magician and diplomat, he began to dream of becoming a great magician himself. When he was 17, the family resettled in New York, and Harry Houdini, as he now called himself, became an apprentice cutter in a tie factory during the day and a magician whenever someone would hire him for an evening or weekend show. Using a friend or his brother Theo as his partner in a spectacular quick-switch trunk escape, Harry played firemen's picnics, boilermakers' soirees and lodge halls.

In June, 1894, he met a young Brooklyn girl named Bess Rahner, and married her after a two-day courtship. The marriage lasted 32 happy years, until Houdini's death.

In 1900, convinced that he was ready for the big time, Houdini took his act to New York. But New York was indifferent. Stung, Houdini told Bess, "Pack your bags. We're going to London." There Harry approached the manager of the Alhambra Theatre—the city's most important music hall—showed him his scrapbook and asked for a tryout. The manager was unimpressed by Houdini's success with American handcuffs. "Go down to Scotland Yard," he said, "and if you can get out of *their* handcuffs I might give you a try."

Houdini went to "The Yard," and persuaded a detective superintendent to put him to the test. The detective led Harry to a pillar, handcuffed him to it, put on his hat and announced that he was going to lunch. "Wait a second!" Harry yelled after him. "I'll go with you!" Handing the opened handcuffs to the astonished inspector, he took his arm and led him through the door.

The story made every paper in England, and soon Harry's fame as "the man no fetter, no lock, no restraint can hold" spread all over Europe. In 1905, he came back to New York a celebrity.

The year 1913 marked a turning point for Houdini. His mother, who had been a profound force in his life, died while he was en route to Copenhagen. Unable to reconcile himself either to her loss or to his failure to be at her deathbed, he swallowed his skepticism and began to visit mediums and spiritualists in the hope of communicating with her. Each medium he visited proved a charlatan. The final straw came when, during one séance, a voice—speaking in Oxford-accented English—assured Harry that she was his mother and that she was happy in the "other world." Houdini's mother had never learned much English, and what little she did speak was unmistakably tinged with a Yiddish accent. Furious, Houdini launched into a savage crusade which made him the terror of every table-rapper and séance fraud.

In 1923, at the age of 50, Houdini began to talk of retirement. His popularity, bolstered by film appearances, had never been higher. Yet he was filled with an impending sense of death. He saw omens in strange happenings: the unexplained sound of his mother calling his name, the bizarre reactions of animals in his presence. In New York, on a rainy night in October, 1926, he phoned Joseph Dunninger, the famous magician and mentalist, and asked him to come to his house. When Dunninger arrived, Houdini explained that he wanted Dunninger to help him take some boxes to a storage place on the other side of the city. As they were driving away, Houdini suddenly told Dunninger to turn back. They arrived before the house, and Houdini got out of the car. He stood silently in the rain and then got back in. "I just wanted one last look," Houdini said. "I'll never see it again alive."

Houdini left soon after on a U.S. and Canadian tour. In Montreal, he gave a lecture at McGill University on the fakery of spiritualism. His talk infuriated local mediums, who were unanimous in denouncing him. On the morning of his final appearance in Montreal, he was lying exhausted on the couch in his dressing room when several students who had been at his lecture arrived. One of them, who wanted to sketch Houdini, had been invited. The others had come without invitation. Suddenly, one of the uninvited guests began to question Houdini's views on spiritualism. Too tired to argue, Houdini tried to placate the visitor, but only succeeded in arousing him. "Is it true," the man cried, "that you are so strong you can take a punch anywhere on your body without injury?" Houdini mumbled vaguely, and before he could prepare himself the man began raining sledgehammer blows on his solar plexis.

Although badly hurt, Houdini refused to show it; in fact, he went onstage for that day's performance. But the next few days were a confusion of agony as he seemed to weave in and out of consciousness. In Detroit, he collapsed and was taken to Mercy Hospital, suffering from a ruptured appendix and peritonitis. Bess, who had also been sick, now joined her husband in the hospital. On October 20, a fading Houdini struggled with his final problem. "Mother never reached me," he gasped to Bess. "If anything happens you must be prepared. Remember this message: 'Rosabelle, believe.'" Shortly afterward, Houdini was dead—strangely enough, on Halloween.

But his death did not end the story. Throughout the years that followed, the same mediums whose tricks Houdini had so industriously exposed began reporting that they were the recipients of messages sent by Houdini from the Great Beyond. "If Houdini keeps this message stuff up," commented Will Rogers, "he's going to put Western Union out of business."

For the next ten years, Bess, on the anniversary of his death, sat in their home before a candle-lit portrait of the master, and waited for his signal. It never came. In 1936, ten years after his death, she extinguished the light.

But among magicians there are still some who go out each year at Halloween to the place where Houdini is buried. And there they wait, hoping for a sign that the unconquerable Houdini has been able to make his greatest escape.

Grand Eccentrics

Tumultuous Tallulah

by Anita Loos

I HAVE spent a lifetime fashioning fictional ladies in novels and on stage and screen. Some of these characters, like Lorelei Lee in *Gentlemen Prefer Blondes*, have done right well by themselves and by me. Yet I had one favorite character who would scarcely have been believed if she had appeared in fictional form: Tallulah Bankhead, the legendary actress.

Tallulah was the blithest, most vital spirit I've ever encountered. She was witty, gregarious, outrageous — and never dull for one solitary moment of her tumultuous life. Everything about her was uniquely hers: her vivid personality, her husky voice, even her name. "Tallulah is a name to inflame the flank of a Pullman car, to blow on a bugle," her friend Richard Maney said. "It is a name to rally the tribesman to battle, to summon the faithful to prayer."

Perhaps the most striking facet of Tallulah's antic personality was that sultry voice and the conversational gushers that went with it. A cynic once described her voice as sounding like "a man pulling his foot out of a bucket of yogurt," but the low, throaty tones beguiled millions. So non-stop was her conversation that columnist Earl Wilson said you had to make a reservation five minutes ahead of time to get a word in with her. Both her scorns and her loyalties were fierce, and her friendships were all-consuming, prompting librettist Howard Dietz to sigh, "A day away from Tallulah is like a month in the country."

I first met Tallulah the day she arrived in New York, a slim

15-year-old beauty from Alabama intent on becoming an actress. She was chaperoned by her beloved Auntie Louise. When they sought an appropriate place to live, fate unaccountably led them to the Algonquin Hotel on 44th Street. It was as if Alice had walked smack into Wonderland without having to go down the rabbit hole. For, on her first day in New York, Tallulah was under the same roof with the aristocracy of stage and screen—John and Ethel Barrymore, Douglas Fairbanks and many others. At the time, Constance Talmadge and Conway Tearle had come on from Hollywood to do a movie script of mine, and I was with them.

Tallulah had no letters of introduction or any training to back up her theatrical ambitions. She had only her fresh young beauty and an unusual gift for mimicry. Her first move was to take up a post in the hotel lobby where she could sit and gaze at the show folk. But her rose-leaf beauty was so dazzling that in no time at all the show folk were gazing back. She confided her acting ambitions to our director, John Emerson, and he forthwith gave her a role as an extra in our movie. Tallulah was so exhilarated that at first we put her down as a stagestruck youngster, too pretty to be anything but dumb. She soon set us straight!

At the Algonquin, she met Alex Woollcott, the waspish drama critic who presided over the Algonquin's celebrated Round Table. Shortly afterward, he condescended to take Tallulah to an opening night. She sat demurely through the first act of a turgid Maeterlinck drama. Then, nudging Woollcott, she murmured, "You know, there's less in this than meets the eye." Next, she attended a bad movie put out by an independent producer. "What I don't see," she mused, "is what the producer has to be independent about." These quips launched her reputation as one of the lively wits of our time.

Tallulah came of a distinguished southern family. Her uncle was a Senator from Alabama, and her father was Speaker of the House of Representatives. Her conversational binges, often compared to filibusters, may have been a legacy from these Dixie lawmakers. In any case, she soon became the darling of the literati who gathered at the Algonquin. Her achievements, however, did not keep pace with her personal splash. She got a few small parts on Broadway, but failed to evoke any huzzas among audiences.

Tumultuous Tallulah

It was in England that Tallulah won stardom. She went there on the advice of an astrologer and got a role in a trifle called *The Dancers*. Her ebullient performance turned it into a long-running hit. At the tender age of 21 she was the rage of London.

I was living there at the time, and had a chance to see Tallulah's impact. Her admirers would queue up more than a day in advance of an opening performance. Her daring clothes, her tossing mane of honey-colored hair, her prowling walk and numerous beaux were the talk of the town. Her portrait was painted by famed artist Augustus John. She hobnobbed with Lloyd George and Lord Beaverbrook, with Ramsay MacDonald and Lawrence of Arabia. Once she invited Colonel Lawrence to a party, explaining, "I adore brave men." "What if he declines?" a friend asked. "He isn't *that* brave," she growled.

The staid British loved her uninhibited behavior, and she, in turn, loved to shock. Once she did cartwheels for a block on Piccadilly at 3 a.m. Like the ladies she sometimes portrayed, she was a hussy with a heart of gold, a gentler Jezebel. "I'm pure as the driven slush," she liked to say. When reminded that the biblical Jezebel was thrown to the dogs, Tallulah retorted, "Yes, but first she rode with kings and princes."

After eight years in London, Tallulah was lured back to her native heath by a movie contract. I was in Hollywood writing scenarios, so our paths crossed once again. For a time we both stayed at the old Hollywood Hotel, where a number of elderly people—as nice as they were dull—lived in retirement. None of us who worked in films ever paid them much notice. But Tallulah did. She used to sit on the porch while a little old lady taught her to crochet. Tallulah had no intention of ever crocheting anything, but she patiently let the lady teach her, out of pure kindness. "You can say all you want about the wickedness of film stars," the old lady told me, "but that little Bankhead girl is as sweet and unspoiled as if she lived in Des Moines."

Later on in Hollywood, I had a house with a pool, and Tallulah used to come to swim. Always ahead of her time, she believed in bathing in the buff. But it happened that a new house was being built next door, and when Tallulah plunged into the pool in the altogether, the construction crew would happily climb a scaffold to enjoy the show. I was busy at the studio at the time, and didn't know of Tallulah's antics until my new neighbor called to complain that work on his house was lagging alarmingly. I explained the situation to Tallulah, who obligingly donned a suit for her swimming thereafter.

After the Hollywood interlude, Tallulah returned to Broadway. "Miss Bankhead, I've heard a lot about you," columnist Walter Winchell greeted her. "Well," quipped Tallulah, "it's all true."

Tallulah's performing was so rollicking that she kept many a rickety vehicle going long after it might have expired. "I have seen Tallulah electrify the most idiotic, puerile plays," novelist Arnold Bennett observed. But she did get a few really good roles. As the cruel and rapacious Regina Giddens in *The Little Foxes*, she was hailed as a genuine dramatic star. She also scored a notable success as Sabina in *The Skin of Our Teeth*. Other ventures were less successful. When she played Cleopatra, one critic stilettoed, "Tallulah Bankhead barged down the Nile as Cleopatra—and sank."

The frenetic Bankhead career was further complicated by matrimony. After a brief courtship, she married a handsome actor named John Emery. She hurled herself into marriage with her customary total involvement. One night Emery was telling her about an argument he'd had with a man. "Oh, if I'd only been there," Tallulah said. "Why didn't you kill the louse?" With that, she hauled off and hit Emery in the eye.

Tallulah's eccentric whims and endless ebullience created a strain that eventually unraveled the matrimonial bonds. "It was like the rise, decline and fall of the Roman Empire," Emery sighed later.

Tallulah was extravagant in everything she did. She was a rabid baseball fan, and when you visited her, you always found several radio sets blaring—usually tuned to a game. Although she loved to drink, she went on the wagon one year in the hope that the sacrificial gesture would inspire her beloved New York Giants to win the World Series. It didn't.

Nevertheless, after the Allied disaster at Dunkirk in World War II, Tallulah again went on the wagon, vowing that she would not drink until Hitler was defeated. Recalling the futility of this tactic with the baseball Giants, a friend pleaded, "For heaven's sake, Tallulah, start drinking or we'll lose the war."

Ambition was never allowed to interfere with play in Tallulah's code, and I have often thought that she lived her life

Tumultuous Tallulah

as many of us would have if we had only dared. Her friends were athletes and bartenders, prelates and policemen. Although a deep-dyed southerner, she was chummy with heavyweight boxing champion Joe Louis and trumpeter Louis Armstrong. And she had rowdy camaraderie with newspapermen. When a magazine printed that she was 45 years old, she was furious. "Do I *look* 45?" she asked columnist Irving Hoffman. "Not anymore," Hoffman replied.

In the early 1950s, NBC asked Tallulah to star in a radio program, *The Big Show*. Thus millions of people who had never seen her on stage or screen were introduced to her inimitable voice and barbed asides. On one program, Frank Sinatra asked her why the flag in her apartment was at half-staff.

"It's for my dahling Giants," she intoned. "They lost the pennant."

"Oh," said Sinatra, "I didn't know you liked the national pastime."

"Dahling," she said, "I *am* the national pastime."

Tallulah was always beset by insomnia, and often spent the wee hours listening to a radio program called Big Joe's *Happiness Exchange*. Big Joe's program consisted of interviews with down-and-outers. Their harrowing tales never failed to touch Tallulah's heart, and before long the program became a two-way broadcast with Tallulah on the phone exchanging bits of philosophy with Big Joe and his derelicts. In later years, at dinner in her New York apartment, one could expect to meet not only old friends from the theater or Hollywood but also lonely outcasts who had appeared on Big Joe's program.

When Tallulah died in 1965, I was asked to deliver the eulogy. As I stood in the pulpit of St. Bartholomew's church on New York City's Park Avenue, reminiscing lovingly but frankly about Tallulah, a funny thing happened. Smiles began to light up the congregation. At first, I was startled. Smiles at a memorial service! Then I thought: how appropriate. Tallulah, who had brought laughter to so many, would have loved it. Looking out over the motley collection of hundreds of her friends—actors, athletes, down-and-outers she had befriended—I could almost hear her throaty, unforgettable voice prompting, "Dahling, tell them about the time I . . ."

Even though I delivered her eulogy, Tallulah herself once best summed up her life in the words of Edna St. Vincent Millay:

My candle burns at both ends;
It will not last the night;
But ah, my foes, and oh, my friends,
It gives a lovely light.

Is That *Really* Walter Matthau?

by Maurice Zolotow

As a UNIVERSAL STUDIOS tour bus was slowly winding past the stars' bungalows, the guide pointed to one tenanted by Walter Matthau, who had just completed his part as a scruffy bookmaker in *Little Miss Marker*. "Why, there he is now," she cried, as a tall man in a beautifully tailored silk suit shambled out the door toward a Mercedes sedan. "Look, folks! Walter Matthau—*in person!*" The bus halted. The visitors gawked.

Matthau looked at them, shaking his head sadly. He seemed to be tortured by a moral decision. Suddenly, he raised an arm and shouted in his distinctive nasal voice, "I am *not* Walter Matthau. This whole thing's a fake. Get your money back!"

Although the disappointed visitors marveled at the man's resemblance to the real Matthau, the guide just couldn't convince them that it *was* the star. So convincing is he as an actor that he can even successfully play Matthau *not* being Matthau.

Matthau the comedian of films is also a comedian in everyday life who loves people and loves even more to fool them. In 1966, when *Current Biography* inquired about his family background, he invented a fictional surname, Matuschanskayasky, and a father who had been a Catholic Eastern Rite priest in Tsarist Russia—before running afoul of Orthodox authorities by preaching papal supremacy. *Current Biography* printed the melodramatic story and for years newspapers retailed this fictional background as the real thing.

Though he has one of the most distinctive faces in the history of motion pictures, Matthau's protean personality somehow makes it exude a feeling of familiarity, reminding the most diverse people of their own favorite uncles.

"Anybody with a bulbous nose and beady eyes looks like me," he once remarked. "It's a fairly ordinary physiognomical phenomenon."

Matthau has a beautiful vocabulary and pronounces words impeccably. He loves language as much as he loves having fun with people, and his comic genius stems from both sources. People who expect him to be like the beer-swilling Little League coach he played in *Bad News Bears*, or the analphabetic old vaudevillian of *The Sunshine Boys*, are taken aback by his elegant discourse. He sprinkles his conversation with bits of French and German; though he knows only a few hundred words of either, his ear is so sharp that his accent fools even natives. In a scene he improvised in *Hopscotch*, he rapidly switches from French to German to an English cockney accent.

He loves hard crossword puzzles, and does the New York *Sunday Times* crossword in 20 minutes—using a pen. On one of his first dates with Carol, his wife of 21 years, he arrived with a puzzle and asked her, "What's a three-letter word for beverage?"

A neophyte, she at once replied, "7 Up." He immediately fell in love with her.

We were dining once at La Serre, a swanky French restaurant in Los Angeles, and I ordered a bottle of Perrier sparkling water as an aperitif. Walter told the waiter, "Bring him a 94-cents plain." He elucidated: "In poor neighborhoods in Brooklyn and the Bronx, where I grew up, we had what they call candy stores, and for a nickel you could get a glass of soda with any fruit flavor, but if you could afford only soda water without the syrup, you asked for a 'two-cents plain.'"

Walter in real life is as many-faceted as his language and his comic autobiographical inventions. He is devoted to classical music, particularly the works of Mozart. As a child he wanted to be a major-league baseball player—also a wrestler, a sportswriter, a general—and he still follows the games. He is a noted wagerer on football and basketball games and a devoted but (by his own admission) poor poker player, though some of the stories about him—partly based on his own tales—are exaggerated. As Jack Lemmon, his closest friend, insists, "His gambling is only a little hobby, something that keeps him rooting, that makes a game more interesting."

Lemmon smiles, remembering something. "Walter and I once watched a football game together," he continues, "the

Is That *Really* Walter Matthau?

Jets against the Vikings. The odds were 5 to 1 on Minnesota. Walter couldn't enjoy the game unless he had a little bet going, so he pestered me until I agreed to steal his money. I bet him $100 to his $20. He took the Jets. I knew there was no way he could win.

"Well, the Jets were a miracle team. They won. I forked over the hundred dollars. Walter was as happy as a clam. Know what he did? He went to Tiffany's. He bought a sterling-silver tray, must have cost him three, four hundred. Then he had it engraved, I WILL NOT BET ON MINNESOTA, 12 times, all over the tray. Another two hundred for the engraving. So let's figure he laid out over five hundred dollars because he won one hundred. And he gave *me* the tray. That's Walter for you. It is not the winning or the losing, it is getting joy out of living, it is having a wonderful time."

Walter possesses the rare gift of making any situation more interesting. Brian Garfield, author of *Hopscotch*, recalls a meeting with the star and some movie executives: "Matthau just walked in, fixed us with that lugubrious stare and—realizing we all knew about his serious heart surgery—said, 'My doctor just gave me six months to live.'" The assembled group sat in stunned silence. "Then, still scowling, Matthau said, 'And when he found I couldn't pay the bill—he gave me another six months.'"

Matthau loves to act. He makes at least two films a year when many stars are content with one, and he would like to make four. For a friend, executive producer Jennings Lang, he even agreed to do a walk-on, but on two conditions: "First, my salary goes to charity. I don't want to put a price tag on our friendship." Lang mulled it over and said, "I think I can meet your first demand." Second, Matthau insisted: "I want no credit or billing." They compromised on his fictional name. Thus, viewers of the disaster epic *Earthquake*, who briefly saw a droll drunk with an oddly familiar face in one scene, searched the credits only to find the actor identified as "Walter Matuschanskayasky."

Matthau can play any role—sophisticated lover, morose conniver, illiterate mucker—with total charm. "Walter's is the greatest actor's face in the world," Jack Lemmon rhapsodizes. "It is the map of every human emotion, and therefore he can do everyman and everything. If he were ever to tamper with his perfect face it would be like rewriting 'To be or not to be.'"

Matthau was born in 1920, on the Lower East Side of Manhattan, where many poor people could afford only the two-cents plain at the candy store. His father was seldom at home. His mother, Rose, a strong, courageous woman with a sharp sense of humor, went out to work in garment factories. Walter made his own way on the streets of New York, getting through school, taking odd jobs, selling refreshments in Second Avenue theaters.

He also played basketball, boxed, ran in track events in high school. He lived a varied life even then. He read and memorized Shakespeare, acted in settlement-house plays, even won a national spelling bee in 1937. At the same time, he learned to play poker and shoot craps.

In 1942, he enlisted in the Army Air Corps and saw action in Europe. After his discharge he studied at the New School's Dramatic Workshop in New York on the GI Bill, and began getting work in summer stock. In 1955, in his first film, he was an evil saloonkeeper, and the Hollywood *Reporter* described him as "one of the most insolent bullies ever seen on the screen." He was insolent and bullying in minor parts for another ten years and, though he was constantly employed on Broadway and television, it looked as if he would never get his name above the title.

Then, in 1964, he and Carol attended a party at which Neil Simon, who had already written two Broadway hits, was also a guest. For several months, Simon had been mulling over the plot for *The Odd Couple*. When he spied Matthau (he had seen him in several plays), the amorphous characters and scenes suddenly began to jell. He walked over and said, "I'm writing a play, and I think you'd be great as the star of it." Simon confided to me that he intuitively composed the character of Oscar Madison, the happy-go-mucky slob, around Matthau. Yet when Simon sent the finished script to Matthau, Walter begged to play the other part, finicky Felix, the divorced man who rooms with Madison and tries to clean up his apartment.

"Oscar Madison's too easy for me," he said. "That part—I can phone it in. But Felix Unger—that would really be acting for me."

"Tell you what, Mr. Matthau," Simon replied, "why don't you 'really act' in somebody else's play and just do Oscar Madison in mine?"

The Odd Couple, which ran on Broadway for two years,

made Matthau a star—at the not-so-tender age of 45. With *The Fortune Cookie*, a wonderfully comic movie made with Jack Lemmon in 1966, he became a national institution. When the film was almost finished, Matthau returned from a dinner party and, during the night, felt ill. *Aw, damn, this is a heart attack,* he thought. He was out for three months, but they held the picture for him.

The scene completed just before the attack showed Walter running upstairs to Lemmon's apartment. "You see me going upstairs weighing 198 pounds," Matthau says, "and I walk in—after this long convalescence—and I'm 160."

"But no one knew," I said. "How did you do it?"

"I just *acted* 40 pounds heavier," he said, grinning.

The Movies' Master of Suspense

by John Culhane

ALFRED HITCHCOCK resembled a gargoyle on a medieval cathedral, looking down with wry amusement on the modern city below. His double chin, pouting mouth and puckish eyes came into play on his naughty cherub's face as he answered questions. Why, for example, did he no longer use a certain actress?

"The difference between *ack-tors* and *die-wreck-tors* is . . .," he began, in his lugubrious tone, then paused and blinked. "*Ack-tors* stand on the side of the camera where the passage of time usually *hurts*." Long pause and pout. "*Whereas die-wreck-tors* can stay on the side where it *may help*."

Time certainly helped Hitchcock. He stayed at the top of his profession from *The Thirty-Nine Steps* in 1935 until his death on April 29, 1980, at the age of 80, becoming a multimillionaire and living to see the greater portion of his 54 films achieve critical as well as popular success.

When I first interviewed Hitchcock, I was disconcerted by his long pauses while he was answering questions. But I realized afterward that when you answer a question you end the suspense—and Hitchcock always hated to end the suspense.

According to Hitchcock, his power to create suspense had its roots in childhood anxieties. It began when a father sent his five-year-old son down the street to the police station with a note. The chief of police read the note and locked the boy in a jail cell. Five minutes later, the jailer let the child out and sent him home with these words: "That's what we do to naughty little boys."

Alfred Hitchcock told that story throughout his life. He insisted that he was that little boy and that he could never forget

The Movies' Master of Suspense

"the sound and the solidity of that clanging cell door and the bolt."

Almost all of Hitchcock's best pictures lock us in a cell for several minutes with some of our worst fears: of heights, in *Vertigo*; of falling, in *North by Northwest*; of hurtling down a road in a car whose brakes have failed, in *Family Plot*. In the end he lets us off, as if warning: "That's what we do to naughty little boys and girls."

"I usually have the theme of the innocent person who is in danger," Hitchcock told me. "Then I build up the suspense—will he get caught, will he escape, will he get killed? It is sometimes said that I make mysteries, but you make a mystery by withholding information, which I rarely do. I create suspense by *giving* information to the audience that makes them worry."

After a certain amount of suspense, however, Hitchcock would give the audience relief in laughter. The entire harrowing rescue of their son by Doris Day and James Stewart in *The Man Who Knew Too Much* takes place while another couple waits for them at their hotel for a social engagement. When the reunited family finally returns, Stewart says casually to his neglected guests: "Sorry we were gone so long. We had to go over and pick up Hank."

Since 1926, each of his films included a cameo appearance of Hitchcock himself. By the late 1940s, his fame was so great that he had to make his appearance early or the audience would be distracted looking for him instead of losing themselves in the action. "Hitch," as his friends called him, was shaped like a larger member of the violin family, and he took advantage of this, appearing with a cello case in *The Paradine Case* and boarding a railroad car carrying a double bass in *Strangers on a Train*.

The most difficult picture to get himself into was *Lifeboat*, because every scene had the same few people in the boat in the middle of the ocean. His first notion was to film himself as a dead body floating past the lifeboat, but he was afraid he'd sink. Hitchcock's solution was to show himself in an ad in an old newspaper found on the boat. The ad was for a fictitious diet drug called "Reduco." It showed "before" and "after" photographs of Hitchcock, who had just dieted from 300 to 200 pounds in real life. When the film came out, Hitchcock was deluged with letters asking where to get "Reduco."

His television series, "Alfred Hitchcock Presents," increased his fame. In the weekly show telecast between 1955 and 1965, Hitchcock's line drawing of his own profile would appear on the screen and then, to the macabre lilt of Gounod's "Funeral March of a Marionette," Hitchcock would match his own profile to that of his caricature, turn to the camera and say, "Gooood evening." Viewers loved the stories and delighted in Hitchcock's kidding his sponsors: "As you can see, crime does not pay—even on television. You have to have a sponsor. Here's ours, after which I shall return."

Born in London on August 13, 1899, the son of William Hitchcock, a successful greengrocer, and Emma Whelan Hitchcock, young Alfred received what he later described as "a strict religious upbringing." He attended St. Ignatius', a jesuit secondary school in London, where the priests maintained order through corporal punishment. Disobedient boys were hit on the hands with a hard-rubber cane. To add psychological distress, the boys had to choose their punishment time: morning break, lunch time, end of the day. Hitchcock noticed that most put it off as long as possible—keeping themselves in suspense all day long. Once, when young Alfred finally held out his hands, the priest gave them a light tap. Thus Hitchcock found that suspense can have a surprise ending.

Later, he included in his films scenes in which the anticipated ill does not materialize—and an unanticipated ill does. In *Rear Window*, when Grace Kelly hunts for clues in the apartment of Raymond Burr, she is caught by the murderer, and then saved by the police—who arrest her as a burglar.

Hitchcock's father died when Alfred was 14. The boy quit St. Ignatius' and, after studying mechanical drawing at an engineering and navigation school, he became a technical clerk at Henley's, an electrical cable company. For pleasure, he took a course in drawing and sketching, and by his 20th birthday, his artistic talent had taken him to Henley's advertising department. When he read that an American movie company, Famous Players-Lasky (later Paramount), was opening a studio in London, he drew up a portfolio of designs for silent-film titles and won a job writing and illustrating them.

The first complete film that Hitchcock directed was *The Pleasure Garden*, a murder melodrama made for Gainsborough Pictures in 1925. His assistant director was a young English film editor named Alma Reville. In 1926, she became Mrs. Alfred Hitchcock. Over the 53 years of their marriage—in addition to raising their daughter, Patricia—Alma provided screenplays, adaptations and continuity for many of her husband's best films.

Hitchcock went on to direct the first British sound film, *Blackmail*, in 1929, and his British films of international intrigue of the '30s—*The Thirty-Nine Steps*, *The Secret Agent*, *Sabotage* and *The Lady Vanishes*—made him world-famous.

David O. Selznick brought Hitchcock to Hollywood where his first American production, *Rebecca*, with Laurence Olivier and Joan Fontaine, won the Oscar for Best Picture of 1940. He was nominated for best director five times—for *Rebecca*, *Lifeboat* (1944), *Spellbound* (1945), *Rear Window* (1954) and *Psycho* (1960)—but he never won an Oscar. When the American Film Institute gave him its Life Achievement Award in 1978, it may have been with some stored-up resentment that Hitchcock, in accepting it, intoned: "Man does not live by murder alone. He needs affection, approval, encouragement and occasionally, a hearty meal."

It is true that for years audiences—including critics—were too busy being entertained to realize that Hitchcock was also one of the greatest artists at telling a story in a *movie* way, that is, almost completely with pictures in motion. Cary Grant carries a glass of milk upstairs to Joan Fontaine in *Suspicion*. Is the milk poisoned? Hitchcock hides a light in the glass to make the milk glow and, even though it turns out that the milk isn't poisoned, the glow makes the very glass look guilty.

Hitchcock planned virtually every shot, drawing it for a story board that looked like a comic strip. The famous scene in *North by Northwest*, in which Cary Grant is attacked by a low-flying crop-duster amid a shelterless stretch of fallow Indiana fields, was all drawn on the story board and played by Grant shot-for-shot—running and falling and rising and running some more. In the shower sequence in *Psycho*, there were 78 separate shots—all sketched in advance—for that 45-second scene. "When Hitch got his finished script," said Anthony Shaffer, who wrote the screenplay for *Frenzy*, "he considered the picture 99-percent finished. But, of course, he still had to shoot it."

Hitchcock's meticulous approach to film-making extended to the preparation of the musical score after the film had been shot and edited. When Hitchcock hired composer Ron Goodwin for *Frenzy*, the director was so specific that he even suggested the scoring for the "sparkling early-morning music" of the opening: woodwinds and glockenspiel. ("If he hadn't directed me," said Goodwin, "I would have written something with a macabre lilt to it"——but Hitchcock wanted no hint of the horror to come.)

Hitchcock was a great practical joker, who used his pranks to satisfy his lifelong curiosity about how people react in extraordinary, or suspenseful, circumstances. When Goodwin first called on the director, he found Hitchcock sitting in his usual Buddha-like pose, hands quietly folded over his enormous abdomen. Beside him, on a table, was a hatbox.

"Hitchcock opened the box and pulled out his head," says Goodwin. "I mean, it was a perfect latex replica of his own head.

"'What do you think of that?' he asked me.

"'Very nice,' I said. What *do* you say when someone shows you a perfect replica of his own head?"

Before he died, Hitchcock made one final joke at death's expense. Though he and his wife, Alma, had become American citizens in the 1950s, Hitchcock was knighted in 1979, by Queen Elizabeth II of his native England. The British consul general came to Universal Studios to announce the honor. "I hope," commented Sir Alfred, "that when the queen's tapping me on the shoulder—she won't let the sword slip."

How the 2000-Year-Old Man Became a Movie Giant

by Maurice Zolotow

MEL BROOKS is a compact man with sad blue eyes, black hair and a wide, stretched mouth out of which emanates a stream of jokes, wild and lunatic. He exhales gags as nonchalantly as air. Until ten years ago, this crazy quipster was known and loved mainly by a small circle of show-business celebrities. He had a reputation as an inventor of bizarre lines and sketches for television comedian Sid Caesar, and he and Carl Reiner had recorded some impromptu question-and-answer sessions that became hit comedy records.

Brooks' most famous impersonation is of a 2000-year-old man with a thick Jewish accent:

Q. *Did you know Napoleon?*

A. *Yes.*

Q. *How did you meet him?*

A. *Well, I had this summer cottage on Elba. I ran into this village guy on the beach. He was crying. I told him, so they took France away from you. Don't cry. Go back and recapture it.*

Q. *So you were responsible for his defeat at Waterloo?*

A. *Who, me? Nah, I'm not responsible. You don't listen to every nut on a beach who tells you to go take France back.*

In 1974, Mel Brooks finally found in the movies the audience which had been seeking his kind of insane humor ever since the Marx Brothers and Laurel and Hardy ceased making comedies 30 years ago. With *Blazing Saddles* (a crazy Western-type comedy), *Young Frankenstein* (a crazy horror-type comedy), *Silent Movie* (a crazy silent-movie-type comedy) and *High Anxiety* (a crazy Hitchcock-suspense comedy), Brooks became one of the hottest personalities in pictures. Co-author or author of all his films, he directs them and often is also one of the stars.

In a time when the movie industry deals heavily in disaster, sex, blood and misery, Mel Brooks dared to return to the early exuberance of cinema, to the world of Mack Sennett and custard-pie hurlers and clowning triumphant over form.

So come with me into the world of Mel Brooks and get your mind off predatory sharks, burning skyscrapers, intergalactic wars and the rotten people of the world.

Mel Brooks' office is an enormous corner suite in the executive building on the Twentieth Century-Fox lot in West Los Angeles. To visitors, interviewers and colleagues, Mel distributes Raisinets—pellets of chocolate-coated raisins. He munches them himself, and he gave some to me. Why Raisinets? "Well, what did you expect, tea and cucumber sandwiches? Sherry and biscuits? Here we give Raisinets."

One of his interviewers spurned the Raisinets. Mel said he should at least take a few boxes home for his children. "No," the man said. "Chocolate is bad for teeth."

"Are teeth so good for chocolate?" snarled Mel.

I was coughing. A chewed Raisinet stuck in my throat. "Eat them, eat them, they're good for you," he chortled. "They are nutritious. Whatever damage the chocolate is doing, the raisins are correcting. There's iron in them."

"Iron?"

"Yes. The only problem is that you can't stay in the water too long if you're a Raisinet eater because you rust."

"Mel, how do you overcome the rust problem?"

"I DRINK OIL!" he cried at once.

This impromptu exchange brings out two points about Mel's comedy. One, it arises out of everyday situations. Two, it is a comedy of exaggeration, wandering eerily between fantasy and reality.

In his films, this instinct for surrealism becomes a moment in *Silent Movie* when Brooks, as a Skid Row bum, drinks from an enormous whiskey bottle—maybe ten feet long—carried by a crew of fellow drunks. Or in *Young Frankenstein* when the hunchback finds his hump slipping from side to side. Or in *Blazing Saddles* when a chain-gang boss tells the prisoners to sing a typical black work song, and they render Cole Porter's "I Get a Kick Out of You," accompanied by Count Basie's 24-

How the 2000-Year-Old Man Became a Movie Giant 117

piece orchestra sitting on a flatcar out in the Western badlands of the 1880s.

(Parenthetically—and, as Mel Brooks would say if he were writing these sentences, why shouldn't it be, since this is a parenthesis after all—Mel used to be a professional jazz drummer, and loves jazz of the Ellington, Armstrong, Basie genre. He writes his own movie theme songs and admires the singing of Sinatra, Crosby, and Fred Astaire, who he thinks is a master of phrasing and tempo. When he drives around town, Mel likes to play tapes of Astaire singing. His car, by the way, is a Honda. He used to drive a Buick. He says that where he grew up in Brooklyn, Buick was *the* Jewish car.

("So," I inquired, "has the Honda become a Jewish car?"

("No," he shot back. "The Honda is for tall people who want to look short."

("But, Mel, you *are* short."

("You see, it works, it works.")

Mel Brooks is never at a loss for a riposte. After paying him a minimal $500 for a guest appearance on a television show, executive producer David Frost said to Mel: "I guess you're giving the fee to your favorite charity."

"Yes," Mel rasped. "I'm donating it to my left pocket." (In truth, he is a charitable person who tithes to charities and makes many personal benefactions.)

Movie critics do not, Mel believes, sympathize with, or understand, what he is doing. Asked once, "What do you think of the critics?" he answered, "They're very noisy at night. You can't sleep in the country because of them."

"Isn't that crickets you're talking about? I meant critics."

"Oh, critics! What good are they? They can't make music with their hind legs."

Mel Brooks was born Melvin Kaminsky, youngest of four brothers, in a poverty-stricken Jewish quarter of Brooklyn, N.Y., in 1926. His father, Maximilian Kaminsky, an immigrant from the Baltic seaport of Danzig, was a process server who died when Mel was three. His mother's name was Kate Brookman. (Mel took her maiden name and shortened it to Brooks when he went into show business.)

Mel's comedy has been seen by some as the reaction to a fatherless home and a Jewish "ghetto" environment. He sometimes falls into this pseudo-profundity himself. "Look at Jewish history," he once told *Newsweek*. "Unrelieved lamenting would be intolerable. So for every ten Jews beating their breasts, God designed one to be crazy and amuse the breast beaters. By the time I was five, I knew I was that one."

But Mel Brooks is definitely not in the tradition of "Jewish humor," such as that of Sholem Aleichem and Isaac Bashevis Singer. His comedy relates more to the brashness of frontier American humor, for example, to the early sketches of Bret Harte and Mark Twain.

How did raw American frontier humor come to infect this kid from Brooklyn? Through the silent movies. Through the crude silent-movie comedies of Mack Sennett, Fatty Arbuckle and other clowns.

When Mel was a boy during the 1930s, a dozen or so cafés and restaurants on and off the Coney Island boardwalk showed silent movies to attract customers. There was no admission. You sat down, in a semi-darkened room of round tables and wooden chairs, ordered a hot dog and a root beer, and you could watch a flickering classic by Chaplin or see the Keystone Kops. As long as you had something on the table, they didn't throw you out. I know. I was taken to such places by my mother, as Mel was by his.

"I fell in love with movies right there," he told me. "Outside, life was dirty and hard. My mother had to work ten hours a day to support the family. Kids beat me up because I was a shrimp. I knew I was ugly and no good. But in here, in the dark, I could eat a knish (they didn't have Raisinets) and drink root beer and it was beautiful. This was much better than real life. Who needs real life?

"Later, when I was old enough to go to pictures alone, I had a big diet of Western movies and talking pictures in a dump neighborhood theater. My mother was always sending an older brother to drag me out. Sometimes I went there when it opened, 11:30 in the morning, and stayed until nightfall, starved to death, a splitting headache, but I couldn't take my eyes off the screen. This was my school—the movies."

He also attended Eastern District High School, graduating in 1944. Then he spent 2½ years in the Army, a good part of the time in Europe with a combat-engineer outfit assigned to move ahead of the armies and repair broken bridges and power stations. Of that experience, Mel says, "It was very unhealthy work."

After his discharge, Brooks became a professional drummer.

How the 2000-Year-Old Man Became a Movie Giant 119

He also started saying clever things and got laughs. Then in the Catskill Mountains one summer he fell in with another musician, a tenor saxophonist named Sid Caesar. They became friends. Or, rather, Sid Caesar became a king of television comedy, with "Your Show of Shows" (on the NBC network from 1950 to 1954), and Mel Brooks was his court jester.

Brooks, at first, was barely tolerated by the rest of the show's staff. He was always late. He was always impudent and impertinent, a restless, nervous person. He couldn't sit at the typewriter. But he could, running about, spew out great Rabelaisian jokes which were perfect for Caesar. And if you didn't like this Brooks idea or gag, he had ten others.

When "Your Show of Shows" ended, Mel went through a long period of defeats and struggle. He wrote a Broadway show which flopped. He couldn't get a comedy-writing job because he was known to be cantankerous. His first marriage was breaking up. (He later married actress Anne Bancroft and they have one of the most enchanting man-woman relationships I've ever known.) He was suffering from severe neurotic symptoms, and underwent analysis for six years.

His symptoms were relieved, and he began to get some emotional maturity, though he was still hard-pressed financially. In 1965, Brooks and Buck Henry concocted the "Get Smart" television series, but Mel decided he wanted to direct and write movies, and write novels. He started writing a satirical novel, *Springtime for Hitler*, which eventually metamorphosed into his first film, *The Producers* (1967).

The Producers died at the box office, and it took three years to get another backer for a movie: *The Twelve Chairs*, a satirical comedy set in Russia. It laid a colossal egg, and it took four years to get out another film. This one, *Blazing Saddles*, made his fortune.

Now, after the successes of his recent films, Mel Brooks is able to write his own ticket in Hollywood. He oversees every aspect of his films, even to the decibels of the sound track. How this man, whom I first met when we were both young, a man who was wild and undisciplined and erratic and, yes, also lovable and whimsical and outrageously funny, how this Mel Brooks became the disciplined and orderly person he is today, I don't know.

But that's what happened. An even greater miracle is that along the way he has not lost his spontaneity, his creative lunacy, his love of life and people. He gets his hard work done in an office which is usually full of friends and colleagues and amid phone interruptions. How does he do it? Maybe it's the Raisinets.

As I was leaving Brooks' office, I admired a picture of him in a blazer and yachting cap. "Handsome man, isn't he?" said Brooks. "If only I looked like him, I could be a movie star!"

This Was Toscanini

by Samuel Antek

A GREAT symphony orchestra, brought together from the far corners of the world, sat in tingling silence on the huge stage of Studio 8-H in Radio City, New York. I was a violinist in that newly formed NBC Symphony, and we were awaiting, that December day in 1937, the first appearance of our conductor.

Suddenly, from a door on the right side of the stage, a small, solidly built man emerged and walked to the podium. Our first impression was of crowning white hair and an impassive, square, high-cheekboned, bemustached face. He was dressed in a black alpaca jacket with a clerical collar, formal striped trousers and pointed, slipperlike shoes. He gestured a faint greeting with both arms, then, in a rough, hoarse voice, called out, "Brahms!"

He looked at us piercingly for a moment, then raised his arms. In one smashing stroke, the baton came down. Thus began my first rehearsal with Arturo Toscanini, "the world's greatest conductor."

That morning, with each heart-pounding timpani stroke in the opening bars of Brahms' First Symphony, our 70-year-old leader's baton beat became more powerfully insistent. As we in the violin section struck our bows against our strings, I sensed, more than heard, the magnificent new sounds around me. Was this the same music we had played so often before? With what a new, fierce joy we played!

"Cantate! Sostenete!" he bellowed as the music reached its first great climax. "Sing! Sustain!" This was the first time Toscanini's battle cry was flung at us, and for 17 years we lived by those words.

Toscanini often said, "Any *asino* can conduct, but to make music is *difficile*." He was always St. George fighting the dragon guarding the musical treasure. What a sense of excitement and discovery each rehearsal brought, as the "Old Man" found in a long-familiar work a note, an accent, a nuance hitherto unnoticed or glossed over by routine or carelessness. Under his baton, time-wearied, shopworn pieces regained their original luster and shone anew. "Routine—the death of music!" Toscanini would wail.

I cannot recall his ever making a gesture that was purely mechanical and not closely identified in mood or movement with the expression of the musical phrase as he felt it. He conducted the music, not the orchestra. For a very hushed effect, he would bring the tip of the index finger of his left hand to his lips as though saying, *"Sh! Sh!"* For even greater expressiveness, he brought his left hand over his heart and indicated an undulating motion, as though playing a wide cello vibrato. "Play with your hearts, not your instruments!"

When the music became particularly poignant, as at the end of the Funeral March of Beethoven's *Eroica*, he would crouch slightly, lean toward us, and indicate with his baton the merest suggestion of a still precise, flowing beat. "Weeping—weeping!" he would cry out.

Toscanini never spoke matter-of-factly. Excitement and dramatic expressiveness filled his phrases. I could feel each member of the orchestra straining every ounce of technique to attain the sound and mood the Maestro wanted. Always when we played with him, the sound that emerged differed as completely from what we had formerly played as does refined gold from the original ore. We would nod to one another, beaming with satisfaction and almost disbelief.

There were two Toscaninis: the conductor at rehearsals and the conductor at concerts. At rehearsals, he would shout, bellow and sing. At concerts he seemed to freeze. I often had the impression that he wished he were invisible so as not to come between the audience and the music. He never smiled at a concert. Sometimes, if a particular passage fell apart, he would shake his head as if saying, "Well, we failed!"

At other times, if a player or a section did something especially displeasing, his head would rock balefully as though to say, "Wait till I get my hands on you!" And if a player made a wrong entrance or played indifferently (at least in Toscanini's opinion), Toscanini would actually shake a clenched fist at the hapless wretch.

No conductor more grudgingly accepted recognition from audience and orchestra alike. Many times, at rehearsals, men would spontaneously break into applause when a particular phrase shone with unusual brilliance. Toscanini never acknowledged these compliments. "No! Is not me!" he would say almost angrily. "Is in the music, just before your eyes."

Few, if any, conductors knew scores as Toscanini did, or even approached his genius for laying bare the flesh and bones of an orchestra's effort. Unerringly, he could put his finger on just where and how a passage had been muddied. "You know," he would say, stopping suddenly, "you play—I hear something—but is nothing—is a big *pasticcio* (mess). Come, we study." Each line would be gone over separately. When all was put together, so delicate, well-timed and sensitive was the balance that every note spoke. "Everything so clear I can touch it!"

One of Toscanini's most enigmatic qualities was the almost unbelievable combination of saint and demon. As he stood on the podium at rehearsals, he looked the personification of a venerable saint. His face was transfigured with a spiritual light as he worked on a passage of surpassing beauty. Then, suddenly, like a thunderbolt, the saint would flee and the demon lash out at the orchestra in a language to rival that of a longshoreman.

Toscanini had one favorite Italian curse that he used without much provocation. He would hurl it with particular relish at a fellow Italian, saying, "You are Italian. Good! I don't have to explain!" Once, however, when he started to use this epithet, he caught himself and put his hand over his mouth. Several women were in the hall. He made a grimace, glared at the player and shouted, "*Hmmmmph!* You know what I want to call you, but—"

The rehearsal went on, until the mistake was repeated. Now Toscanini bellowed, "*Zuccone!* I tried to control myself, but you won't let me. You are a—!" Out came the epithet in fullest glory. He glared triumphantly at the player. A moment later he was his angelic self again. If any other conductor had spoken to an orchestra the way Toscanini did, he would have been brought up before the musicians' union on charges of "misbehavior"!

In 1950 the NBC Symphony went on tour, giving concerts throughout the United States. We saw great snowcapped mountains, vast deserts and exciting cities. But, as the tour progressed, we realized that the greatest wonder of all was on the train with us—our incredible 83-year-old Maestro. His zest and enthusiasm astounded us all. Once, in Sun Valley, I came upon him at ten o'clock in the morning, stretched out full-length on the lawn of the hotel, drinking a toast in champagne to the beautiful mountains!

In Atlanta, an incident occurred that illustrated his almost mystical attitude toward music. As we entered the huge auditorium that morning, we were greeted by the sound of hammering. In the center of the auditorium workmen were busy erecting a ring for the prizefights that were to take place that night. Our concert was to be played the following night. All the noise stopped when Toscanini came to the stand and during the brief rehearsal. But, as Toscanini stepped off the podium, the workmen reappeared and a foreman walked past the Maestro with his hat on. Toscanini stopped abruptly.

With a flick of his baton he knocked off the foreman's hat. *"Ignorante!* Take off the hat! Is a church here!" The man, dumb with amazement, looked around at the prizefight ring and stared at the Old Man in perplexed terror. "Yes! *Ignorante!"* rasped the Old Man. "Where is music is a church! Off *stupido!"*

As a conductor, Toscanini stood like a colossus astride the musical horizon. For me, this principal genius lay in his capacity to transform music-making into an epic experience. Those of us who had the proud privilege of playing with him until the NBC Symphony was disbanded in 1954 felt that we had undergone a spiritual regeneration. Making music became the very noblest of professions and aspirations. This was the miracle of Toscanini.

The Manorial Air and Larcenous Eye of W. C. Fields

by Corey Ford

W. C. FIELDS, whose old films are still shown on TV, is generally acknowledged to be the supreme comic artist of his time. In my opinion he was the funniest man who ever lived, even funnier offstage than on. His drawn-out rasping voice was the same, of course, but he had an infectious giggle, a falsetto he-he-he-he like the chirp of a cricket, which I never heard him use in his professional work. His everyday speech was extravagantly florid. The stilted phraseology of the English romanticists—"betwixt" or "forsooth" or "hither and yon"—came naturally to his lips, and he was the only person I've known to start a sentence with the word "Likely."

That occurred, for instance, on a night when Fields and I were having dinner at Chasen's in Hollywood. Sabu, the Elephant Boy, made one of his elaborate entrances, clad in Indian robes and followed by two white-turbaned Sikh bearers (probably from Central Casting). Bill, who was facing in the other direction, swung his head slowly around, his gaze moving like the beam of a revolving harbor light until it fixed on Sabu with a baleful glare. Then, in an aside which could have been heard clear to Santa Barbara, he growled, "Likely the little mahout will mistake my nose for a proboscis, and climb on my sho-o-ulder!"

I never knew how much of what Fields said was factual. He constantly embellished his stories with new imaginative touches. It didn't matter. Bill could have recited the alphabet and had me rolling on the floor. "Got the theater in my blo-o-od," he would drawl. "My Great-Uncle Fortescue used to be a Swiss bell ringer at Elks' smokers. Ah, yaas, poor old Uncle

Fortescue. Run over by a horsecar in Scollay Square, Boston, after attending a musi-*kale* at the Parker House."

Now and then he would dwell on his early boyhood in Germantown, a suburb of Philadelphia. He was born William Claude Dukenfield, the son of "poor but dishonest parents." His father made a scanty living hawking vegetables from door to door. Much against his will, young Bill was forced to ride the grocery wagon and help peddle the produce.

Mr. Dukenfield was a firm believer in discipline, and whacked his son regularly, whether he deserved it or not. Once, at the age of nine, Bill sneaked past the ticket taker at the local vaudeville house, and was fascinated by a juggling act. Filled with enthusiasm, he stole some lemons and oranges from his father's cart to practice the new art. "By the time I learned to keep two of them in the air at once," he admitted, "I'd ruined several dollars' worth of fruit." His father took stern measures to cure him of this expensive habit. He concealed himself in the stable, caught his son in the act and gave him a parental beating.

One afternoon when Bill was 11, he left a rake in the yard, and Dukenfield stepped on it, banging his shin. Seeing that Bill was observing him with amusement, he picked up the rake and bashed it over the boy's head. Bill resolved to square accounts—"I rejected certain measures which might have elicited the attention of the coroner," he said—and settled on the simple solution of hiding on a ledge above the stable door, poising a heavy wooden crate. His father entered, Bill flattened him—and left home, never to return.

Bill eventually developed the skill he had acquired with his father's oranges and lemons into a spectacular vaudeville act which he climaxed by balancing 25 cigar boxes end on end with a rubber ball on top. He employed no patter. "His comedy," *Variety* observed, "speaks for him."

Fields' very appearance evoked laughter from an audience: the manorial air that was so obviously false, the too benign smile, the larcenous eye. He had the round, ruddy face of a dignified and slightly felonious country squire. Its most prominent feature was the celebrated red-veined nose, which would grow redder, like a warning light, if he felt he was being victimized—as often happened, because he had so many prejudices.

His distrust of doctors was legendary. He termed the members of the medical profession "dastardly fee-splitters. When doctors and undertakers meet, they always wink at each other."

He found bankers even worse. In order to outwit their cunning designs, he deposited sums of money in banks scattered all over, even stepping off a transcontinental train to open an account in a small town while the engine was taking on water. Bill finally had over 700 bank accounts or safe-deposit boxes in such far-flung cities as London, Paris, Sydney, Cape Town and Suva. He insisted that his system not only insured him against conniving bankers, but also made it difficult for income-tax agents to collect revenue for the government, which he likewise mistrusted. "Uncle Whiskers will strike down even a child and take away its marbles," he glowered.

Children were another of Fields' pet phobias. "Of course I like little tots," he would protest righteously, "if they're well cooked." Baby LeRoy, with whom he made several films, was his particular aversion. Convinced that the infant was deliberately plotting to steal scenes from him, he would eye him with dark suspicion, muttering vague threats under his breath. Once he succeeded in spiking Baby LeRoy's orange juice with a surreptitious shot of gin, and sat back amiably while director Norman Taurog tried in vain to rouse the youngster from his stupor. "Walk him around, walk him around," Fields advised professionally from a corner. When Baby LeRoy had to be taken home and the shooting postponed till the next day, Fields was jubilant. "That kid's no trouper," he jeered.

Fields' attitude toward women was courtly, even a trifle old-fashioned. If someone started a bawdy anecdote in mixed company, he would make some excuse to leave. And he would remove his hat punctiliously in an elevator or rise promptly to his feet if a woman entered the room. One hot afternoon, Bill was sitting stark naked behind his desk when his manager, Billy Grady, and a female companion burst through the door without warning. Ever the gentleman, Bill stood up politely and extended his hand, and then blinked in surprise as the woman gasped and departed in haste. He greeted members of the fair sex with such cavalier terms of endearment as "My little chickadee" or "My little glowworm" or, in a romantic scene with Mae West, "My little brood mare."

It was his dislike of birds—another of his innumerable prejudices—which led him to sell his Toluca Lake home, an imposing mansion with broad green lawns sloping down to an artificial lake. The shallow water was populated by numerous swans, which used to roam over the premises and hiss at him, an unforgivable affront to an actor. Whenever Bill spotted one of his web-footed adversaries cropping his grass, he would place a golf ball in position and drive it accurately at the intruder with a No. 4 iron, whereupon the outraged bird would flap its wings and chase him up the lawn and into the house. Once Bill borrowed a canoe and pursued a large swan all over the lake, until he dozed off after his strenuous efforts and the swan paddled up behind the canoe and nipped him. "The miscreant fowl broke all the rules of civilized warfare," he complained later.

Although pictured by the public as a lush who indulged in wild drinking sprees, Fields had nothing but contempt for the thick-tongued, staggering drunk, and would order a friend from his house if he became tipsy. "Gives drinking a bad name," he said. His own capacity for alcohol was enormous—his household staff estimated that he consumed two quarts of martinis a day—but I never saw him show the slightest effect. Before setting out for an afternoon on the links he would secrete a dozen miniatures in the pockets of his golf bag. "I always keep a supply of stimulant handy in case I see a snake," he liked to explain,"—which I also keep handy."

Fields appeared in every edition of the *Ziegfeld Follies* from 1915 through 1921. Then, in 1923, with the musical comedy *Poppy*, the former "tramp juggler" graduated into an authentic and expert comedian. He played the role of Eustace McGargle, a magnificent fraud who gained his livelihood by fleecing the local yokels at a country fair. The grandiose eloquence and unctuous smile of the mountebank, urging innocent farmers to participate with him in the shell game, and the aside, "Never give a sucker an even break," established the pattern which Fields pursued the rest of his life.

His film debut occured in 1925 in a motion picture of *Poppy* (retitled *Sally of the Sawdust*). It was hailed as a comic masterpiece, and he followed it with many others.

Bill had the ability to turn his prejudices to comic advantage. After acquiring a car, he developed a persecution complex about road hogs who, he was convinced, were out to get him. His sequence in *If I Had a Million* gratified a long-standing thirst for vengeance. With the million dollars that he inherited in the story, he purchased a number of second-hand cars, hired

The Manorial Air and Larcenous Eye of W. C. Fields 129

a flock of intrepid drivers and set forth at the head of the column, his eye peeled for the first offender to cut across the center line. When he spotted a culprit, he would signal one of his commandos to wheel out and ram it. Sometimes Fields would take part in the fray himself, giving a blood-curdling yell of exultation as headlights shattered, wheels came off and fenders crumpled.

Fields insisted on writing his own screen plays, which he would dash off on the back of an old grocery bill and sell to the studio for $25,000. Then, since his contract specified that he had the right of story approval, he would notify the studio that he had rejected the script and compose a second one for another $25,000. (Director Norman McLeod told me that Fields built up his take on one story to $85,000.) After the script was finally approved and paid for, he would toss it aside and ad-lib on the set as he went along.

Fields was also successful—and dangerous—on radio. On the "Lucky Strike" program, he referred to his son "Chester" for several weeks, until his sponsors belatedly realized that "Chester Fields" might be doing them no good.

For most of his years in Hollywood, Fields occupied a rundown Spanish mansion on De Mille Drive, north of Hollywood. He had an abiding fear of burglars, and his solution, of which he was inordinately proud, was the installation of an intercom system throughout the house. Loudspeakers were concealed everywhere: in the pantry, down in the cellar, inside chandeliers, under washbasins, behind pictures, and back of the knocker on the front door, a carved woodpecker which the guest activated by yanking a string. If he heard a suspicious noise during the night, he would pick up the microphone and bellow, "Stand back, I've got you covered!" and then go back to bed, confident that the intruder would remain with arms raised until morning.

During World War II, on my way out to the Pacific on Air Force duty, I stopped off to see Bill, whose health, I had been told, was failing. As I stepped up to the door and reached for the string of the knocker, the woodpecker yelled, "*Let* go of me, Ford!" in Bill's snarling voice. (He had a telescope, I learned later, with which he could spot any approaching visitor.)

It was the last time I ever saw him. Two years later, on a rainy Christmas—a holiday he pretended to abhor—W. C. Fields died.

Psychologists analyzing Fields' humor have concluded that his prejudices and fears were due to a basic hostility toward his father. Well, maybe it's true, and yet I feel with E. B. White that "Humor can be dissected, as a frog can, but the thing dies in the process and the innards are discouraging to any but the pure scientific mind." I prefer to think of Fields as a comic genius who defies analysis, unequaled among America's funnymen, the one and only.

Here's Steve Martin... Maybe

by Maurice Zolotow

WHEN Steve Martin started out as a stand-up comic in the 1960s, his favorite opening line was, "Hi, folks, this is Steve Martin... I'll be out in a minute." Now one of the hottest comic actors around, he sometimes behaves as if he is still waiting for the real Steve Martin to be out in a minute.

Between scenes of his M-G-M movie, *Pennies From Heaven*, he remarked, "Here I am, the star of this twenty-million-dollar singing-and-dancing movie, playing a serious dramatic role, a romantic hero, and you know something?" He looked around as if to make sure M-G-M owner Kirk Kerkorian was not nearby, and whispered hoarsely, "I can't sing. I can't dance. And I can't act."

Though rich, handsome and famous, Steve doesn't emanate that rich, famous, handsome aura. A woman cornered him one day, stared hard at him and announced, "I have one of those life-size cutouts of you."

"How wonderful!" Steve responded, feigning joy. (He loathes the six-foot photographic cutout his fans purchase, but likes the royalties from their sale at $10 apiece.)

"I wanted to see if you look like him," the woman continued.

"Who?"

"The cutout."

"Do I?"

"Absolutely not!" she snarled.

But there's always the other Steve Martin just a minute away. That Steve can outshine a life-size cutout. And he can act. Above all, Steve Martin is an actor.

In one of the big musical numbers in *Pennies From Heaven*

he sings, "That's the story of—that's the glory of love."* But it's not really Steve Martin singing. It's the other Steve Martin brilliantly imitating Bing Crosby.

During his spectacular rise to celebrity status in theaters and television from 1976 to 1980—he was a frequent guest host on TV's "Saturday Night Live"—he was not so much a comedian as an actor playing the part of a comedian, a "wild and crazy guy."

His impersonation of a comedian was *very* convincing. When he went on a 50-city tour in 1978, appearing in 20,000-seat arenas, dizzy fans came to his sellout concerts wearing weird Steve Martin appurtenances—arrows through the head (actually arrows with curved shanks that snap *over* the head), rabbit ears sprouting from craniums, twisted balloons around necks. They knew all the Steve Martin punch lines. "Well, ex-*cuuuuse* me," they screamed playfully with him when the lighting crew didn't give him the proper spotlight.

In 1979, U.C.L.A. students named Steve "Entertainer of the Year" and started lining up three days before the award ceremony to make sure of getting in. Another human sea of arrow-headed and rabbit-eared crazies laughed themselves into manic euphoria.

Professional critics were slower to appreciate Steve Martin, actor. His first movie, *The Jerk*, about a sweet-natured slob, opened in 1979 to unenthusiastic reviews, which the public ignored. By mid-1981, *The Jerk*, produced for $4.5 million, had grossed over $110 million.

The public even liked Steve Martin's impersonation of an author. His "book" *Cruel Shoes*, a flimsy 128-page work with wide margins, many photographs and nonsense essays with titles like "How to Fold Soup" and "The Confessions of Raymond to His Goldfish," sold 500,000 copies in hard-cover, a million in paperback. Stubborn to the end, reviewers dismissed it as piffle.

Steve's habitually serious manner and mien make it hard to tell which Steve Martin is going to emerge at any given minute. He is a vegetarian and doesn't smoke or drink. But recently he was observed puffing cigarette after cigarette. Why? "My doctor told me I had a tar deficiency," he replied gravely. (It

---

*Copyright MCMXXXVI Renewed by Shapiro, Bernstein & Co., Inc. Used by permission.

turned out that he portrays a smoker in *Pennies From Heaven*—so Steve was practicing.)

Once, in Juarez, Mexico, Steve approached a street vendor and asked the price of a broad-brimmed straw hat. "Four dollars, señor," the man replied. "I'll give you six dollars," Steve said. Out of habit the vendor shot back, "For you, I make it three." "No, I'll give you eight," Steve said. The vendor by now was confused. "What, señor?" "Okay," Steve said, "I'll give you ten dollars or nothing!" The Mexican shrugged and took the money.

Sometimes Steve even acts the big star. His agent, Marty Klein, drives a navy-blue Rolls Royce Silver Shadow. It was a gift from Steve. During the hard years, when Steve had trouble getting a split week in a low-class dive, Marty would often be the only one in the audience laughing. To cheer his client up, Marty would say, "Don't worry, Steve. Someday you'll make it big and buy me a Rolls Royce."

So Steve did.

Martin was born in August, 1945, in Waco, Texas. His father, Glenn Martin, was a professional actor and drama coach at Baylor University. The family moved to Southern California when Steve was five, and his father went into real estate. When Steve was eight, his parents took him to the Monte Montana Wild West Show. From then on his destiny was sealed; his vocation as a performer had found him.

By the time he worked up his impersonation of Monte Montana twirling a lariat (he is still a skilled twirler), Steve had become enthralled by a magician he saw at a traveling carnival. Soon he was doing a 30-minute magic act for family and friends.

Seeing Tony Curtis play the role of Houdini in the film of that name sharpened his dream of becoming a professional magician—and an actor. Then Disneyland opened in nearby Anaheim. At ten, Steve got a job there selling guidebooks after school and on weekends, walking the two miles from his home. Five years later, he was doing a magic act at Disneyland's Golden Horseshoe Revue.

With characteristic dedication he learned juggling and ventriloquism; he taught himself to play the banjo by reading an instruction book and practicing four hours a day. While at high school and later at college (he attended three universities without getting around to graduating from any), Steve began working small coffeehouses and clubs. His act consisted of one or two banjo numbers and some magic tricks with increasingly comedic twists.

He had, for instance, a rabbit he extracted from a hat. He would make its ears twitch, cuddle it and suddenly throw it to the floor—where it bounced. It was a realistic-looking fake stuffed with a rubber ball.

One day Mason Williams, head writer for the Smothers Brothers TV show, saw Steve's act. He was impressed with his material and hired him to write for the show. Soon Steve was making $1500 a week as a comedy writer, but he took club bookings at every opportunity because what he really yearned for was to get out in front of an audience.

Agent Marty Klein caught his act and became convinced that Steve Martin was a future star. Steve was off and running—into years of failure and endless touring through small towns. Occasionally he did curtain-raisers in Las Vegas for big acts like Ann-Margret.

During those struggling, on-the-road years, art was bachelor Steve's solace. When playing a college town, he would spend all day in the university library reading books on American art. Through his love of painting, the young man from California became a cosmopolitan. He discovered the richness of the American experience through the paintings of Thomas Eakins and Winslow Homer, among others, and has become a serious collector of 19th- and 20th- century American art.

Always in Steve's character there has been a streak of comical insanity that skews his experiences into a fabric of farcical patterns. He once persuaded a leading art dealer to rent him a gallery for a one-man show. He put on an exhibition of invisible paintings and invisible sculpture. Each empty frame and pedestal had a title such as "Still Life with Rabbits" or "Unfinished." Steve got tremendous publicity on TV, and the art critic of the Los Angeles *Times* wrote a serious review of the show.

Meanwhile, Marty Klein was hearing from fellow agents that he was wasting his time, that Steve Martin did not have it. Then in 1976, Home Box Office taped Steve's show at the Troubadour in West Hollywood. Seen by nearly two million cable-TV subscribers, it was a sensation. Guest appearances on "Saturday Night Live" and on Johnny Carson's show followed. Steve Martin made the cover of *Newsweek*. Stories began to appear about his studies in philosophy and existentialism; of how Wittgenstein's famous tractate on logic had convinced him there was no meaning in meaning, and so he had become a comedian of the absurd.

Two years ago, Steve bought a large Spanish-mission-style mansion in Beverly Hills and redecorated the interior in contemporary, stark-white, Le Corbusier-style. The real function of his home is to provide a place where he can hang the paintings he so loves.

In 1980, after headlining at the Riviera Hotel in Las Vegas, he decided to call a temporary halt to his stage career. He began marshaling his great energy, willpower and formidable talent to become one of the movie superstars of the decade.

The new, real Steve Martin will be out in a minute, folks. Maybe.

The Sounds of America

The Queen of Country Music

by George Vecsey

> *But here in Topeka the rain*
> * is a-fallin',*
> *The faucet is a-drippin' and the*
> * kids are a-bawlin',*
> *One of them is toddlin' and*
> * one is a-crawlin',*
> *And... one's on the way.**

FOR NEARLY two decades country singer Loretta Lynn has been traveling the roads of America singing songs like this in her clear, plaintive voice. They are honest songs, funny songs, sad songs. Songs of hard times, sickness, children, shaky marriages, unrequited love. And they have built a special bond between Loretta and the women of middle America. No other country singer touches them the way Loretta does.

She was the first woman ever named "Entertainer of the Year," the top honor in country music. Almost every one of her 50-odd albums has sold more than 300,000 copies. She is the first country musician to have an autobiography hit the bestseller list—*Loretta Lynn: Coal Miner's Daughter*, later made into a movie, for which its star, Sissy Spacek, won an Academy Award. The film went on to become one of the top ten grossing films of 1980 and was shown on television. Loretta has done her own television special and appeared on "Fantasy Island."

---

*"One's on the Way," words and music by Shel Silverstein. Copyright © 1971 Evil Eye Music, Inc., New York N.Y. Used by permission.

A second volume of her autobiography is being planned. And while men like Johnny Cash, Buck Owens, Roy Clark and Charley Pride are recognized on national television, among women Loretta Lynn has been the clear favorite for more than a decade.

Why is this woman with the attractive figure, blue Irish eyes and dark Cherokee hair so popular? Partly because she embodies every woman's desire to be respected and treated equally. "I ain't no better than anybody else," she confides to her audiences, "and there ain't nobody better than me." She doesn't tell women to "stand by your man," as one popular country song puts it. She tells them to "stand *up* to your man." As she says, "There ain't no double standard in the eyes of the Lord." But most of all she touches so many women because there is something about her that convinces them that "she knows our life," and she is "just like us." And indeed she is.

Loretta Lynn was born Loretta Webb, the second of eight children raised in poverty in Butcher Hollow (pronounced Holler), Ky. Her father worked in the coal mines when they were open and, during the Depression, on federal work projects. Loretta's mother kept the family healthy with country common sense and folk remedies.

Life was hard in Butcher Hollow—"one of the most backward sections of the country," Loretta says—but she is very proud of her people. She had to walk several miles to a school, and her few companions were mostly relatives in neighboring cabins. The children who lived in the coal camps down the hill were like sophisticated city slickers to her.

Even as a girl, Loretta liked to sing old mountain folk songs about train wrecks and tragic romances to her younger brothers and sisters. Her father would hoard the charge in his battery-operated radio for Saturday night, when she and the family would listen to the rollicking sound of "Grand Ole Opry," the nationally broadcast show from Nashville, Tenn. The next day, Loretta's clear child's voice would rise into the mountain pines, mimicking what she'd heard.

When Loretta was 13, she was spotted by a baby-faced ex-soldier, O. V. "Doolittle" Lynn, nine years her senior. Bidding for her pie at a community auction, he won the right to escort her home. Within a month, the insistent young man proposed marriage. Although it was not usual for Kentucky mountain girls to marry before the age of 14, Loretta was eager for a

The Queen of Country Music 141

new way of life, and her parents could not dissuade her. Wearing borrowed clothes, she and Doolittle were married by a justice of the peace.

Loretta became pregnant shortly after marriage and had some rocky times with her husband. Eager to get away from the coal mines, Doolittle got a farming job in Washington State, where he had lived as a child, and Loretta soon followed. It was a major step for a pregnant, shy 14-year-old who had never been more than ten miles from home. "I was scared to get on that train," she recalls. "But he was my husband, and I wanted to be with him."

By the time she was 18, Loretta had four children—two boys and two girls—and she was working practically around the clock. She learned to cook (winning first prize at a state fair) and parked her babies on a blanket while she picked crops. Her husband worked as a mechanic and lumberjack, and got a new nickname—"Mooney"—when his fellow loggers discovered he had lugged moonshine back in Kentucky.

There were few diversions for these hard-working country people. On big occasions, Mooney would take Loretta to a tavern for a few beers and some country music. He had heard Loretta singing along with the radio, so he bought her a cheap guitar and suggested that she could entertain in local clubs and earn a few dollars.

Loretta never dreamed that she would perform onstage. She began by imitating Kitty Wells, then the top woman in country music, but soon began making up her own lyrics. When Mooney marched Loretta out for auditions with local clubs and radio shows, the frightened housewife received warm applause.

A local merchant agreed to sponsor a record of a song she had written, "I'm a Honky Tonk Girl," and she and Mooney traveled to Los Angeles for a date with studio musicians. The record was issued on something called the "Zero" label, a newly created name. Leaving their children with a friend, the Lynns traveled and slept in their old jalopy, distributing the record and photographs of Loretta to country disk jockeys. When they picked up a station on the car radio, they would head for the town. Loretta would put on her one presentable dress, knock on the door of the station, and try to get the disk jockey to air her song. The record began to be played from the West Coast all the way to Nashville, and moved into the country-music hit parade.

On October 15, 1960, Loretta was permitted to sing the song on the "Grand Ole Opry's" Saturday-night radio jamboree. Later she signed for a tour and got a contract with Decca Records (now MCA). About a year after going on the road, the Lynns moved their family to Nashville, and Loretta was named 1961's "Most Promising Female Singer."

The girl with a poor Kentucky education had a touch of poet in her. She fashioned songs from incidents in her own experience. One night, a woman confided that her husband was seeing another woman. Loretta took one look at her and blurted, "Why, honey, she ain't woman enough to take your man." Emboldened, the woman went off to reclaim her husband. Meanwhile, Loretta scribbled down the words: "You Ain't Woman Enough to Take My Man." That song is now one of her trademarks and, she recalls, the woman who told her of her troubles is still "married to that same guy."

Today, traveling the country in a huge, well-appointed bus, Loretta Lynn puts on some 125 shows a year. She gears them, she says, for a certain type of housewife. "The men have lots of pretty singers to cheer for. But I think about the housewife who's watching the kids all week. I was like that for a long time myself. That woman saves up her money to have a good time at my show. That's why we always give 'em their money's worth."

There are always fans, wherever Loretta goes, who feel that they must meet her, see her up close, and that if they do their lives will somehow be different. They constantly write, too, for advice on how to run their lives. Loretta seems amused by this, since she has had her own share of problems. (She feels guilty, for instance, about leaving her children while they were growing up—it is her one regret about going into singing.) Many of the fan letters are as touching as Loretta's songs. One woman in Denton, Texas, wrote after reading Loretta's autobiography: "I identified with you, for I too remember flour sacks, outhouses and not having enough to eat. But until I read your book, I was always ashamed of it all."

Life gets monotonous on long tours, with the band and the background singers crammed into the buses and Loretta secluded in the back of one of them. She suffers from periodic migraine headaches. Often she stays up half the night, humming songs into a tape recorder. After 20 years on the road, she doesn't know, or care, what state she is passing through. The blinds in her room remain drawn; all she knows is the hum of the air conditioner and the rumble of the wheels underneath.

How long can she keep up the touring grind? Loretta insists she could "quit tomorrow" and stay home. But she doesn't feel comfortable on her brief visits to her ranch and Hurricane Mills, 65 miles southwest of Nashville, and admits that her only true home is in the back of the bus—being accessible to her adoring fans.

In addition to television and recording dates, Loretta has added Lake Tahoe, Las Vegas and Reno to her heavy concert schedule. Country musicians need constant live exposure. And, Loretta says, she would miss walking out onstage, all dressed up in her sequin-studded pantsuit, and seeing those housewives, in their own finest outfits, waiting to hear songs written by Loretta—about *them*.

The Man Who Put the Top Hat on Jazz

by John Reddy

THE WHITE HOUSE had never seen anything quite like it. The greats of the jazz world, and a ricky-tick piano player named Richard Nixon, were playing and singing up a storm in honor of Duke Ellington's 70th birthday. The President tinkled out "Happy Birthday" on the piano in the East Room, then presented Ellington with the Presidential Medal of Freedom. "In the royalty of American music," Nixon said, "no man swings more or stands higher than the Duke."

At this, the Duke kissed the President twice on each cheek—the ultimate Ellington accolade. And the party rocked along until the wee small hours, with the famous guests playing Ellington tunes and the Duke sitting in at the piano. "I've never seen the place like this," an elderly butler said as he poured champagne. "It sure has soul tonight."

That lively bash in April, 1969, was the most spectacular of a host of celebrations for the birthday of the remarkable pianist, conductor and composer. After the party, a friend remarked that Ellington looked tired. "Well, why not?" asked the Duke. "Did *you* ever blow out 70 candles ten nights in a row?"

Actually, Ellington, who died at the age of 75, was almost never tired. Although the deep-scooped pouches under his eyes, the comfortable paunch, the long, somber face gave him an air of world-weariness, he was robust and incredibly active and creative into his 70s. A devout hypochondriac ("Man, fresh air can *kill* you"), he nonetheless bounced along on a grueling schedule, playing one-nighters with his band, traveling 52 weeks a year to all corners of the world. "I don't believe in the generation gap," he said on his 70th birthday. "I believe in the regeneration gap. Each day you regenerate, or else you're not living."

In many ways, Duke Ellington's story is the story of jazz itself—perhaps the most American art form. In more than half a century of composing, he wrote over 6000 songs, ranging from such standard hits as "Mood Indigo" and "Solitude" to sacred music and long, harmonically complex tone poems such as "Black, Brown and Beige." He composed the music for Broadway shows and several movies, and he sold nearly *20 million* records.

Honored by four U.S. Presidents, Queen Elizabeth and Pope Pius XII, Ellington conducted the London Philharmonic, the orchestras at the Paris Open and at La Scala in Milan, as well as the symphonies of Hamburg, Stockholm and Toronto. He appeared with many major U.S. symphony orchestras. Although he never finished high school, he was awarded honorary degrees by eight universities, including Yale and Brown. ("A doctorate is wonderful," he said. "It means that somebody obviously is listening. But if I write some music, and *I* hear it, that is my reward.")

Ellington did not escape racial slights, but he rose above them. In the 1930s, when his band first toured the South, hotel doors remained firmly shut. Ellington solved this situation by traveling in two private Pullman cars and a baggage car. "At each station," Duke recalled, "the natives would come by and say, 'What's that?' 'Well,' we'd say, 'that's the way the President travels.'"

Like Joshua before Jericho, Duke brought the walls of prejudice tumbling down. "The best way for me to be effective is through music," he contended. "Social protest and pride in the history of the Negro have been the most significant themes in what we've done." He pointed out that he wrote a song titled "Black Beauty" in 1928. "Now 'Black is Beautiful' is the latest thing," he said with a trace of irony. Ellington was particularly proud of a 1963 show called *My People*, in which, through music and dance, he traced the last 100 years of the Negro experience in America. One song, called "King Fit the Battle of Alabam," recounted the dramatic confrontation between Martin Luther King and Birmingham's segregationist police commissioner Bull Connor.

Ellington was giving a benefit concert at Carnegie Hall for Mississippi's Tougaloo College when he received word of Dr. King's assassination. He went into his dressing room and locked the door. After some moments alone, he returned to the stage and called on a white clergyman friend in the audience to say a prayer in King's memory. Then he continued the concert.

Edward Kennedy Ellington was born in Washington, D.C. He had a loving and deeply religious upbringing. His mother was a Baptist, his father (a butler at the White House) a Methodist, and his mother insisted he go to *both* churches every Sunday. He often spoke of his mother's powerful influence on him. "She used to say, 'Edward, you are blessed,'" Ellington recalled. "She told me I'd never have to worry—so I never have."

Both his parents played the piano, and at the age of seven he started taking lessons. The teacher soon gave up on him, however, because he wouldn't practice scales. Still, by the time he was 14 he had composed his first song, "Soda Fountain Rag," inspired by the fact that he worked at an ice-cream parlor. He had also picked up the nickname "Duke" because of his aristocratic bearing in his starched soda-jerk's outfit. When he was asked to play that first song, he'd say, "I can't. It's too difficult."

After a few years of playing with small bands around Washington, Ellington made his way to New York. There he received the nearest thing he ever had to formal musical training. He was befriended by a legendary black violinist named Will Marion Cook, who had studied and been widely acclaimed in Europe. "I'd ask him questions about music," Ellington said. "And when I got the answers, it was the equivalent of a semester's education. Then he'd say, 'You gotta go to the conservatory.' And I'd say, 'Dad, I don't want to go to the conservatory because they don't teach what I want to learn.'"

Eventually, Duke organized a small band that played around New York. They got their first big break in 1927, broadcasting over national radio from the Cotton Club in Harlem. Jazz was just coming into its own then, and Harlem was a swinging place. They had some great sessions, which the Duke recalled fondly. "There'd be 'Willie the Lion' Smith and James P. Johnson. I'd take a shot at the piano, and so would Fats Waller. The Lion would put his cigar in his mouth and stomp over to the piano. 'Get up,' he'd say. 'I'll show you how it's *supposed to be.*' And he would!"

Although 1929 was the year of the Wall Street crash, Ellington's stock continued to rise. He starred in Florenz Ziegfeld's *Show Girl*, with music by George Gershwin. He and the band also went to Hollywood to make two movies, and in the early 1930s they toured Europe, where Ellington's music was compared to that of Ravel and Bach.

Duke was a brilliant pianist, but he has always said that his orchestra was his instrument. "We write music for the cats in the band," he said, "and what comes out is us." His complex harmonies and unusual instrumental combinations produced the warm, lush sound that was the Ellington style. Over the years, he progressed from writing popular standards like "Do Nothing Till You Hear From Me," to longer, more complex symphonic pieces such as "Reminiscing in Tempo" and "Such Sweet Thunder." In everything he composed he took the music of black America—ragtime, gospel and blues—and endowed it with elegance and grace. "He put the top hat on jazz," one critic said.

This is especially true of such evocative music as "Harlem Air Shaft," which captures in melody the vivid sights and sounds of the Negro ghetto. "So much goes on in a Harlem air shaft," Ellington said. "You hear people making love. You hear gossip floating down. You hear people praying, fighting, snoring. You smell dinner. I tried to put all that in 'Harlem Air Shaft.'"

The Duke could compose under almost any conditions, but he functioned best with a deadline. He wrote "Black and Tan Fantasy" in a taxi careening through Central Park on his way to a recording session. "I wrote 'Mood Indigo' in 15 minutes, and 'Solitude' in 20 minutes while standing up," he said.

In the mid-1960s, Ellington was playing a smoky nightclub in Redwood City, Calif., when he was approached by Canon John Yaryan and Dean C. Julian Bartlett of Grace Cathedral in San Francisco. They proposed that he do a sacred concert at the cathedral. "I was shocked," Duke said later. "How was I going to stand up in that big cathedral and make a noise? I said, 'You better wait. Let me get myself together.' Later on, I said, 'Okay, let's go.'"

The sacred music posed one of the greatest challenges of Ellington's long and productive career. Always religious (he read the Bible every night), he was determined to produce music of reverence and beauty. "I said to myself, 'Here's you, Duke Ellington, and there's that great big cathedral. You can't slouch, man. You've got to write stand-up-straight music for a cathedral.'"

The concert, with the cathedral choir singing Ellington's music, and a tap-dancer dancing before the altar, was an enormous success. The Duke later performed it in other famed cathedrals, including St. John the Divine in New York and Coventry cathedral in England, as well as in leading synagogues, with the Ellington music sung in Hebrew. "These concerts are really musical sermons, statements of eternal truths," Ellington said. "It's a deeply religious and joyous performance. And why shouldn't it be? One form of worship is to offer in the service of the Lord that which you can do best."

Ellington could have retired a wealthy man but he kept up his arduous schedule until he died. Once in his early 70s, he flew in from a series of one-nighters in the West Indies for a recording stint in a New York studio. During the three-hour session, he alternated between playing the piano and bouncing off his stool to conduct, swinging his arm choppily to the tempo, then crouching in the middle of the circle of musicians, beckoning gently to his sidemen as though softly coaxing the music from their instruments.

About midnight, the Duke was finally ready to leave. He would catch a bite to eat, he said. Then he and Harry Carney, his amiable saxophonist who had been with him for 41 years, would drive through the early-morning hours to reach Cleveland in time for an engagement the next night. Harry would take the wheel, as he had on thousands of other nights, leaving Ellington free to compose.

"Harry and I don't talk much," Duke said as he left the studio. "I just dream and write, and I keep thinking that the thing coming up tomorrow is the big one. Who knows what direction it will take?"

W. C. Handy: Father of the Blues

by Carl B. Wall

ONE EVENING in 1956 residents of Brooklyn's Home for Aged Colored People assembled to lend ear to a gentleman who had been billed as "guest speaker." They were astounded when, instead of a discourse on the pleasures of growing old, the guest lifted a golden trumpet to his lips and began sending a spirited rendition of "St. Louis Blues." As the buoyant notes bounced off the ceiling, wrinkled faces crinkled in smiles, hands began clapping in rhythm to the song that many of these oldsters had first danced to more than 40 years ago.

The "speaker" was William Christopher Handy, patriarch of America's song writers, composer of the immortal "St. Louis Blues" and many other hit tunes. That night, he was putting into practice one of his favorite adages: "If you want to be happy, make others happy." Despite an illness which had confined him to bed for several weeks, he had insisted on keeping the engagement. "This is going to help me just as much as it's going to help these old folks," he had said to his doctor.

His physician refrained from pointing out that Handy, then 82, was probably older than most of the inmates of the old folk's home. Not that it would have done any good. The venerable musician refused to recognize the passage of the years. Others may grow old, but he only became "mellower." Another handicap he ignored was his blindness.

W. C. Handy, affectionately referred to by some as "De Lawd of Tin Pan Alley," was one of the truly legendary figures of the American entertainment world. Until his death in March, 1958, his cheerful face was unlined, his vibrant, youthful laughter would fill a room. As head of the Handy Brothers Music Co. he still handled all important details of the business, which netted him an income of about $40,000 a year. He traveled around each year, visiting music dealers, speaking at fundraising dinners, appearing in benefits. He devoted a major share of his time to the W. C. Handy Foundation for the Blind, an organization he established in 1953.

In 1956 when he was hospitalized by a slight stroke, one of his friends asked, "Why don't you take it easy, W. C.? Let somebody else do all this charity work."

W. C. grinned. "It's what the Lord wants me to do," he said. "I can't quit now."

Behind this driving urge to help others lay the facts of Handy's life. To the millions who have danced to his music, he seemed a fabulous genius who effortlessly created undying hits like "Beale Street Blues," "Memphis Blues," "St. Louis Blues"—and lived happily ever after on the royalties. The real story is very different.

Born in Florence, Ala., with a love of music in his heart, Handy met with parental disapproval as early as his 12th year when he brought home a guitar he had purchased with hard-earned savings. "A guitar!" his father gasped. "One of the devil's playthings. Take it back where it came from! Git!"

But the youthful Handy made forbidden rhythm by scraping a nail across the jawbone of a horse, or humming through fine-tooth combs. He roamed the woods, cataloguing sounds. Robins were a warm alto. The mockingbird trilled cadenzas. Even the far-off bellow of a bull, the deep-throated whistles of steamers on the Tennessee River echoed in his imagination as musical notes. He bought an old cornet for $1.75 and practiced on it secretly for years.

As a young man he went to work in the Bessemer, Ala., steel mills for $1.85 a day. When depression closed the mills in 1893, he roamed the country as a wandering musician, sleeping where he could: on the cobblestones of the Mississippi levee, in vacant lots. He worked at anything—with a street-paving gang, as janitor in a singing society hall in Henderson, Ky., where he studied music under the society's maestro.

His first break came when he was offered a job as cornetist with W. A. Mahara's Minstrels at six dollars a week. After several successful seasons, Handy organized his own dance

W. C. Handy: Father of the Blues

band in Memphis. It was a good one, but many a dance was played by Handy's band on horns and fiddles released for the evening by an indulgent pawnbroker. At 40, Handy considered himself a failure. A married man now with a family of four small children, his income averaged about $2.50 a day.

Suddenly came a turnabout. On a September evening in 1914, Handy locked himself in a rented room with a piano in the Beale Street section of Memphis and feverishly jotted the notes of a melody that had been haunting his brain for 20 years. It was a plaintive, poignant song, and it began with those words now so familiar: "I hate to see de evenin' sun go down." "St. Louis Blues" swept the country. Every mail brought at least one royalty check; over one miraculous week-end more than $6000 flooded in.

In 1918 Handy opened his music-publishing office in New York. At first, business boomed, but with the general tightening of the economy after World War I, sheet-music sales began slipping. Handy's royalties fell to a trickle. He was forced to lay off most of his staff, devote his Sundays to bookkeeping, his nights to arranging scores. He refused to quit.

Through all these dismaying days the "Father of the Blues" kept his lively sense of humor. There was, for example, the episode of the grand piano, which had been mortgaged. Handy, lacking the payment due on the loan, had the piano moved from his home to his Broadway office, where he could continue working on a new song. He soothed the office landlord, who had been threatening to evict him, by suggesting that the piano could be considered security for back rent. Then one day the finance company sent its men to pick up the piano. A hassle ensued.

While the landlord and the movers tried to argue each other down, Handy, his eyes twinkling, calmly picked out experimental chords. When the movers began shoving the piano, Handy looked up and bellowed, "Dammit all, how do you expect a man to work with all this fuss going on?"

Then he turned to the landlord and demanded: "Why don't you pay these buzzards the few dollars they want so I can get back to work? All I got to do is get this tune finished and you'll get your money. It'll be a hit, I tell you. Just listen!"

With that he began to play "Sundown Blues," and soon both the movers and landlord were tapping their feet to its catchy tempo. The incident ended with the landlord advancing the money for the loan and adding it to the rent due.

But business continued to fail. And, quite suddenly, Handy was plagued by excruciating eye pains. Within a few months he was totally blind, the result primarily of overwork, worry and nervous strain. To the doctor, he said, "It's my own fault, isn't it? My father used to tell me to wear life like a loose garment—but I've worn it too tight around me. All I've thought about was success, the things money will bring."

Then he continued, "But I promise God here and now that if I ever see again, that's what I'll do for the rest of my days—wear life like a loose garment.

The first shock of blindness brought Handy close to despair. He would sit by himself with tears streaming from his sightless eyes. One night he asked his wife, Elizabeth, to read to him from the Book of Job. As her soft, clear voice read those majestic passages, he gradually relaxed. Bible reading became a regular evening ritual.

Once again he began to pick out chords on the piano. It was in those days that he first arranged sacred songs such as "They That Sow in Tears" and "I'll Never Turn Back No More."

In those years of blindness, Handy discovered the generous hearts of his friends. Bill Robinson, the famed dancer, and scores of others helped with cash and in a hundred other ways. One afternoon a printer for whom the composer had once done a good turn put two $1000 bills in his hand with a murmured, "And don't worry about paying it back."

Then one unforgettable morning, the Handy family awakened to a vigorous rendition of "St. Louis Blues." W. C. had found his golden trumpet and was again sending with all his heart. He had emerged from the depths. His health improved rapidly and, after an operation on his eyes, his vision miraculously returned.

Reopening his Broadway office, he began patching together his shattered business. Gradually his affairs prospered. "Aunt Hagar's Blues," a song he had written years before, suddenly became a hit. But Handy, now in his early 50s, was determined to follow the advice of his father to "wear life like a loose garment." He dedicated himself to sharing with others. Even as he was paying off his own debts, he advanced grocery money to impoverished song writers, paid hospital bills for unemployed musicians, contributed to scores of private charities. And the more he interested himself in others, the more his own business picked up.

A torrential talker, Handy became a good listener. One evening he listened patiently to a man named Robert Clairmont, a stranger whom he had typed as a Greenwich Village drifter. "Why don't we give a concert in Carnegie Hall showing the evolution of Negro music?" Clairmont said.

"An excellent notion," Handy replied. "But those things cost a bundle of money—$3000 at least."

"All right," the stranger promised. "I'll bring you the money Monday morning."

Clairmont proved to be an unusual man: a successful broker with a yen to express himself outside the stock market. The resulting concert, one of the first "glorifications of the blues," was a tremendous success. Paul Whiteman and other fine orchestras began arranging symphonic interpretations of blues music, too. Royalties poured in from record sales, and Handy was freed forever from financial worry.

Toward the end of 1939, Handy's vision again started to fail, but this time he accepted approaching blindness with equanimity, refusing to let it halt any phase of his work. In 1953, the New York State Commission for the Blind honored his charitable work in that field with a citation which paid tribute to "the man of 80 years whose magnificent spirit reflects the words of his famous song, 'I hate to see de evenin' sun go down.'"

Handy himself perhaps best expressed his own philosophy when he said: "Life's a lot like playing the trumpet; you got to blow something into it to get something out of it."

Sousa Marches On!

by Ann M. Lingg

ON A NASTY November day in 1896, John Philip Sousa was pacing the windswept deck of the S.S. *Teutonic*. The collar of his heavy coat turned up, his cap pulled down over his eyes, he was in near panic.

He and his wife, Jane, had been ending a delightful working vacation in Europe when he read in a week-old Paris newspaper that his manager and trusted friend, David A. Blakeley, had suffered a fatal stroke in his Carnegie Hall office. Moreover, Sousa, 42, had never handled his own business affairs. How could he manage without Blakeley?

Now he looked up. The sky was as gray and gloomy as his mood. Only the ship's American flag provided a touch of color, its pole a steady marker in a drifting universe. Suddenly, as he paced back and forth, a melody seemed to rise from the waters beyond—a melody that floated briskly along like a flag in a spanking breeze. It was a good melody, inspiring, strong. It made him step to its rhythm. An imaginary band played it in his ears.

The melody stayed with Sousa for the rest of his trip. And on Christmas Day, he wrote it down, calling it "The Stars and Stripes Forever."

Had he never written anything else, Sousa would still be famous. The march became so popular the world over that foreigners sometimes still mistake it for our National Anthem. Experts say that its firm-beat optimism makes it the finest military and patriotic march ever composed.

Sousa soon became a legend, and his very name kept people

Sousa Marches On!

guessing. He was rumored to be an immigrant, and "Sousa" was said to stand for his initials, S. O., plus the destination—U.S.A.—that he had scrawled on his luggage. Actually, he was a genuine American product. His ancestry was Portuguese and German, but he was born in Washington, D.C., near the Capitol, one of ten children of Antonio and Elizabeth Sousa, on November 6, 1854. Papa Sousa played the trombone in the U.S. Marine Band, and little John Philip used to hang around the barracks grounds. One of his earliest impressions was of the parade marking the Civil War's end. Weaned on patriotism and band music (he learned to play several instruments, notably the trombone and violin), he always credited this early exposure for his infatuation with marches.

When John Philip was 13, his father apprenticed him to the Marine Band to keep him from running away with a circus. He quit after several years to tour with theater companies and variety shows. In 1876 he was concertmaster to Jacques Offenbach, who had come to America from Paris to conduct at the Philadelphia Centennial Festival. At 25, married to a Philadelphia debutante and sporting a pirate's beard for dignity, Sousa was rehired by the Marine Band, this time as its leader, the youngest ever.

Within 12 years, he built the Marine Band into a first-class concert organization, and wrote numerous marches for it. "Semper Fidelis," ordered by President Chester A. Arthur and dedicated to the Marines, is still played at all parades and official functions of the Corps. In 1889 he composed "The Washington Post," to celebrate a massive public-school essay contest sponsored by the newspaper. The light and festive beat of the new march took America by storm, and before long even dance bands had picked it up. Until then, the traditional two-step had been considered a dry and boring dance. "The Washington Post" pepped it up, and soon the two-step craze was on.

Sousa introduced his own concert band in 1892 at the Columbian Exposition and World Congress in Chicago. From there it went on tour to win audiences that soon were the largest in the country. The band made 32 transcontinental tours and hundreds of shorter trips, went to Europe five times (once as far as Russia), and in 1910-11 circled the globe, trailing headlines. All in all, Sousa and his men covered 1.5 million miles, and were seen and heard by more than 50 million people. His business acumen need not have worried him: in spite of paying out some $28 million in salaries and transportation costs, Sousa became a wealthy man.

Wherever he went, the zip and verve of his conducting captivated audiences. While he stood with feet firmly planted, the upper part of his body literally acted out the music. To some people he seemed to be swimming or dancing or fencing; others said he handled his baton like a whip or an eggbeater. At the climax of a march, he would swing his right arm up and down like an Indian club, throwing audiences into virtual hysterics with what became known as "the Sousa swing."

By the early 1900s, Sousa had made for himself a big place in the musical life of the nation. Advertised everywhere in veritable P. T. Barnum style, his face was probably more familiar to people across the land than that of any other American. He was less successful, however, in his fierce one-man war against the phonograph. Although he had been one of the first to make recordings, he did not like machines and the "mathematical system of megaphones, wheels, cogs, discs and cylinders." "Canned music is as incongruous by a campfire as canned salmon by a trout brook," he once wrote (thereby introducing the term "canned music" into our language).

Sousa never revised this opinion, even though recordings did extremely well by him. "Your phonograph is all right" was all he could be moved to say as an endorsement for the Victor Talking Machine Company. In May, 1923, when the nearly septuagenarian and slightly deaf Sousa was introduced to the nearly octogenarian and almost completely deaf Thomas A. Edison, the two were soon embroiled in a shouted argument about recordings.

In 1914, he signed up with the Hippodrome Variety Theater to supply musical entertainment twice a day, and a feature show on Sunday nights. These Sunday programs became big events, with such legendary singers as Emmy Destinn, Nellie Melba, Julia Culp, Olive Fremstad, Maggie Teyte and John McCormack appearing on the Hippodrome's New York City stage with the master himself.

Although the movies eventually superseded vaudeville, and the tango replaced the two-step, the nation's fancy for marches was unaffected. "Marches will be the music of the world as long as men like to keep in step," Sousa predicted confidently. In all, he wrote over 100 of them (in addition to operettas, symphonic poems and songs).

During World War I, in his 60s, he was called upon to train military bands. The work with young people proved to be a fountain of youth for Sousa, and his fund-raising concerts and parades earned him the title "Pied Piper of Patriotism." His wartime activities netted him two honorary doctorates as well, and the rank of lieutenant commander in the Naval Reserve.

As the '20s roared around him, he traveled far and wide (though now in his 70s) to encourage the growing school-band movements. His conducting grew more sedate after he fell from a horse in 1922, fracturing a vertebra. Though he was constantly in pain, the March King carried on in his sturdy, refreshingly old-fashioned way. "The first you'll hear of Sousa's retirement is when you hear 'Sousa dead,'" he remarked. Death did finally overtake him on March 6, 1932, in a hotel room in Reading, Pa., where he suffered a heart attack after a rehearsal and banquet. He had written seven new marches the year before.

Sousa lives on in people's minds as one of the great Americans, above and beyond the call of music. In 1954, his centennial year, a bill was passed by Congress to make "The Stars and Stripes Forever" the national march, "to be used for the appearance of high federal and state government officials, other than the President, on public occasions." And on November 1, 1973, Sousa was elected to the Hall of Fame for Great Americans (the only other musicians there being Stephen Foster and Edward MacDowell).

His inclusion there seems fit and just. The impact of his stirring marches shows no signs of fading. Fads may come and go, but John Philip Sousa will forever remain a symbol of sturdy, optimistic Americanism. Sousa marches on!

Beautiful Friends

Bing Crosby:
A Road Buddy's Memories

by Bob Hope

IT'S FUNNY how many times the most lasting friendships of our lives begin in a moment so incidental we scarcely recall it. Bing Crosby and I shook hands outside the Friars Club on 48th Street in New York one autumn day back in 1932. He was already a recording star and had one of the most popular radio shows in the country. I was a comedian fresh out of vaudeville and nibbling at a Broadway career.

Two months later I was emceeing a variety show at New York's Capitol Theater, and Crosby was the lead singer. It was the first time our names appeared together on a marquee. Across from the theater there happened to be a watering hole to which Bing and I repaired each evening between shows. We started kidding one another, then developing little bits to work into the show. The crowd in the bar loved it. Who can define what the chemistry was between the easygoing crooner from Tacoma via Spokane and the erstwhile boxer and vaudeville hoofer from England via Cleveland? It was just there.

On our respective radio shows during the 1930s, we both fostered the "Hope-Crosby Feud." He took potshots at my nose ("like a bicycle seat"), my golf and even my jokes. I fired back at "Ol' Dad," the aging star, ribbing him about everything from his "groaning" to his rapidly thinning hair and jug ears.

One night he walked on, unexpected, during my radio show. "Tell me, Bing," I said, "with so much hot air and those ears, why don't you take off?" He replied, chuckling, "The downdraft from your nose prevents it."

Bing could kid around about those very things that made

other stars founder in a morass of vanity. He once wrote regarding my incessant razzing over the hairpiece Paramount made him wear in his films: "Robert Hope, of the non-classic profile and the unlissome midsection, is sometimes goaded by a knowledge of his own lack of physical charms into referring to me as skin head. I don't have to specify what it means. It's generally known that for screen purposes I wear a device the trade calls a scalp doily."

By the time I got to Hollywood and signed with Paramount, Crosby had already made his mark in movies. By then, too, ol' Cros was also a little mad about horses, though the ones he bought weren't necessarily mad about winning races. The first horse he owned was named Zombie, and it ran true to its name. Bing often averred that his losing stable was purely an altruistic gesture for my benefit, a charitable source of jokes. "Hope is always short of good material," he said.

Bing's penchant for horses eventually got us together in the movies. Wanting to be sure he had good seats at the finish line, Crosby had in his grandly casual way purchased a big interest in the Del Mar racetrack, near San Diego. To boost attendance, he helped stage lavish parties at the track's Turf Club, and invited film and radio personalities to entertain. I was included in one of these Saturday-night forays, and Crosby and I did a little reprise of our clowning from the Capitol Theater days. The old chemistry was still there. Only this time a Paramount producer was in the audience, and he said, "We've got to get these two boys together in a picture."

The result was a zany film called *The Road to Singapore*—the first of seven "roads" we traveled on film, usually in pursuit of the lovely Dorothy Lamour. It was Bing who saw the possibilities for ad-libbing in the script. I can still see Cros drawing thoughtfully on his pipe between takes as he studied new ways to butcher the script. Sometimes we'd shout back and forth between our dressing rooms, trying our new bits. Poor Dottie Lamour, who had studied her lines like the pro she was, couldn't recognize a single phrase to cue on.

Crosby always loved words, liked to trip them mellifluously over his tongue. He had a soft-spoken way of circumlocution larded with erudite words and foreign phrases that was part of his trademark (Crosby would have loved those last two sentences.) I remember a scene in *The Road to Morocco* in which we were having trouble with a French policeman. I began ad-libbing and asked Cros, "Can you talk French?" "Certainly I can," he replied and directed an effortless stream of Gallic at the policeman. Later I discovered he had recited a short French fable about a crow and a piece of cheese—a classic piece of high-school French that was indelibly imprinted in Bing's brain.

It's no big secret how long I panted after that Barbie-doll-sized gold statue they call Oscar. In fact, it was a running gag between Bing and me, especially after he won one as best actor for his portrayal of Father O'Malley in *Going My Way*. Once, during the filming of *The Road to Rio*, the script had me down on my knees, clutching at Crosby's coattails, crying, "Don't leave me! Don't leave me!" As the take drew to a close, Crosby solemnly pulled his Oscar from beneath his coat and handed it to me. The sound stage broke up.

If you want biographical detail on Harry Lillis Crosby, there are several books around (including Bing's own, *Call Me Lucky*) that trace his career from the early days in Spokane to his place in the pantheon of popular entertainers. You can read all about Crosby playing drums with an outfit called the Musicaladers, about his big break with the Paul Whiteman band and the forming of a trio called the "Rhythm Boys." Then, at the fabled Coconut Grove in Los Angeles, Bing began singing solo, and the music business was never quite the same.

The mischievous kid from the big Irish family who had wanted to be a professional baseball player became a recording star before there *were* recording stars. It's estimated that he sold more than 400 million records and recorded more than 4000 songs. Then there were the movies, and the radio and television and concert appearances.

But nobody has to remind us how big Bing was. I just like to recall the *way* he was.

For all his celluloid escapades, for all his celebrity, Bing was a private man and he let it be known quite firmly that he intended to live "*outside* the fan magazines." He had the magnificent opportunity to love and be loved by two extraordinary women: his first wife and mother of his four eldest sons, Dixie Lee, who died of cancer in 1952; and Kathryn, the beautiful and vivacious lady who was his wife the last 20 years of his life, bearing him two sons and a daughter.

The public loved him because they saw in him an absolutely

ordinary guy who had become very rich and very famous—yet never left his real self behind. Who but Bing could be refused a room at a posh hotel when he came in from a hunting trip all bearded and bedraggled? And it was just like him, too, to be caught by the Paris police who found him dozing next to a "Keep Off the Grass" sign, a newspaper tented over his face to shut out the sun. He loved singing and show business, but he always let it be known that he might just rather be playing golf, fishing a good trout stream or hunting pheasant with a Labrador at his side.

Make no mistake, though, Bing was serious about those things he believed important in life—family, church and giving his time, talent and money to a world he felt had been pretty good to him. He was a devout Catholic, but he didn't wear his religion on his sleeve. When director Leo McCarey approached him about playing the part of the young priest in *Going My Way*, Bing was concerned that the Church might find the idea of a "crooner" in the role offensive. Only after McCarey assured him that a number of priests had reacted favorably did Bing agree. The result was the portrayal of Father O'Malley that further endeared him to millions.

Bing also had to be practically coerced into recording "Silent Night" and "White Christmas." When Decca asked him to do "Silent Night," he refused, saying it would be like "cashing in" on religion. He relented when it was arranged that the proceeds would go to orphans being taken care of by American missions in China. Later, during the Second World War, Bing and his troupe toured military camps on funds from "Silent Night." It was his next-biggest-selling record to "White Christmas."

"White Christmas," sung by Bing. What more can you really say? Who isn't touched with a wave of nostalgia when he hears it? But again, everyone had to twist Bing's arm to get him to sing it in the film *Holiday Inn*. He said it might be interpreted as commercializing Christmas. He was finally persuaded, and he sang it like nobody ever will again. It became one of the biggest hits of all time, a special tribute to the man who loved to take his kids caroling in the neighborhood every Christmas.

I don't suppose anyone will ever be able to calculate the total amount of money Crosby gave or raised for charitable causes. He loved golf, particularly when he was playing to raise money for a hospital, school or some other worthy cause. And he sacrificed time, money and even physical stamina to do charity benefits—so much that someone called him a one-man "itinerant foundation."

Once we played a charity golf match together in Indianapolis during World War II. I was scheduled to go from there to South Bend for a War Bond rally at Notre Dame. I asked Bing to come along, and he did. The crowd roared with delight at his unexpected entrance. Then he flew on to Chicago, while I stayed in South Bend to do a show at a Navy installation the next day. It was my birthday, and darned if Cros didn't fly back to surprise me onstage with a cake.

He liked those casual surprises. I was in London once doing a benefit for a boys' club, and asked Bing, who was also in town, to appear. It was unlikely he could make it, and I didn't really promise that he'd show, but the word got around. That night the audience called to me, "Where's Bing?" I joked with them, saying it was late for such an old man to be out. Suddenly there he was, leaning against the proscenium grinning at me between puffs on his pipe. The crowd went nuts. It was the first time Bing had ever been on the stage in England. He sang for 40 minutes as the audience shouted out their favorites.

In December, 1976, Bing and his family began a charity concert tour that showed the world he could still sing like nobody else. Clive Barnes wrote in the New York *Times*, "He lives his songs. He never plays any role other than himself. This is what is so touching."

That was Bing all the way. A natural. One of his old buddies from Spokane said that when Bing was a boy, you could always tell he was coming because you'd hear him singing or whistling. Well, thanks to records and films, he'll never leave us. That's a reassuring and pleasant thought.

Bing loved his dad, and said of him, "He was a cheery man. He liked everybody and I think everybody liked him, which is a better epitaph than most men have."

It's Bing's epitaph, too. If friends could be made to order, I would have asked for one like him.

High Priestess of the Dance

by S. Hurok

SHE WAS the worst poker player I ever met. When she held a good hand, she hummed, chattered or gazed around the room with such elaborate unconcern that everyone knew she had a pair of aces. With a poor hand, she was so glum you would think the world was ending.

This was the Anna Pavlova I knew. To the world she was the greatest of ballerinas, a legend in her lifetime. Even today, her name is known to people who never attended the ballet or who are not even interested in it. To them, she was a shimmering, unreal person with a greatness that time has not touched. But to me, she was one of the warmest, most vital human beings I ever knew.

People today who know her only in terms of old—and bad—film clips of her dancing, think of her as remote as the farthest star. That exquisite mask of a face, with its great dark eyes and camellia features, and its expression of cold, chiseled melancholy, made her seem dehumanized. Remote and ethereal, she was a dying swan, a ghostly maiden, a fairy princess; in her filmy white costume, severe hairdo and deadly white makeup, she was a creature not of this world.

That was Pavlova to the public. Yet in all the 57 years I have been presenting great artists to the world, I have never known anyone with such a zest for life.

I'll never forget the first time I met her. I was already well-known as an impresario, yet I was so star-struck by her that I used to stand in back of the audience at the old New York Hippodrome every night and watch her dance. One night, a

High Priestess of the Dance

friend offered to take me backstage to meet her. Mentally, I rehearsed a little speech in English, then in Russian. But when I got to her dressing room, I was too tongue-tied to speak. She extended her hand and I numbly bent to kiss it. When she invited me to join her at supper, I could only nod. My dream of meeting my idol had come true—and I had not uttered a word.

What sort of restaurant do you think she would pick, this high priestess of the dance? I imagined her in some exquisite setting, nibbling at a plover's egg. Instead, she chose the outdoor café at Palisades Amusement Park in New Jersey, where she polished off a two-inch steak, French-fried potatoes and ice cream. Pushing back her chair at the end of dinner (I had only picked at mine), she grinned and said, "Let's go and have some fun."

Pavlova's idea of fun turned out to be a tour of the amusement attractions. She giggled at our reflections in the funny mirrors, shrieked as she went careering down the roller coaster, and finally dragged me onto the dance floor, where she did a very creditable fox-trot.

This was the woman whose incomparable grace caused playwright John Van Druten to liken her to "the wind passing like a shadow over a field of wheat." But Van Druten never saw her swimming. Pavlova loved the water, but in it she was clumsy beyond belief. She was all arms and legs, all going in different directions. On the diving board she was even worse. This thing of beauty, as insubstantial as a shaft of light onstage, would hit the water with a spread-eagle splash, throwing up spray like a miniature tidal wave. Every time she dived, I shuddered.

Anna Pavlova never had children of her own, but it was to youngsters that she was most vulnerable. She maintained a home in Paris for about 30 Russian refugee children. She watched over the girls in her company like a mother hen and felt personally responsible for their welfare. At holidays or birthdays, each received a carefully chosen present. In 1923, she sent relief packages to Russia under the Hoover Plan, and I can still remember ballerinas from the Bolshoi and Maryinsky theaters queuing up to receive food parcels from Pavlova in America. Even today, her name is revered there, although she left her homeland in 1913.

But it was to the world outside Russia, particularly America, that Anna Pavlova gave her finest gift. More than anyone else, she brought ballet to the millions. In one year alone, she gave 238 performances in 35 weeks, playing 77 towns and cities across the United States. In the course of her career, she traveled 500,000 miles, dancing to untold millions of people. And, mind you, this was not by airplane.

In all the time I managed her, she never missed a performance. Once in Jackson, Miss., I thought I would have to cancel her appearance. The theater was an old garage and it didn't even have a stage—just a platform. There were no dressing rooms, only a few curtains hung in a cellar full of rats. But she never complained. "I want people to see me dance," she declared, and cheerfully performed. In Montgomery, Ala., there was such a big hole in the roof that rain poured in, soaking costumes and scenery, and Pavlova pirouetted in puddles. "It is wonderful," she said to me in the intermission. "We don't need lights; the lightning comes inside to us."

Yet she was not a plaster saint. Many a fusillade of ballet slippers and pungent Russian invectives were flung at an unlucky manager. And she could be a martinet. Once, when the company was playing in Washington, D.C., through an oversight no class or rehearsal had been scheduled the day of the opening. That night, ten minutes before the curtain went up, Pavlova ordered the entire company to line up onstage, single file. Slowly, deliberately, she asked each one, "Have you practiced today?" All said no. "I am a dancer," she said in glacial tones. "You are dancers. I practice while you do nothing. So. We will have a lesson now." And, with the audience stamping on the other side of the curtain, Anna Pavlova delayed the opening for half an hour while she held class for the entire company.

Anna Pavlova was born in St. Petersburg in 1881. Her father died when she was two, and her mother was very poor. They often lived on nothing but cabbage soup and rye bread. At ten she was accepted as a pupil at the Imperial Ballet School in St. Petersburg, where they fed the emaciated little girl cod-liver oil to fatten her up.

Tsar Alexander III and his empress occasionally visited the school and had tea with the children. One day the Tsar took

High Priestess of the Dance

one of the youngsters on his lap. Little Anna burst into a fit of jealous weeping. The Tsar asked her what was wrong, and she sobbed that she, too, wanted to sit on the royal lap. Grand Duke Vladimir picked her up, but she kept on howling, insisting that she did not want a substitute.

The dance that was the most emotional experience for Anna Pavlova was one that she had choreographed herself. It was called "Autumn Leaves." I remember how her eyes would be filled with tears when she came offstage after dancing it. She had dedicated it to a young man she had known in Russia and who had drowned. "Autumn Leaves" was a memorial from Anna Pavlova, the woman who loved him.

"You must have loved to be a great artist," she once told me. "You must know all about love—but you must learn to do without it."

Far from being remote, Anna Pavlova enjoyed having people around her. She had a beautiful home near London, and people like George Bernard Shaw and Feodor Chaliapin were frequent guests. She enjoyed entertaining, and planned every party in minute detail.

Her kindness was legendary. When business was bad—as it once was in Chicago—she refused to be paid. "I want no money," she told me. "If you can, pay the boys and girls in the company." One year, on their way to Cape Town, South Africa, the company was disconsolate at being away from home at Christmas. In fact, they would be crossing the equator on December 25. But she had a surprise. As the ship crossed the equator, she called everyone into her suite. There was a large Christmas tree she had stored in the hold of the ship; it was fully decorated, with presents for everyone scattered under its branches.

Once, when she was dancing in Rio de Janeiro, she was furious because the curtain didn't work properly. Refusing to finish the performance, she stormed offstage. At the stage door, she was stopped by a woman with a little girl. The child asked why she was leaving. When she explained, the child began to cry: "But mother promised me that you would dance the swan!" The woman explained that she had brought her daughter to the theater for a birthday treat. Pavlova bent down, kissed the little girl, and promised that she would return. Ten minutes later, she was back onstage, dancing for her.

The ballet she danced for the child, "The Dying Swan," was of course, the one with which the public still associates Anna Pavlova. In it, with apparently effortless movements, she depicted the agony of death. She is remembered for it not because of her incredible technique but because of the compassion in her artistry.

Soon after her death, conductor Constant Lambert led a memorial performance of "The Dying Swan" in London. With the first notes, the curtain rose on an empty, darkened stage. A spotlight played on the ballerina who was not there and followed her unseen presence across the stage. The London audience rose to its feet and stood in silent tribute as the orchestra played the Saint-Saëns music with which she is forever identified.

The last time I saw Anna Pavlova was in the autumn of 1930. I was in Paris, getting ready to sail back to New York. She telephoned me from London, where she was dancing, and asked me to embark from Southampton. Naturally, I agreed.

Although the weather was damp and chill, she came to the ship, examined my stateroom, made sure that my bed was comfortable, and instructed the purser to take good care of me. As though I were a child, she told me what to eat, to be sure to exercise, and to get lots of sleep. The other people present tried to hurry her off the ship, fearing that she might catch cold. She wheeled on them. "Be still!" she said with a break in her voice. "Maybe it's the last time I see him."

It was. Three months later she was dead. She died in The Hague of double pneumonia. At three o'clock one morning, she awakened in a fever. She called her maid and asked her to unpack the swan costume. She asked that her manager be notified that she was well and could resume rehearsals the next day. An hour later, at age 49, Pavlova was dead.

The spring after she died, I went to London. It was my first time in Europe in years without seeing her. I went to Golder's Green Crematorium, not far from where she had lived, and I remember asking the watchman where her ashes were. "East Wall, 3-7-11," he said.

That was all that was left of Anna Pavlova. There, on the stone walk in front of East Wall, 3-7-11, I placed a small bunch of violets.

They were her favorite flower.

The Round Table's Blithest Spirit

by Marc Connelly

WHENEVER I encounter one of life's little frustrations, like ballpoint pens that don't start writing when I do or taxicabs that dissolve in the rain, I think of my friend Robert Benchley and usually wind up laughing at the situation and myself. Benchley had a rare ability to extract humor from his own encounters with the minor disasters and major banalities of life. Like most of us, he was confused by such everyday perils as income taxes, after-dinner speakers and financial transactions. Yet his reactions were so lively and wry that he could transform a frustration into an essay or a movie short that would make millions of people laugh.

I first met Benchley through a common bond: we were both unemployed and broke. It was in New York City at the onset of the 1920s, and he had lately left *Vanity Fair* magazine in a burst of indignation because the magazine had fired his friend Dorothy Parker. They took working quarters together in a cluttered cubicle in the Metropolitan Opera House and were occupied with desultory literary odd jobs. On the door was a sign saying, "Utica Drop Forge and Tool Company." Originally Mrs. Parker had suggested the simple legend: "Gents." Their cable address was PARKBENCH.

"We had considered taking smaller quarters, but Mrs. Parker vetoed the idea," Benchley said on my first visit. "She's right. Anything smaller than this would be adulterous."

Benchley did not look the part of a merry-andrew. He had a moon face, a toothbrush mustache and a well-upholstered figure. He commuted to the New York suburb where he had a wife and two sons, and was active in social-welfare work. Yet he was the blithest spirit of all the group that gathered at the Algonquin Hotel in those years.

All of us were occupied in some fashion with the arts. Benchley was soon rescued from the ranks of the unemployed by being taken on as drama critic by the original *Life* magazine. He was admirably suited to the task, for he loved the theater and was always as much performer as writer.

One day at lunch a disgruntled actor, his ego bruised by abrasive reviews by Benchley, Mrs. Parker and Alexander Woollcott, suggested that our raffish literary group put on a show and let the actors criticize *us*. We accepted the challenge forthwith, and began whipping up a show called *No Sirree!*, in which we not only would write the songs and acts but would perform them as well. Recalling the aplomb with which I had seen Benchley orally satirize human foibles, I urged him to do something for the show.

The solitary performance of *No Sirree!* was presented on April 30, 1922. In a cab en route to the theater, Benchley jotted down some notes for his performance. Then, at an unplanned point in the show, he wandered uncertainly onstage. "I shall take but a few minutes of your time this evening," he said, smiling nervously, "for I realize that you would much rather be listening to interesting entertainment than to a dry financial statement."

The audience stirred restlessly, and several people eyed the exits.

"But I *am* reminded of a story," he persisted, "which all of you have probably heard." Benchley, it developed, was pretending to be an assistant treasurer of a club, delivering a hopelessly unbusinesslike report to the members. As he bumbled along in a mixture of confusion and bravado, interrupting himself with false chuckles, getting tangled up in his meandering syntax, it began to dawn on the audience that his apparently fumbling performance was actually a classic parody of the inexperienced public speaker caught between terror and the love of the sound of his own voice. When he exited, bumping into the proscenium, he brought down the house.

This inspired bit of folderol, "The Treasurer's Report," was to transform Benchley's life. Irving Berlin saw it and promptly hired him for his *Music Box Revue*. Benchley received bids

The Round Table's Blithest Spirit

from the movies. Later came his syndicated column, a radio show and a steady stream of books. His performance had revealed to the public what his friends already knew—that Benchley was one of the funniest men alive.

"Just to meet him was a tonic," humorist Frank Sullivan once said. "Spending an evening with him was a boon. That was his cross. There just wasn't enough of him to go around."

He was not only funny himself; he was also the ideal audience for *your* story or joke. He would listen with a look of eager glee, chuckling in anticipation of your point. And when you had finished, he would explode in a booming, infectious laugh—"a New Year's horn of a laugh," playwright Ben Hecht called it—that made you feel you were the wittiest person in the world. "Because he was so interested in you," a friend said, "you seemed to become more interesting."

It was impossible to pay a dinner check when you were with Benchley. Even if you got your hands on the tab, he would slip the waiter a large bill and murmur, "Don't pay any attention to my nephew. He spent his allowance last night at the roller rink."

Basically, he believed that all financial transactions were booby traps for the unwary. Once I spent a night with him and his wife, Gertrude, at their home. The normally merry and witty Benchley seemed unusually pensive. "That bank of mine is very strange," he said, finally. "I went there this morning because I needed a loan. And do you know something? They gave it to me just like that."

The next day he went to the bank and withdrew his account. "I don't trust a bank," he muttered, "that would lend money to such a poor risk."

His erratic financial methods made him the despair of banks, but he was so cheerful about it all that the bankers could never stay angry long. When endorsing checks he would add friendly little messages like "Banker's Trust, I love you." Once, while out on the town, he cashed a check, first writing on the back, "Having a wonderful time. Wish you were here."

Benchley moved into the Algonquin Hotel, but soon found that his friends made it almost impossible for him to get any work done. When he announced that he was moving to a new hideaway, the manager of the Algonquin protested that he would take measures to keep friends from coming up to bother Benchley. "You might keep them from coming up," Robert sighed, "but you wouldn't be able to keep me from coming down."

He would put off writing as long as possible if there was congenial company at hand. Once he wrote a magazine article titled "I Like to Loaf." The editor received it two weeks late with the explanation, "I was loafing." Another time Robert sat down to write a magazine piece, pecked out the word "The." Then he got stuck. Disgustedly, he went downstairs, where he met some pals and spent a cheery hour or so. When he returned to his typewriter, the solitary "The" still stared accusingly at him. He sat disconsolately trying to think of something more, then suddenly added, "...hell with it"—and went back to rejoin his friends.

I doubt if there ever was an apartment like Benchley's retreat at the Royalton, across the street from the Algonquin. Magazines, books and other impediments were strewn everywhere in grand disarray. There was also a sagging sofa which Benchley called "The Track." When he felt like a snooze he would say, "Well, guess I'll take a couple of laps around the track"—and lie down on it. Although designed as a hideaway, the place was soon filled, as James Thurber said, "with men who wanted to get his ear, hear his laughter and his talk, and cry on his shoulder."

Benchley always had a low regard for his own talents. "It took me 15 years to find out that I had no gift for writing," he once grumbled. "But I couldn't give it up because by that time I was too famous." When someone complimented him on his style he said, "I don't know enough to have a style. I know, at the most, 15 adjectives."

Actually, his combination of nonsense, non sequiturs and inside-out logic gave him a style unique among humorists. In books like *My Ten Years in a Quandary and How They Grew;* After 1903 *What?;* and *From Bed to Worse,* he wrote some of the funniest things ever written by an American. "The Benchley plan is to knock you over with a feather," playwright Jean Kerr says.

Despite his admitted dislike of buckling down, Benchley produced an amazing amount of work. Besides writing a dozen books, countless columns and magazine articles, he wrote or appeared in 47 movies, some of which still adorn the late-evening TV shows, and 48 movie shorts, including the Oscar-winning apotheosis of insomnia, *How to Sleep*.

Much of Benchley's humor was a case of art imitating life—Benchley's life. Some of his most amusing remarks were impromptu. Once, coming out of a Hollywood restaurant slightly befuddled, he asked a uniformed man to call him a taxi. "I'm sorry," the man said coldly. "I happen to be a rear admiral in the U.S. Navy." "All right, then," Benchley said cheerfully, "get us a battleship."

He loved practical jokes—never cruel jokes, but fey, nonsensical pranks. Once he left an envelope at the door of Grant's Tomb. A passerby who found it was startled to discover inside a note reading, "Please leave one quart Grade A and one pint whipping cream. U.S.G." On a trip to Venice he cabled a friend, "Streets flooded. Please advise."

Benchley was born in Worcester, Mass., and had a solid, conservative New England upbringing. From his earliest years, however, he had a cockeyed outlook on life. At Phillips Exeter Academy, when he was assigned to write a paper on how to do something practical, he wrote "How to Embalm a Corpse."

While at Harvard, he and a friend were walking one day through exclusive Louisburg Square. Smitten by inspiration, he stepped up to a house and knocked on the door. A maid answered. "We've come for the davenport," Robert said briskly. The confused maid let them in; they picked up a davenport and carried it across the square to another house. Again they knocked and were greeted by a maid. "We've brought the davenport," Robert announced. "Where shall we put it?" The bewildered maid indicated a place in the living room. Benchley and his friend deposited it there and went happily on their way.

After college Benchley had a dreary procession of jobs, including one organizing clambakes for a paper company. Yet he never lost his determination to be a writer. When he was trying unsuccessfully to get started, he worked as a volunteer, checking housing conditions in Harlem and as leader of a Lower East Side boys' club called the Seagull A.C. Later, when he was famous and occupied with many things, he also constantly tried to help people who were down on their luck.

He always retained his New England conscience, and a flinty sense of integrity—and, for all his love of fun, he could get angry. He resigned from the Harvard Club of New York because it rejected a man for writing a book about socialism. He moved out of a Hollywood hotel when it refused to let a black musician friend of his visit him in his room.

But even Benchley's anger could take a whimsical turn. During his time in Hollywood, we once had adjoining bungalows at a pleasure dome called the Garden of Allah. One night, trying to place a long-distance call, he couldn't raise the switchboard operator. Whereupon he stalked into the lobby and turned all the furniture upside down. Then he left a note for the sleeping operator. "Let this be a lesson to you," it said. "I might have been having a baby."

In November, 1945, Benchley suffered a series of hemorrhages and was taken to a New York hospital. Scores of his friends rallied round to give blood, but he lapsed into a coma and died. Suddenly the world seemed a duller place. "There's nobody like that around any more," John O'Hara said. "There's nobody who even comes close."

Someone recalled what Robert had said after George Ade's death: "When a great humorist dies, everybody should go to a place where there is laughter, and drink to his memory until the lights go out."

Those of us who loved Robert decided to do exactly that. Groups gathered at two restaurants he was devoted to, 21 in New York and Romanoff's in Beverly Hills. We reminisced about him and the funny and kind things he said and did. Those of us in New York telephoned the group in Beverly Hills, and everyone had a favorite Benchley story, gay or outrageous, to exchange. Finally it was time to go home. The lights had gone out.

Richard Tucker:
Brooklyn's Caruso

by Robert Merrill

I WAS SCARED STIFF that December evening in 1945 as I waited backstage to make my debut at the Metropolitan Opera House in New York. Suddenly, a hand gripped my shoulder. I turned to see a short, stocky figure with intense brown eyes and radiant grin.

"Relax, Bob," said Richard Tucker, who'd made his own Met debut only 11 months earlier. "You're pretty terrific, you know, or you wouldn't be here tonight. Me, too. So let's go out and give that audience everything we've got. They'll love us!"

His confidence braced me. Next thing I knew, Licia Albanese, Tucker and I had sung our way through *La Traviata*. A storm of applause greeted us. Then Tucker was shoving me—a 26-year-old kid from Brooklyn—onto the stage alone to receive an ovation.

Such was my introduction to the man whom top critics would soon call "the American Caruso," and whom *Time* magazine would proclaim the "greatest tenor in the world." For nearly 30 years, until he died on January 8, 1975, at the age of 61, Tucker remained among opera's top stars. He sang 715 performances at the Met, in 30 leading roles.

I was privileged to sing more than 200 performances with Richard, to have him as one of my best friends, and to discover time and again the open secrets of his greatness. To begin with, of course, he had that rare golden-velvet voice which, as a reporter once remarked, sounded as though he were "fresh off the boat from Naples." Because he was quick to agree that he was a wonder of a singer, some people got the impression he was arrogant. But we who knew Richard well knew there was nothing vain about him. He was guided by one simple notion: he believed that his voice and the breaks that made him famous were gifts straight from God. "How else," he'd wonder, "could somebody like me have come so far?" His talents, he felt, were simply entrusted to his stewardship, to be shared with as many people as possible.

This explains why Richard Tucker never set foot on a stage without giving his absolute best. And it explains why I, six years younger and inclined sometimes to be a bit easygoing, could not have had a better partner. Not long before his death, I complained, "Dick, why do we have to do so many difficult numbers in our joint concerts? Why don't we program some less strenuous things?"

"Bob," he replied, "people don't come to hear big-time opera stars sing easy pitter-patter songs any more than they come to see big-league ball players bunt. So let's keep going for the home run every time!"

Too many artists think that the world owes them a license to be temperamental, inconsiderate and generally beastly. Not Tucker; he had a king-size concern for others. Down-and-outers knew he would always lend a helping hand. To keep from disappointing an audience, he'd undergo almost any ordeal. Once, scheduled to appear in New Orleans, he found that a storm had grounded all planes. He stayed at Newark Airport for 36 hours, hoping for a break in the weather, then finally took a train to Cincinnati, and from there a plane that got him to New Orleans one hour before the opera. Exhausted, he nevertheless sang flawlessly.

Although phenomenally busy with a schedule that brought him well over $250,000 a year, Tucker couldn't resist taking on charity performances. Admirable enough—except that sometimes he absentmindedly agreed to sing free on nights when he was already booked. In 1972, Richard inadvertently stood up 16,000 paying fans at a Hollywood Bowl gala while singing gratis in Israel!

Richard was an outspoken believer in the American system. "Look what it did for me!" he'd say. His given name was Reuben Ticker, and he was born in a Brooklyn ghetto, the fifth and last child of poor Romanian immigrant parents. The Tickers couldn't afford a radio, much less music lessons. To help put

Richard Tucker: Brooklyn's Caruso

food on the table, Ruby dropped out of high school and became a runner on Wall Street.

But, as Tucker always told it, two "miracles" intervened in his behalf. When he was six, his family had moved to Manhattan's Lower East Side, where a neighbor, hearing Ruby singing in the street, suggested that his parents take him to Samuel Weiser, cantor at the Allen Street Synagogue. Weiser immediately began grooming the boy as a soloist—free voice lessons!

The second miracle happened when Ruby was 20, a $25-a-week salesman of silk linings for fur coats, singing party gigs for $5 bills, and studying to become a cantor. He met Sara Perelmuth, the 19-year-old daughter of a food caterer (and sister of operatic tenor Jan Peerce). It was practically love at first sight. Shortly after their marriage, in February, 1936, Sara took her husband to his first opera—and changed his career. Reeling with the music's glory, Ruby decided, "This is for me!"

Six years later, having scrimped to take voice lessons at night, Ruby adopted the stage name Richard Tucker and entered the Metropolitan Auditions of the Air, the Met's annual contest-search for new talent. He sang his heart out, but did not win. The defeat and its aftermath gave him his best talking point in later encouraging struggling young artists. "Never let a failure get you down if you've done your best," he would say. "If you keep trying, *somebody's* going to notice you."

Edward Johnson, then general manager of the Met, remembered Richard's all-out auditioning effort so well that two years later, when he needed a tenor, he sought out Tucker, who had become a cantor at the Brooklyn Jewish Center. So, on January 25, 1945, Tucker made his Met debut in Ponchielli's *La Gioconda*. An hour or so later, taking 16 curtain calls, he was a celebrity.

Richard was among the first singers to prove that you didn't have to be European-trained to become an international opera star. Indeed, a snobbish element at the Met always derided him for being "too American." This clique noted that he was stocky and overweight (so, of course, was Caruso); that he never lost his Brooklyn accent, and sometimes bruised the language he sang in. Also, some felt that his acting left something to be desired. To the last charge, I always felt like yelling, "Even if it were true, you'd be missing the point! Tucker is a great *singer*—and that's what opera is all about."

To protect his voice, Tucker sacrificed a lot. In order not to talk too much before a performance, he'd spend the whole afternoon at a movie. He'd deny himself many of the football and baseball games he loved because, he said, "I can't resist hollering myself hoarse." Most important, he worked up gradually to the more demanding operas.

"A lot of young singers take on the tough ones long before they're ready," he said. "That's why they don't last." To sing Canio, the clown in *Pagliacci*, the throat-racking role that had been Caruso's signature, Tucker waited, painstakingly building up to the part, for 25 years!

Richard claimed he wasn't superstitious; yet he never undertook anything new and difficult without having his wife go through a quaint Jewish custom, the Kayn Ayin Hora. Half pecking, half kissing him on the cheeks, Sara would incant, "Poo-poo-poo," to drive off evil spirits and bring him good luck. The night of January 8, 1970, as Richard waited to perform Canio at the Met for the first time, her Poo-poo-poos were unprecedentedly intense. When the final curtain fell, the bravos roared like surf. Later, in the dressing room, even his severest critics—Sara and their three sons—were speechless and weeping from the power of his performance.

Richard was as square as they come, and proud of it. With him, his family was No. 1. His chauffeur-driven Cadillac bore the license plate RST-3, which stood for "Richard and Sara Tucker—and three sons." His favorite spot on earth was with the four of them at their ranch-style house in Great Neck, Long Island, and he turned down many a profitable tour with the explanation, "I'm a father, ya know, and am needed at home right now."

Every year, during the fall High Holy Days and the spring Passover services, he took time off to officiate as cantor at synagogues scattered from Great Neck to Israel. In 1967, when U.S. forces in Vietnam were short of Jewish chaplains, he journeyed there to hold services. Twice he turned down invitations to sing in Russia because the Soviets wouldn't agree to two conditions: that he be permitted, when not busy elsewhere, to sing for Russian Jews in their temples; and that all proceeds from his concerts be donated to needy Jews in that country.

Richard Tucker: Brooklyn's Caruso

But Richard was first and last an American, and a remarkably tolerant one. After all, a "messenger" on business for the Almighty, he felt, doesn't quibble about religious differences among mortals. He was a relied-upon fund-raiser for Catholic schools and charities. A standard fixture at the annual Al Smith Dinner to raise money for charity cases at New York City's Catholic hospitals, Richard would close these affairs—as he closed our concerts—with a whole-hearted rendition of "You'll Never Walk Alone." Moved to tears, Terence Cardinal Cooke, Archbishop of the Diocese of New York, would leap up and hug Richard, and on this highly charged emotional note the dinner would end with floods of additional contributions pouring into the hospital coffers.

Tucker was a man of warm, unpredictable impulses and humor. To ease our tension, we fooled around a lot onstage. I'll always remember how one night, when I was in the middle of a long dying scene, he heckled me by asking, "When are you gonna kick off? I have to catch the 1:40 to Great Neck."

I'll remember, too, a chaotic scene when Dick was learning a new role from his voice coach and, at the same time, dictating letters to a secretary, posing for publicity pictures, conferring with an agent about a concert engagement, and bending an ear to a rabbi who wanted him to sing somewhere else for nothing. I begged him—all his friends begged him—"Dick, slow down!" But he couldn't. "I'll be the first to call it quits," he would promise, "when I can't deliver my best to the public."

That time never came. At an age when most singers are completely washed up, Tucker stayed as powerful as ever. "You keep young," he said, "by learning and doing new things." He continued to learn two entire new operas every year, and in 1973, at the age of 60, triumphed in the new role of the old Jew Eleazar in Halévy's *La Juive*, in New Orleans and in London. He also continued to take his gift to scores of out-of-the-way U.S. towns. "Why," he'd ask, "don't American artists sing and play in Kalamazoo?"

We happened to be in Kalamazoo the day he died. It was a bleak, gray afternoon, but we were having a fine time at rehearsal. About 1 P.M., we finished, and I told him, "I'm going to take a nap."

"I am, too," Richard said, "a little later. Right now I've promised to hear this local girl sing."

It was the last time I saw him alive. While writing a recommendation for the young singer, he collapsed with a heart attack.

Last rites were spoken for him from the great red-and-gold stage of the Metropolitan Opera House—the first funeral ever held there for a singer. Nine months later, his Catholic friends eulogized him at the first memorial service ever held in New York's St. Patrick's Cathedral for a Jew.

Soon, his family and friends organized The Richard Tucker Music Foundation, Inc., an active, non-profit organization which continues to aid young singers in their careers. But Richard needed no more durable memorial than the one he assured for himself. For, as a Scottish poet once wrote: "To live in hearts we leave behind is not to die."

A Gift of Laughter

by Allan Sherman

SHORTLY after we moved to the Bel Air section of Los Angeles, my wife, Dee, and I began to notice that angels were playing music outside our bedroom window every morning. From somewhere, we didn't know where, came the sound of a harp. And then one day, over the tall fence that surrounded our lot, flew a badminton shuttlecock. I went next door to return it. The man who answered the door was Harpo Marx.

But it was not the Harpo Marx known to generations of moviegoers around the world. Without his makeup—the fright wig, the battered hat, the long coat, the klaxon horn—he was a sweet, dignified, baldheaded, little gentleman with smiling young pixie eyes.

When I was a small boy, growing up in the wreckage of a broken marriage, I used to cut school and pay a dime to sit all day and most of the night in the movie houses. The whole world was poor then. There was something going on called the Depression, something a child couldn't understand—but I knew it was bad. And in the middle of all the badness there were these movies—the Marx Brothers pictures, and they made you scream and jump with laughter, and the world wasn't so poor then. As long as you could smile, you knew things were going to get better.

I saw them all—*A Day at the Races, A Night at the Opera, Monkey Business, Horse Feathers, Duck Soup, Animal Crackers*—I saw them all, not once but over and over again until I could do the jokes by heart. I could go flapping around with my knees bent low like Groucho, with a pencil in my mouth like a cigar, leering and making my eyebrows go up and down.

I was never too good at imitating Harpo, though. I could make big eyes and roll them around, and I could flub my lips. But there was always something about him I couldn't imitate. Now I know what it was. It was the simplicity of the man, the beauty inside, the thing that God gives to maybe one in every 50 million of us: the ability to see and to laugh and to give joy to others in a way so special that you *can't* imitate it.

Harpo was a child who never grew up. He was the best part of a human being, the innocent part that sees things with wonder. He could see where the reality is, inside all of us, where there is a warm place, bubbling with fancy and laughter and music and playfulness and love. Most of us get so scared, so civilized that we invent a disguise for ourselves, and we walk around looking serious and acting self-important, and we call it Grown Up. So here we all are in our Grown Up suits, busy doing our Grown Up jobs, rushing our children to get Grown Up as fast as possible; and where has all the fun gone to, and why does the music sound so far away?

Well, Harpo Marx had the good sense and the great gift never to Grow Up, and that was the soul of his comedy. Harpo made eyes at pretty girls the way we all wish we had the nerve to do; and he invented harps out of broken pianos, and piccolos out of strands of spaghetti; and wherever he was, there was music for everyone, and laughter. And when he was sad he was so terribly sad that we could see that there is even something funny in that, and so we laughed and forgot some of the things that made *us* sad. Comedy makes you *feel good*, and that is what Harpo Marx did.

Harpo had a home in Cathedral City, near Palm Springs, but he had rented the house next door to us for the summer to escape the desert heat. I was still an unknown (and often unemployed) TV producer, and I didn't have much to offer Harpo except a sight of the Second Largest Rubber Tree in the Western Hemisphere, which grew in my yard. I told him about it. He came over one afternoon to admire it and pick up a few free samples of raw rubber, and he came often after that.

I remember especially the time we were entertaining friends whose little boy was in a wheelchair. Suddenly, Harpo came creeping around the fence in full costume, flubbing his lips and honking that nutty klaxon horn and whistling that shrill whistle with two fingers in his mouth. And for a while that

A Gift of Laughter

little boy escaped from his prison of pain in the wide world of laughter.

We often went over to Harpo's, too. In fact, a measure of the size of Harpo's heart was that he gave parties so that the celebrities of Hollywood could hear his unknown neighbor sing.

One night Dee and I were walking next door to Harpo's house when an enormous white Cadillac drew up alongside of me. It stopped. The driver said, "Excuse me, boy. Is this the Marx party?"

The speaker was Jack Benny. Beside him was Mary Livingston. In the back were George Burns and Gracie Allen.

"Yes, Mr. Benny," I replied. "It's that house right there."

"Will you take care of the car, boy?" Jack Benny asked.

"Sure, Mr. Benny."

He gave me a one-dollar tip and I parked the car. Then I walked back to Harpo's house and mingled with the celebrities. Mary Livingston did a double take when she saw me. "Look," she told Jack, "there's the parking boy."

"It's all right, Mary," Jack explained. "Harpo is a very democratic person."

At this party were all five Marx brothers and many other leading comedians. They were stunned when Harpo asked me to sing some of my parodies. As I was leaving, Gracie Allen said to me, "With all your talent, you shouldn't have to park cars for a living, young man."

At the end of that summer Harpo moved back to Palm Springs. Meanwhile, my first record had been brought out, and my world was turned upside down by its success. But one thing never changed—my friendship with Harpo. And in the turmoil brought on by sudden riches and popularity his simplicity surely helped save my sanity. Take the day I went up to have lunch with him and Susan at their beautiful Cathedral City home.

There were a lot of flies around that day, and I told Harpo about a new way of getting rid of them. You suck them up in a vacuum cleaner, right out of the air, *poof*! Well, Harpo had one of those tremendous factory-type vacuum cleaners, and he thought this was a marvelous fly-removal method. When he turned the thing on, it made a sound like a hundred jet planes all at once. There followed the most beautiful and insane scene I have ever seen in my life: this lovely little baldheaded 75-

year-old man who had had five heart attacks went running around and leaping up and down like a kid with a wild new toy, trying to suck up flies in that vacuum cleaner. And he never got *one*. *Not one*. And he was glad, and so was I. Because Harpo never wanted to kill a fly anyway.

It was at that lunch that I worked up the courage to ask Harpo to do a concert with me. Astonishingly, he agreed, and we scheduled a show on January 19, 1963, at Pasadena Civic Auditorium. It made show-business history. That night when I walked into my dressing room I found a note written on plain brown wrapping paper. It said:

Dear Allan,
   Tonight, as I retire from show business, I pass on to you the advice Bernard Baruch gave to me years ago when I was starting. Baruch said, "If you want to succeed you must always remember three things..."
   I would gladly tell them to you, Allan, but unfortunately I have forgotten all three.

With great affection,
Harpo

So this was Harpo's last public performance. After Harpo had done his act and played the harp and shuffled off, I walked on stage and took the microphone and said, "Ladies and gentlemen, Harpo Marx has been delighting the world for 56 years. And what you have just seen—these beautiful minutes we have just spent with Harpo—this was the last—it was Harpo's final..."

By now I was blubbering so badly I couldn't talk. Three thousand people sat there in Pasadena Civic Auditorium, watching a short, fat man with glasses crying like a baby. I couldn't pull myself together, and I couldn't leave the stage either. The audience began to mumble. They didn't know what was going on.

And then from the wings Harpo wandered out, and the audience began to applaud. Harpo waved his hand to stop them, and then he took the microphone from my hand, and for the first time in 56 years, this lovely little man that so many people thought was a deaf-mute spoke, on a stage, in his costume. "Allan," he said, "you're too emotional."

Harpo was an old pro, and he knew you don't just stand on

A Gift of Laughter

a stage like an idiot and cry. He turned to the audience and said, "Now! As I was about to say in 1907..."

They roared. Harpo went on talking, and almost every word got a tremendous laugh, as the audience realized with delight how articulate he really was. Harpo said, "Say. I *like* this talking business. I think I've found a whole new career."

Then he told them he really was leaving show business, and there were yells of "No! No!" and there were many people in the audience weeping. Harpo handed me the microphone and began to amble off the stage, but they wouldn't let him. The standing ovation lasted six or seven minutes. I never expect to see anything like it again. It was an outpouring of love, from children and grown ups, love gathered over the years for this man who had spoken so eloquently in every language without saying one word.

Twenty-one months later this beautiful, funny man was dead. He left more than a monument, and more than a fortune. He left us all a gift of laughter.

The Personal Touch

Katie and the Hard Hats

by Garson Kanin

WHEN KATHARINE HEPBURN arrived in New York for rehearsals of the musical, *Coco*, she took an intense interest in every department of the production: casting, scenery, costumes, choreography, lighting and, of course, the theater itself.

Experienced professionals know that plays have failed because they were in the wrong theater, one that was too large or too small, or simply not right. Kate has played virtually every size and shape of theater but was anxious to become acquainted with the one that had been booked for *Coco*: the Mark Hellinger on West 51st Street. Producer Alan Jay Lerner and co-producer Freddie Brisson took Kate to see it a few days after she reached New York.

After walking on the stage to study the auditorium and walking about the auditorium to study the stage, Kate announced, "It's a fine theater, but we can't use it. What else is available?"

The management was speechless. Theaters, especially sizable ones for musicals, are not easy to come by in the shrinking world of Broadway. Moreover, the deal for the Mark Hellinger had taken months to arrange. The idea of changing theaters was out of the question.

Finally, Brisson said, "What are you talking about?"

"What's the matter with you people?" Kate responded. "Can't you see anything?"

"Like what?" asked Alan.

"Across the street," said Kate, patiently, "they're beginning the construction of a skyscraper. They're excavating now. It means two things. That this theater is going to be very hard to get to, and it's going to be impossible to play the Wednesday matinee. I don't care how good we are, we can't compete with riveting."

Everyone (probably including Kate) knew that they were committed to the Mark Hellinger, but Kate wanted to make her point. As it happened, she was correct on both counts. As construction progressed, the company did its best to work against the increasing noise, but it was soon apparent that large sections of the audience, particularly those on the left side of the house toward the rear, were having a tough time at Wednesday matinees.

Kate, as Coco, had several numbers in the first act that she was able to belt out successfully, even against the racket. But toward the end of Act One came a delicate scene during which she sang the moving title song. Finally, at one matinee, Kate found it impossible to perform the number properly in the overwhelming presence of the noise from across the street.

The following Wednesday, she left for the theater an hour early. She went directly to the construction site, found the supervisor's trailer and asked to see him. He was up on the structure, but Kate made the matter seem so urgent that an assistant led her out onto the job. Wearing the mandatory hard hat, she found herself facing the supervisor.

"Look here," she shouted. "My name is Katharine Hepburn and I work across the street."

The astonished supervisor gaped at her. "Holy smoke!" he said. "What the hell are you doing here?"

"I have to talk to you," Kate shouted.

Carefully, the man escorted her to his trailer, and Kate explained her problem. "I know you've got to build this building," she said, "but we've got to give a show over there. We can't ask you to stop—but at least you can help us out."

"How?"

"There's one main spot," Kate said. "It's my 'Coco' number. On Wednesdays, that number starts at three-oh-five and goes on until about three-fourteen. Just for that little time, couldn't you possibly hold the hammers?"

"Well, Jeez, I don't know, Miss Hepburn," said the supervisor.

"Sure you could," urged Kate. "Give them a coffee break or something. I'll pay for the coffee."

Katie and the Hard Hats

"Yeah," he said, "but who'll pay for the time? You know what these guys get, don't you?"

Kate gave him The Hepburn Look, and said softly, "You can do it if you want to."

He took a deep breath, and said, "Lemme see what I can figure out."

At 3:05 that afternoon, as the introduction of her soft number began, the world outside fell suddenly silent. The audience may not have been aware of the abrupt change, but everyone connected with the *Coco* company was. Some of those who were momentarily free stepped out into the street to see what had happened. Up and down the structure they saw the workers signaling for silence and looking at their watches. At 3:14 the applause for the number was augmented by all hell breaking loose across the street. The following day Kate made a special visit across the street to thank her new friends.

So it went for week after week. Every Wednesday afternoon at the specified time, the construction gang gave Kate the gift of silence. Then came the afternoon when an outside crew turned up on the corner to make a cable repair. At 3:05, when the building work stopped, the uninformed repair crew continued. Whereupon, from every part of the structure, the shouts rained down.

"Hold the noise, you guys!" "Shut up down there! Katie's on!" *"Quiet!"* In addition to the hollering and yelling, an ad hoc committee went dashing over to enforce the admonition.

At the end of the matinee, Kate was handed a note from the supervisor, explaining that the short burst of noise at the beginning of her number was "not us, but that crazy repair crew—which we have now straightened out!" After that, there were no more interruptions.

The Day I Met Caruso

by Elizabeth B. Rodewald

WHEN I was ten years old I took my first trip alone from Boston to New York. That was along about 1915. I'd been visiting Cousin Hannah, one of my father's family, and as she put me on the noon train she said: "Thy father will meet thee. Since thee's in the parlor car, thee'll be perfectly safe. Just read thy book and do not speak to strangers."

My seat was the first one at the end of the car, right across from the drawing room. The door was open and I peeked in.

"Look, Cousin Hannah!" I exclaimed. "A little room! I wish I had this!"

"Lower thy voice," she admonished me. "Drawing rooms are for large families. People do not travel alone in the drawing rooms unless they are extravagant."

In my experience Quakers had no dealings with extravagance. As the train pulled out I turned away from the sight of Cousin Hannah, in her mole-gray hat, waving good-by. I rolled the lovely, forbidden word around in my mouth. I yearned for extravagance. To waste a whole day, to buy something useless, to be kissed for no reason! There were people who lived like that, but not in our family.

As the train stopped at Back Bay Station I looked out at the crowd waiting on the platform, and particularly at a circle of men and women clustered around a fat man. The women were pretty, with bright hats and white gloves, and flowers pinned to their muffs. Most of the men had glossy mustaches. The fat man wore an overcoat that was plainly extravagant—it had a fur collar. None of my father's coats ever had a fur collar.

The Day I Met Caruso

The fat man was kissed and slapped on the back and hugged. Everyone was laughing and gay. As I watched, I was aware of a procession of bags being carried into the drawing room. For a large family, I thought. The fat man sprang nimbly onto the train step. A woman unpinned the violets from her muff and tossed them to him as the train began to move.

I looked at the drawing room to see the large family, but no one except the fat man went into it. Then the porter came along. Cousin Hannah had given him a tip to take good care of me, so he stopped by my seat.

"You know who's in there, little girl?" he asked, nodding at the closed door.

"No. Who?"

"Mr. Caruso, the opera singer. You ever heard of him?"

"Oh yes!" I said, looking spellbound at the closed door. We had a victrola and I was allowed to play my father's Red Seal records on rainy afternoons. When the voice called Caruso sang to me I shivered all over.

The porter had disappeared and the passengers weren't watching me. Quickly, before prudence could speak, I slipped out of my chair and tapped at the closed door.

"Come in!" roared an enormous voice. I went in and shut the door quietly. Mr. Caruso was arranging playing cards on a table in front of him. I was astonished. In our house only the cook played cards.

"So, a little girl!" Mr. Caruso glanced up briefly and went on with the cards. "You want my autograph?"

"No, I wanted to see you."

Mr. Caruso slapped the cards down. "You do *not* want my autograph?" he exclaimed.

"What is an autograph?" I asked.

"My name written on a paper."

"What do you do with it?"

Mr. Caruso exploded into laughter, and the drawing room shook.

"How do I know?" He spread his hands and rolled his eyes. All of him was laughing. "Show it, sell it, burn it up. Sit down, sit down. We have five hours to waste. We will play cards."

I slid into the seat across from him. "I don't know how," I confessed.

"No cards, no autograph! What do you do?"

"I go to school."

"Of course. But that is not the whole of life, to go to school. You go to the opera, perhaps?"

"My gracious, no!"

"So, why this 'my gracious'?"

"In our house children don't."

"And what kind of house is this?" he asked.

"My father's a Quaker."

"A what?"

"A Quaker, a Friend."

"To be a friend, this is wonderful. But may not friends go to the opera or play cards?"

"No. Friends are quite strict. I mean you're not supposed to have too much fun. The cook plays cards, but she's Catholic."

"I, too." Mr. Caruso began laying one card on another. "It must be Puritans, this religion of no cards. Would you like me to teach you, little Puritan?"

"Oh, yes!" I exclaimed, looking straight into the painted face of Extravagance. She nodded and smiled at me, only it was Mr. Caruso who smiled. He pulled a second deck out of the bag beside him.

"So!" He handed me the cards with a flourish. "These are for you. Now watch what I do."

After an hour we were playing double Canfield. From time to time Mr. Caruso asked a question about life in a Quaker household. I told him about the silent Meeting and how opera was all right for grownups, but children were supposed to improve their minds and go to bed on time. He shook his head at that and began to talk about himself. My head was spinning with new words—Aïda, Rigoletto, Naples, Carmen, Pagliacci....

"You've heard me sing?" he asked, putting a black nine on a red ten.

"Only on a victrola."

"What did I sing for you?"

"La donna è mobile."

"Shall I sing it for you now?" he asked.

"Please!"

He put the two and three of spades on the ace and, without looking up, began to sing. His voice was overpowering. It was

The Day I Met Caruso

like having a waterfall leap into my face. I could hardly breathe. The drawing room was swirling with sound, and the sound made color and the color made light and into the light strode giant figures. I was caught up in something I had never known existed. Suddenly it stopped.

"The ace, put out the ace." A fat forefinger jabbed at my cards. I stared at him blankly.

"I forgot," I said.

Mr. Caruso looked pleased. "I made you forget," he said. "I make you forget again."

All that trip he sang and played Canfield and supervised my playing. Sometimes, when he was choosing between two moves, the singing dropped to an undertone. Sometimes it swelled until I thought the drawing-room door would burst open. I was too young and ignorant to know what I was hearing. I only knew that he was making glorious, extravagant pictures with his voice. Men boasted, fought, laughed and wept. Banners waved at high noon. The smell of roses was sweet in the air. Lovers clung together in the moonlight, and I was part of it all.

It was dark as we approached New York. Mr. Caruso stopped singing and peered out of the window into the distance. "Hell Gate," he announced and swept his cards together. "A bad word?" He laughed and rang for the porter. "Bring in the little girl's hat and coat. Who's meeting you?"

"My father."

"The Quaker father!" Mr. Caruso chuckled. "We will surprise him, this Mr. Quaker." He helped me into my coat and buttoned it gently under my chin.

He turned my brown hat around in his hands, disapproval on his face. "So plain," he muttered. "Like the mouse," he added sadly, setting it on my head.

"It's bad taste to be fancy," I quoted primly.

"Ha!" Mr. Caruso spat out the sound of contempt.

When we got off the train in Grand Central, Mr. Caruso stood smiling—hat atilt, debonair, foreign, extravagant—to be photographed. Then he took my hand and swept me up the ramp. As we came through the gate there was a blaze of glory around us. I saw my father standing a little in front of the other people waiting to meet the train. He looked at Mr. Caruso indifferently at first, then sharply, and called, "Elizabeth!"

I tugged at Mr. Caruso's hand. "My father," I said, sandwiched between two titans. Mr. Caruso turned—an extravagant turn, tilted hat, fur collar, all that coat. People stood still to watch.

"Ah, Mr. Quaker!" His voice was so big it filled the station, yet it wasn't loud. "I bring you back your little Puritan. We have spent our afternoon at the opera. When she plays cards with your cook, do not punish her. I myself taught her to play! And I beg you, buy her a hat with flowers!"

Before my father could answer, Mr. Caruso was off. I looked up nervously, expecting to see my father's face black with anger. Instead he was laughing.

"Wonderful fellow!" he said as we got in the cab.

"I thought thee'd be angry," I said, puzzled.

"What about?"

"I spoke to a stranger. I played cards. And Mr. Caruso is extravagant. He had a drawing room all for himself, and Cousin Hannah says that is extravagant."

"Thy Cousin Hannah," said my astonishing father—kissing me for no reason at all, kissing me and throwing open the gates to all lovely adventure—"thy Cousin Hannah is a narrow-minded old woman!"

Donahue:
Darling of the Daytime Dial

by William Brashler

PHIL DONAHUE may well be America's oldest altar boy. Daily he examines his conscience and turns it into the best thing on TV: a subliminal mix of charm, intelligence and—wonder of wonders in TV land—morality.

Each weekday, he ushers 200 women into his studio, while another 6½ million are within the sound of his voice. He tugs at them, hugs them, touches, talks, listens, prods, learns and shares with them. They reciprocate by making him the most popular and acclaimed talk-show host on daytime television.

"Donahue"—one household word, cut down from "The Phil Donahue Show"—is not Manhattan chic or Hollywood glitter. Each day it is talk generated from a cinder-block studio at WGN-TV in Chicago. Yet by 1979 the show was syndicated to 171 stations, invading over 4½ million households, including the major markets of New York City, where it outstripped local and network competition, Los Angeles and Chicago. It is the most talked-about talk show on daytime television, and the most effective book-selling show on the air.

You wouldn't know it to be there. A telephone sits onstage—a technique long since abandoned everywhere else on television—for call-in questions, and wide aisles are cut in the audience so Donahue can field impromptu questions. The show, which is taped for delayed broadcast elsewhere in the country, is fed live to Chicago audiences (only telephone calls are screened). There is only one topic of discussion a day. It may be divorce, abortion, impotence, Nazism—any one of an exhaustive pool used to fill 235 fresh programs a year. An occasional Hollywood celebrity appears, also for a full hour, and talks about a lot more than just his or her current movie.

By all standards, the show should fail miserably. Donahue has no obsequious sidekick; he doesn't sing, tell jokes, cue the band, fall into banal chatter. Instead, he sustains a mesh of issue and entertainment, the participation and identification of his viewers, in studio and at home, and delivers a constantly high level of tension and debate.

At 10:50, he walks unannounced into the studio. His audience—those 200 women who have come in from suburbs and more distant midwestern towns—spots him, and breaks into loud applause, eyes fastened on him in that celebrity daze normally reserved for Newman or Redford. After all, they have waited up to two years for their tickets and only because of this man.

Part of it is Donahue's presence: his charm, the thick, silver-gray hair, the Irish good looks, the wit. Yet all that would go for zot if every woman in every chair, and each one watching at home, didn't think that he was somehow vulnerable, that they could talk to this guy and he would talk back and they would both reveal something about each other.

He immediately warms to them. The audience, he says, is the show's most precious asset. So he smiles, touches, goes through shticks to make them feel at ease. "Gee thanks, I feel like a big star.... Glad you're here.... I'm so nervous. ... Gosh, you look so much thinner in person...." On and on, until the audience is glad it's there. Then he makes his pitch. "When the show begins, help me out. Get into the act. Show me you care."

And the pitch continues into the broadcast, which opens without any fanfare and almost before the audience knows it. Today he's invited two lesbian mothers and their six children to talk about living together in a family. The studio audience at first is stunned, then troubled, then strangely sympathetic to the two quite ordinary-looking women, whom they find enormously likable, and their children, whom they find incredibly normal.

In minutes, Donahue is running up and down the aisles with his portable microphone, sensing the tension, communicating the concern and bewilderment of his audience to his guests. It is Donahue at his best.

He nods at a questioner, goes to her with the mike, faces her, holds her hand or puts his arm around her back as she talks. If anyone else wooed a female audience like this, he would appear paternal, patronizing and sexist. Donahue does it as a host, a listener, and thrives because of it.

That is his magic. You cannot watch the show without getting the feeling that you have gotten *your* question in, that the woman standing up, unrehearsed and unprepared, is saying what's on *your* mind. Yet it would be little more than video anarchy if Phil Donahue weren't there to make it work.

Donahue wasn't plucked from a modeling agency, a backfield or a canceled situation comedy. Instead, he came up from being a reporter for a string of small radio and television stations, having covered fires, auto accidents and political primaries, to take over a Dayton talk show. The previous show came complete with audience. Donahue decided to keep it. And he soon discovered that the questions he took from them were often better than his own.

Slowly, other stations signed on, and in 1974 the show moved to Chicago's WGN. A national daytime Emmy award in 1977 helped, but only when "Donahue" started killing the competition in New York did critics begin to drool. Donahue took a second Emmy in June 1978, and a third in May 1979, and today the entire industry—and the Nielsen ratings—toast his superiority.

Donahue's technique is not to badger, harangue or hector, though he is capable of all three. Rather, he checks, edits, and calls his guests on their lapses and illogic—all on the basis of his own research. He probes and picks with his "Yes, but—" line of questioning. "Everyone agrees with that, but—," he says when a guest is being evasive. "You know I think you're the greatest, but—," he says to a celebrity who's just said something stupid.

Without being evangelical or pedantic, "Donahue" always shows a moral ingredient—a need to expose laziness, hypocrisy, dishonesty, racism, sexism, pretension. "I think it's important not to preach," Donahue says. "But I reserve the right to express myself, and I feel compelled to bring a guest who speaks in grand terms down to earth. I'm not trying to pronounce my moral values on society. Nobody's that smart. Besides, it's more complicated."

He is a man who has had his own complications, a survivor of a marriage that disintegrated after 17 years and five children. He admits to being an absentee father, a workaholic, a ladder climber so intent on professional success that he neglected his private duties. He retained custody of his four boys after his 1975 divorce—they are now age 15 through 19—and his wife took their only daughter and has since remarried.

On an estimated income of $500,000 a year, Donahue has the money to afford live-in housekeepers and can travel freely with the boys anywhere he or they desire. Yet he is suspicious of too much of anything. Two of his kids work in grocery stores after school; one of them works in a gas station. They know, as Donahue's friends sense, that the old man is a lot more conservative on his own than on the air.

It's just that, on the air, there are a lot of things he can no longer let pass. He especially abhors affronts to women and supports feminism. This sensibility pervades every interview, from questioning newscaster Paul Harvey about what roles he considers "appropriate" for women to asking "est" guru Werner Erhard why most of his trainers are men. "I'm for the women's movement. I think it's good for us, and I don't think it's going to go away."

Donahue has made mistakes. Once, during a show about dentists and dentistry, he took a question from a woman in the audience who spoke authoritatively on the subject.

"You must be the wife of a dentist," he remarked.

"No," she said. "I *am* a dentist." Donahue winced.

Yet his detractors in the feminist world are amazingly few, and his ardent supporters legion. One of them is actress/author Marlo Thomas. After talking with him on a show in 1977, she said on the air, "You are loving and generous and wonderful, and whoever is the woman in your life is lucky." (Ms. Thomas became the woman in his life.)

Donahue is the first to say that he is not a Carson, that he is not a great intellect or a great prosecutor. Perhaps his secret is that he was in Dayton too long to forget. He still signs autographs, poses for pictures, goes through the little amenities that have become a bother to personalities half his size. In short, Phil Donahue still listens.

After each program, he stands at the door of the studio. He smiles and thanks each departing member of the audience, and says he hopes they had a nice time. He remains until the last of the flock has passed, each one assured, each one blessed.

What It Was Like to Kiss Clark Gable

by Mary Astor

BANKS MAKE me feel guilty, automatically. And when a teller gives me a sharp look from behind steel-rimmed glasses and says, "Will you wait a moment, Miss Astor?" I get a crunching feeling in my stomach.

When this happened the other day at my bank in California, the teller emerged from behind her grill. Touching my elbow in a confidential manner, she walked with me toward the entrance. "Tell me," she said, her voice now warm with cello-like overtones, "what was it like to kiss Clark Gable?"

I was startled into blurting the exact truth: "Good Lord, I've forgotten!"

"Oh, you couldn't!" Her face pinked up, and behind the sharp-lady-teller mask I saw yesterday's bobby-soxer.

"Well, it *was* a long time ago, you know."

"Yes, but there was a TV re-run of *Red Dust* last night—didn't you *see* it? I should think that would have reminded you."

I remembered reading in the schedule about the movie's being on around one in the morning, but I hadn't watched it. Yet I just couldn't walk away from that disappointed face. So I smiled confidentially and said, "It's a long story." Let her read into that whatever she wants, I thought.

In the car, my poodle, Jasper, was as usual pantomiming, "What took you so long?" I told him about the lady and about the memories of *Red Dust* she had stirred up:

...That great opening shot of Jean Harlow cleaning the parrot's cage and saying, "Whatcha been eatin', cement?"

What It Was Like to Kiss Clark Gable

...Stage 18 (or was it 16?) on the MGM lot, where the "Indochinese" interiors were filmed—hot (no air conditioning in 1932) and damp from the constant use of rain machines. Director Vic Fleming being tough about our complaints: "Everybody sweats in the tropics—that's the way it is!" A Mason jar full of moths was opened for each scene. They were supposed to flutter and bat their way around the kerosene lamps for realism, but of course they preferred the brighter, hotter lights offstage.

...The early scene where I (playing a young engineer's wife) arrive by riverboat at the rubber plantation. Clark, the handsome superintendent, escorts me with great politeness along the dock to the house, *away* from the camera. Vic stops the first take and says, in front of everybody, "Mary, *please*! Go to your dressing room and take off that damned girdle. We need the bounce!"

...Soon Clark and I fall in love, but—to spare my husband—Clark subsequently convinces me that he's been trifling with me. I find a gun and wound him, but Harlow, a lovable creature of dubious reputation, takes the blame. My husband and I leave. Clark and Harlow contentedly stay.

...What *was* it like to kiss Clark Gable?

We had completed several days on the plantation set—and many shots of Clark carrying me through the mud, gasping from the force of a "monsoon." That particular morning we had just finished the continuation on the stage inside where he, soaking wet, breathless, carries me up the veranda steps into my bedroom.

Fleming says, "Okay, let's move in on a tight two."

In the script it probably read like this. "Close shot: He is about to dump her unceremoniously onto the bed, but her arms still cling. He gives her a look. A faint, cynical smile crosses his face. This is the wife of his employee, but she's been asking for it. He kisses her, gently at first, then fiercely, savagely."

Clark is a good sport and very husky, but it's not practical for him to hold me up for the hour or so the shot will take. So, first of all, a stool has to be found to support most of my weight. Out of sight, of course; they're framing the shot at elbow height.

A prop man and a carpenter shove a stool under my bottom as Clark hoists me up, his right arm supporting my knees, his left around my waist.

From behind the camera, Vic shouts, "Too high! Her head's gotta be lower than his—" The carpenter starts to saw one of the legs.

"Wait a minute! Check it in the finder, first. Let's see where you're going to be, kids. Clark, just before you kiss her, swing her an inch or two, so we get your full face."

We try it.

Vic says, "Too much, too much. Back just a little—" peering through the camera lens.

Clark says, "It's uncomfortable. I'll never hit it right."

"Yes, you will. Just clear that key light on her neck, Clark. See it?"

"Okay, *okay!*"

Meanwhile, the carpenter is taking a tape measurement from the bottom of my fanny to the floor, and getting the legs sawed off the stool. Lighting is being blocked in. There are lots of lights. We're hedged in by them. It's getting very, very hot.

Head cameraman Hal Rossen says, "You can step out now for a minute, Clark and Mary. Give me the stand-ins."

We cool off and have a smoke. I have my usual argument with the makeup man about too much makeup. He pursues me, waving a powder puff like an extension of his arm.

Soothingly he says, "The freckles are coming through on your forehead, Mary. Just let me touch it up with a little bit of pancake."

"Okay, but *no* lipstick. You know what Mr. Fleming said. All that rain, I'd never have any makeup left."

"Looks so naked."

"That's what he wants."

Half an hour or so later: "Ready to try it!" I go back onto the set.

"Clark's on the phone. Step out of the lights a minute, Mary, but don't go 'way."

One of the prop men, in a raincoat, yells from somewhere, "You wanna wet 'em down?"

"Just a rehearsal—no rain."

"Okay, here's Clark. Let's try it now. Everybody settle down. Quiet!" Bells ring; doors are closed. It's not very quiet. Nobody ever quiets down. And it's not really important until

What It Was Like to Kiss Clark Gable   207

that final moment when the sound man says authoritatively, "Speed!" Then it's quiet.

I hoist myself up onto the stool. As Clark takes his position he cracks, "Hey, you've lost weight. What a relief!"

Kneeling under the camera a stagehand points to a light and asks Clark, "This going to be too hot?" "Gee-sus, it *is* hot," Clark replies. "It'll make me squint." "No, it won't. We really need it." "Then what did you ask for?" The man grins and says, "Got anything in the fifth on Saturday?" "Yeah, I gotta honey." "Lemme in on it, huh?" "Sure, later."

Finally Vic comes from behind the camera so that he can talk to us, quietly. And we start to think about the scene. What happened previously, relationships, emotional level, etc.

"Let's just move through it once," Vic says. "The look needn't be very long, Clark. Mary, keep it simple. Real. Just *be* there."

He turns and disappears behind the lights.

"Let's make one, okay?" he calls. "Don't need a rehearsal. Just mean it. Think. Feel." To the camera crew, "Can we go?"

Hal says, "No rehearsal? Well, let me check their position when they kiss. Give us a look, kids."

Clark leans his head close to me, and our lips are barely touching. "How's this?" he says loudly, so Hal can hear over the noise. To me, "Sorry, baby," as I jump a little.

"No good," Hal announces. "We're just getting the top of your head." We maneuver fractional changes, our noses getting in the way.

"Hold it! That's fine, if you raise her just a little—too much, too much. Right there. That's perfect."

Clark whispers to me, "That's where we were in the first place."

The assistant checks his watch. It's getting close to lunchtime. "Okay, can we go? Let's wet 'em down!"

Clark says, "Here we go again, baby."

He helps me down from the stool, and we go just off the set and stand in a bathtub arrangement made of tar paper and two-by-fours. A man in a raincoat turns garden hoses on us. After the heat of the lights, the water feels icy. We gasp and yell as it hits us.

The assistant says, "Let's go, let's go—get 'em while they're wet!" The makeup man pops in to wipe a drop from the end of my nose.

Now it's quiet. Now we do what they pay us all that money for. The great, acquired ability to concentrate, to focus all one's thoughts and emotions on the scene. This is what they'll see up there on the screen in the theaters, although that isn't what you think of at the time. The best way I can describe what happens is with the phrase, "as though"; we think and act "as though." As though at that moment we were in the grip of an emotion bringing us violently together in the first taste of lips....

Somebody's laughing. Out there behind the lights.

Clark jerks his head up, startled, annoyed, and the whole crew breaks into loud guffaws.

Vic says, "Cut it!" and comes in to us. "It's a very hot scene, kids, but not that hot. You're steaming!"

And we are, literally. The hot lights have vaporized the water on our clothes and skin, and it's rising in waves.

After the laughter is over, everybody starts making suggestions at once. Finally the problem is solved. The water has to be heated, of course. We simply stay in position with those hot lights on until we stop steaming, but to prevent our drying off at the same time, the prop man pours warm water over our heads and shoulders.

To the assistant director, who must keep things on schedule, it's all very hurry-up, very urgent. But the situation has given the rest of us the sillies. Somebody says, "Clark, wanna deck of cards? You and Mary could play a hand of gin rummy while you're waiting!"

And all the time the assistant director is chanting, "Can we go? Can we go, fellas?"

There's a muscle in my shoulder that's beginning to complain. "Can I stand up a minute?" I ask.

"No, Mary," Vic says. "We're all set. Don't move out of it. Wet 'em down a little more." The warm water dribbles on our hair. Clark says, "What, no soap?"

"Okay, roll 'em!"

And the scene is shot. Time: about 35 seconds (maybe less) of a hungry look and a kiss (*as though*!).

Vic says, "Print it." It's okay and we go to lunch.

The weird part of it all is that it has never occurred to anyone, including Clark and me, that all the horseplay, all the distractions, might interfere with the "mood," with being able to play a love scene convincingly. That's the way it is.

* * *

What It Was Like to Kiss Clark Gable

So, dear Mrs. Bank-Teller Bobby-Soxer, in answer to your question, "What was it like to kiss Clark Gable?" there isn't an answer. Maybe if circumstances had been different—quite different!—I'd be able to tell you how one afternoon he grabbed me and pulled me behind a door and said, in that wonderful crumbly voice, "Baby, you're for me!" and (sigh) *kissed* me. Then I could have told you what it was like!

The Many Faces of Jack Lemmon

by Maurice Zolotow

ON THE THIRD-FLOOR LEDGE of a Riverside, Calif., hotel, Victor Clooney prepares to leap to his death because his wife has run away. He stares down at the onlookers in the courthouse square, infinite suffering in his gray-blue eyes. His lips quiver. His legs and arms seem to jerk and twitch, even though he is standing still.

Moments before, Jack Lemmon had clambered up the scaffolding behind the false front of the hotel set to start "becoming" the suicidal Clooney, a network-television censor, in director Billy Wilder's film, *Buddy Buddy*. Normally Jack's stunt double, Tom Anthony, would do the jump, but it is only the first week of filming. "I'm still looking for Victor Clooney," says Jack. "I don't feel I've got a character down until I'm in his skin, like a hand in a glove. But Victor Clooney wants to jump *now*, and so I've got to do it."

A thin, nearly invisible wire is snapped to a sort of cummerbund under Jack's shirt. He shrugs resignedly. "Billy says this rig can hold 6500 pounds." Jack weighs 160 pounds wringing wet. At this moment he *is* wringing wet—from perspiration. He seems frightened. Or has he already entered into the soul of the character he is playing and it is Victor Clooney who is frightened?

The camera is ready. From the courthouse square below, Wilder gives Lemmon the signal to jump. Suddenly Jack balks. "Tell Billy I can't do it."

"Why not?" Wilder's voice crackles back on the walkie-talkie.

"Because cameras make me nervous," Jack says, laughing

The Many Faces of Jack Lemmon

so hard he almost goes over the ledge. Wilder has fallen for this same old gag a million times, Jack tells me.

Then Jack is Victor Clooney again. His long, sad-eyed face and twitching body convey fear and anguish. Wilder signals he is happy with the scene. He always is with Jack Lemmon. "Audiences have more rapport with Jack than with any other actor since Chaplin," Wilder says.

Rapport, identification. That is the Lemmon secret. Audiences love Jack whether he is a tragic alcoholic in the classic *Days of Wine and Roses*; Daphne, the "female" musician in *Some Like It Hot*, the comedy that made him a big name; or a wisecracking newspaper reporter in *The Front Page*. He moves easily from the tragic to the ridiculous. And no matter what the situation, he makes us feel we are in it with him. He is the average man as hero.

When he plays the sophisticated lover opposite such stars as Shirley MacLaine and Kim Novak, we know he will slip on a banana peel. All of us who have ever made fools of ourselves feel the bond. We recognize part of ourselves in the young executive on the make in *The Apartment*—and hope that, like the Lemmon character, we have a redeeming streak of decency.

For his efforts Jack has been nominated for seven academy awards. He has won Oscars both for Best Supporting Actor (as Ensign Pulver in *Mr. Roberts*) and for Best Performance by a Male Actor (as Harry Stoner in *Save the Tiger*).

How does he do it?

As Jack gets ready to start a day's filming, he always murmurs, "magic time." The instant the camera rolls he is like Alice going through the looking glass into another world, another existence.

Jack pours himself intensely into being other people. It becomes almost an obsession. It's as if the character possesses Lemmon instead of Lemmon's owning the character. When he played Scottie Templeton, the man dying of leukemia in *Tribute*, he lost weight and played the part at a mere 135 pounds. He didn't have to diet; role identification did it. As an alcoholic in *Days of Wine and Roses*, Jack regularly attended meetings of Alcoholics Anonymous. He also drank so heavily his friends became concerned about him. Preparing for *Irma La Douce*, an amusingly naughty film in which Jack plays a Parisian gendarme who falls in love with a prostitute, he and co-star Shirley

MacLaine spent hours talking to one of Paris's ladies of the evening.

Jack's efforts to get inside his characters by doing some of his own stunts has frequently led to trouble. In *How to Murder Your Wife*, a rusty fire-escape ladder he was descending broke, and he started falling toward an asphalt court. Jack caught hold of a chimney and saved his life. But he strained his chest muscles so badly that it was a year before he could raise his arms without hurting.

Once, Jack's zest to perfect a character won him not only wounds but an important booster. Some of *Fire Down Below*, a 1957 picture he made with Rita Hayworth and Robert Mitchum, was filmed on location in Trinidad. Then the actors moved to London for the interior scenes, and Jack started to lose his suntan. By his standards makeup just wasn't good enough. He bought a sunlamp, forgot to cover his eyes, and fell asleep under it for twelve minutes instead of the intended two. Within five hours he had blisters on his swollen eyelids.

In that state he attended a birthday party for Louella Parsons, then the most powerful Hollywood gossip columnist.

"I was in terrible pain," Jack recalls. "The toasts praising Louella started. My eyes puffed up and I started tearing. Louella saw the tears flowing and said, very loudly, 'Isn't that the sweetest man?' After that I could do no wrong so far as she was concerned."

John Uhler Lemmon III, son of upper-class Bostonians, was born on February 8, 1925, in an elevator going up—after his mother had lingered too long at her bridge club and failed to make it to the maternity ward of Newton-Wellesley Hospital. Jack has been in motion ever since. When he walks he seems to be running. When he stands he seems to be trotting. Even when he is sitting, his hands and face move constantly.

Jack was also born with jaundice. When the nurse saw him, she said, "Well, here's a pretty little yellow Lemmon,"—the first bad Lemmon joke.

In school, he was Jack U. Lemmon. Or, "Hey, Jack, you Lemmon." He fought a hundred schoolyard battles, then accepted it. On a Milton Berle cable-television show, he stepped out of a cabinet in which Milton had placed a beautiful girl. "You put in a peach," Jack told Berle, "and out came a Lemmon."

Jack's parents loved stage shows and movies and took him

The Many Faces of Jack Lemmon

frequently. At age nine he saw a 12-minute short starring Richard Haydn, an eccentric British comedian who did various kinds of snores. At home, little Lemmon started impersonating movie and radio stars as they would sound snoring. He got attention, got laughs.

He got something else. When he became somebody else— say Jimmy Durante or Fred Allen snoring—he felt a strange joy. He had found his vocation, and a way to get out of his shell of loneliness. For he had always been shy, suffering a series of childhood diseases that had isolated him from friends. As himself, he felt like a nobody. As Eddie Cantor or Ed Wynn, he felt like a somebody.

At Harvard University, Jack drifted through his academic work and put his energies into the drama club and the Hasty Pudding Society. He helped write and acted in the society's first postwar show. Then he took off for New York and went through the usual struggles, cheap apartments, starvation diets, before finally becoming a regular on such TV programs as the Kraft Television Theatre, Playhouse 90, Studio One. They were televised live and with little rehearsal time, so Jack had to learn to get into the souls of a diversity of characters quickly.

In 1953, Jack signed with Columbia Pictures. By 1956 he was the studio's hottest personality. Dorothy Blair, a Columbia publicist, arranged a fan-magazine picture spread of superstar Jack and his wife Cynthia Stone at a barbecue, where he met Felicia Farr, a young actress. Jack's and Cynthia's marriage was shaky.

Jack became enchanted with Felicia. After his divorce, he began a long, fiery courtship of her. They were married in Paris in 1962 while he was filming *Irma La Douce*.

Jack's obsession with doing everything his characters do almost wrecked their honeymoon. His character leaps into the Seine. Jack did it and swallowed a mouthful of germs. "I came down with the worst case of amoebic dysentery since it was invented," he recalls. "It sort of put a crimp in the romance. Thank God, Felicia has a sense of humor. We both laughed."

They have been laughing and fighting and loving ever since. Chris, Jack's son by his first wife, is an actor and is close to his father. Felicia has a daughter, Denise by her first marriage. And together they have a smart, lovable daughter named Courtney.

Felicia and the family have the interesting experience of

dealing with a different husband and father every six months or so. When he played Harry Stoner, the desperate, lost protagonist of *Save the Tiger*, Jack became that man so intensely that he would break down and weep hysterically while driving to the studio in the morning. Having become Victor Clooney for *Buddy Buddy*, he started playing golf like a man worried about his wife running away. Result: he hit long drives into the rough. But the movie is basically a comedy. So Jack also made some miraculous recovery shots to the green.

At such bounce-back moments it is hard to believe that Jack's life as an actor has consisted wholly of standing on dizzying ledges, wrenching muscles in falls and getting amoebic dysentery. In *Some Like It Hot* he spends considerable time in an upper berth with Marilyn Monroe and a bevy of scantily dressed girl musicians. Surely *that* must have been pleasurable?

"Are you crazy? Fun?" says Jack. "That upper berth had a very low ceiling. I could hardly breathe. I kept hitting my head over and over again. I had a splitting headache for days."

He pauses. His right hand moves in a characteristic spiraling gesture and he smiles. "I'd rather stand out on a ledge anytime."

Victor Clooney talking? No, Jack Lemmon, actor.

Music Makers
and Dreamers

The Heroic Conscience of Pablo Casals

by Isaac Stern

"I GIVE YOU MY HEART, my fingers and my fiddle," I told Pablo Casals the first time I met him. That was 25 years ago, and I never had cause to take them back, least of all my heart. All my life I had revered Casals, who was two tremendous persons in one—the finest cellist in history and a supreme humanitarian. The uniqueness of every living thing awed him. An outspoken foe of totalitarianism, he traveled thousands of miles crusading for peace, even in his 90s. Despite personal tragedy and loss, he always maintained, "Life is wonderful." As Thomas Mann, the Nobel Prize-winning writer, said, he was "one of those artists who come to the rescue of humanity's honor."

I first met Casals in the small French village of Prades, just across the Pyrenees from his native Spain, where he had exiled himself in 1939 following Franco's victory. There Casals began organizing aid for Spanish refugees and vowed never again to play his cello in a world of war and dictatorship. Later, however, he took heart and played a few times for the refugees.

In 1950, violinist Alexander Schneider talked Casals into appearing at a festival commemorating the bicentenary of J. S. Bach in the 14th-century church at Prades. Then he talked me and a few other musicians into joining them. In that lovely village of red-tile roofs and cobblestone streets, we gave our concerts, and they became an annual tradition.

Between rehearsals, Casals would often sit and talk. He felt that his first responsibility was not to his music but to the welfare of mankind. "To live is not enough," he used to say. "We have to take part in what is good and do our best."

Pablo was born in 1876, near Barcelona, in the village of

Vendrell. His father was the church organist, and the family was poor; but Pablo was a lively, happy youngster. Strolling players came to Vendrell, and the boy was fascinated by their musical instruments, especially the cello. His father made him one out of a gourd and a strip of wood. At 11, he received his first real cello.

Despite Pablo's interest in music, his father wished to apprentice him to a carpenter to learn a trade. But his mother had other ideas. She took him to Barcelona when he was 11, started him on music lessons and left him with relatives. To pay for his classes, Pablo took a job playing at a local café. One night Isaac Albéniz, a leading Catalan composer and pianist, heard him and was so impressed that he brought him to Count de Morphy, a patron of the arts and adviser to the Queen Regent, María Cristina. The queen granted Pablo a small pension, and he studied for nearly three years in Madrid, until de Morphy advised him to move on to the prestigious Conservatory of Music in Brussels.

When Pablo auditioned in Brussels, he was told to sit in the back of the room while members of the cello class played. Finally, the professor said to him sarcastically, "Well, little Spaniard, will you play something for us?" The professor reeled off a list of compositions, and Casals nodded to all of them. "This boy must know everything!" the professor said, and the class hooted with laughter. The professor told Casals to play "Souvenir de Spa," a flashy and difficult piece. When Pablo finished, there was a stunned silence, and the professor said softly, "You will get first prize if you will consent to be in my class."

"No," Pablo told him. "You ridiculed me in front of your pupils."

Pablo, his mother and two young brothers promptly went to Paris. Annoyed, Count de Morphy had the queen cut off Pablo's pension. Without it, life was grim. The only job Pablo could find in Paris was as second cellist at the Folies-Marigny, a music hall that specialized in the can-can. Each day he walked halfway across the city to work and then home, to save the 15-centime trolley fare—enough to buy a loaf of bread. His mother took in sewing. When Pablo fell ill, she had to sell her beautiful long black hair to buy medicine.

Destitute, they returned to Barcelona. There, suddenly, things started looking up. Pablo was offered a teaching post, and he

The Heroic Conscience of Pablo Casals 219

found a job playing cello in the opera orchestra. At 22, armed with a letter of introduction to conductor Charles Lamoureux, one of the musical giants of the time, he decided to try Paris again. At their first meeting, Lamoureux gruffly told Casals to return the next day. Pablo did. This time, Lamoureux, who was writing at his desk, grumbled about interruptions and went on with his work. But as Casals started to play, Lamoureux dropped his pen and slowly turned around to face him. When he finished, Lamoureux embraced him, saying, "My dear child, you are one of the elect."

Pablo quickly became an international figure, commanding tremendously high fees. But his chronic stage fright was almost his undoing. When he made his debut in Vienna, he was so nervous that the bow to his cello sailed out into the audience. In total silence it was passed back to him from one row to another. Later, when his left hand was mangled in a mountain-climbing accident, his immediate reaction was thankfulness that he could never play in public again. (Fortunately for the world, the hand healed in a few months.) "The thought of a public concert always gives me a nightmare," he told me.

To make it possible for poor people to attend concerts, Casals had founded the Workingmen's Concert Association in Barcelona in the 1920s. Eventually it had 300,000 members who paid but a few cents a year for tickets. He also hired 88 of the best musicians he could find to establish a fine orchestra for Barcelona. Until it was able to break even, he made up the $300,000 deficit out of his own pocket.

The Spanish civil war put an end to both the Workingmen's Association and his orchestra. On the night of July 18, 1936, while he was conducting Beethoven's "Ninth Symphony," word came of the impending battle for Barcelona. Casals told his beloved musicians: "I do not know when we shall meet again and I propose that we finish the symphony as an *adieu* and an *au revoir* for all of us."

Just as he had refused to play in Franco's Spain, Mussolini's Italy and Stalin's Russia, Casals would have nothing to do with Hitler's Germany. Three high-ranking Nazis called on him one day in Prades, asking him to play for Hitler. He refused, pretending to be ill. They offered him a private railroad car for the trip. He said that he was too old to travel. Later, the Nazis put his name on a list of their enemies but, afraid of world outcry, they spared him.

Casals was married three times: first to a Portuguese cellist in 1906, second to an American singer in 1914. In 1957, he was married again, to a lovely young Puerto Rican cellist named Marta Montañez, who had come to Prades to study with him. She was 20 and he was 80. They moved to Puerto Rico. There Pablo started the Casals Festival anew, and it has taken place every year since 1958. Nearly every summer he went to Marlboro, Vt., to teach and conduct at the festival directed by a good friend, pianist Rudolf Serkin.

Slowly he came to realize that he alone could not sway governments with his protests. Perhaps his music could succeed where his words could not. In 1960, he first conducted his oratorio called "El Pesebre" ("The Manger"), about peace and world brotherhood, and he offered to go anywhere in the world to conduct it. In 1971 came his "Hymn to Peace," with text by W. H. Auden. He conducted this at the United Nations.

Although he loved the whole human race, children were his special favorites. To my own, who adored him, he was always "Pabbie." But he worried about children growing up in a totally materialistic world. "They know nothing of the wonder of life," he said sadly to me. "To realize that one is unique in all creation—what a privilege!"

Age meant nothing to him. It was only a matter for the calendar. "As long as one can admire and love," he told me at one of our last visits, "then one is young forever." He could never understand people who complained about age. To one such friend, Casals said gently, "You are not old. It is just that you were young a long time ago."

In the summer of 1973, Casals went to Israel. When he arrived in the 90° heat, he looked every one of his 96 years. We carried him, faint and ill, from the plane to his hotel in Jerusalem. Immediately, he demanded a piano. The only one I could find was in the hotel bar, so I had it brought up to his suite. The frail, weary old man sat down, loosened his tie, dropped his braces and started playing a Bach prelude. The color came back to his cheeks. He smiled, and everything was all right again.

Back in Puerto Rico, in September he had a heart attack, followed by lung complications. Impatient at being hospitalized, he pulled out all the intravenous tubes from his arms, flung them to the floor and told the nurse: "Damn it, I will not die!" Incredibly, he managed to survive another day.

Three days of mourning were declared in Puerto Rico, and he was buried in a little gray-granite crypt by the sea. Memorial services took place all over the world, and even in Spain part of his peace oratorio was played in tribute.

The last time that I saw him was late in August, 1973, when he was leaving Israel. I kissed him, and we said that we would keep in touch. I watched him walk across the hotel lobby. He turned and smiled. I waved. We always knew that any time could be the last, so we never talked about good-bys. Instead, my mind was on something that he had said to me years ago in Prades: "How else could I act? A man has to live with himself."

Leopold Stokowski:
The Glamour Boy Conductor

by Andre Kostelanetz

AS THE THRONG of elegantly dressed men and women gathered for the New York Metropolitan Opera's revival of Puccini's *Turandot*, excitement filled the air. That night the featured performers were Birgit Nilsson, Franco Corelli and Anna Moffo. And for the first time, my friend Leopold Stokowski was to conduct this great opera company.

The house lights slowly dimmed and Stokowski appeared—on crutches. When the audience saw him, they began applauding. Stokowski reached the podium, acknowledged what had become a standing ovation, gave his crutches to his assistant and sat down on a stool.

I can still see him sitting there that February evening in 1961. The memory of the crutches vanished as his arms reached out vigorously, caressingly, urgently, drawing from the orchestra the glorious sounds of that opera. There is something about music that awakens hidden sources of vitality and enthusiasm. That night it gave Stokowski, then 78, the energy and zest of a young man.

When I went backstage to congratulate Leopold on the exciting performance, he simply said, "What beautiful music!" But I kept thinking of my friend's great courage and determination. He had broken his hip in December at his apartment while teaching his young sons to drop kick a football. After surgery, instead of canceling his Metropolitan Opera debut, he studied the score the entire time he was in the hospital. Stokowski had never been one to think anything impossible.

Throughout his life Stokowski was brilliant and unpredictable, always doing things his own way. Tall and strikingly

Leopold Stokowski: The Glamour Boy Conductor 223

handsome in his youth, he was known as the "glamour boy of the baton" until one day, during a particularly vigorous movement, his baton broke. From then on he used his hands, and those graceful expressive "instruments" soon became his trademark, along with his china-blue eyes and golden hair.

In 1912, at the age of 30, he took over the then mediocre Philadelphia Orchestra and within ten years made it one of the great orchestras of all time. Much has been written in analytical terms about Stokowski's ability to build orchestral groups with a specific lush sound, full of fire and drive. Frankly, I feel there has been *too* much analysis. One can explain the greatness of Stokowski in a single word: genius. Once, when rehearsing Stravinsky's "Rite of Spring," he stopped the orchestra during a rousing passage; "I didn't hear the fourth trombone," he said. And he was right; the librarian had forgotten to bring out that trombone part, and the fourth trombone was playing the same part as the third trombone.

For 12 years Leopold and I lived in the same apartment building. Our terraces adjoined, and we would often talk. He was not an easy person to know, but this is not to say he was cold. He simply disliked small talk and gossip. He preferred to talk shop—about composers, artists, performances, orchestras.

Once he and I were discussing the art of composition. He said, "You know, the greatest art of all is living itself." Certainly his life was proof of that philosophy. Leopold was interested in everything from politics to electronics. He was an adventurer in life, with insatiable curiosity and willingness to try new things.

At a time when audiences expected only the classic sounds of Bach, Mozart, Beethoven and other masters, Stokowski insisted on new compositions by contemporary composers. "Tradition," he said, "is a form of laziness." There are close to 100 works now in the so-called standard repertory which Stokowski originally introduced to American audiences. Such pioneering made him one of the most controversial and exciting figures in the musical world.

Leopold's audiences weren't always appreciative of his efforts. In 1919 he introduced Philadelphians to Scriabin's "Poem of Ecstasy," and many in the audience rose and walked out. In 1922, he gave the American premiere of the "Rite of Spring." Leopold, who early developed the practice of talking directly with the audience before a performance, said, "Frankly, I can't imagine you liking this on first hearing." And he was right.

My friend's interest in new works was matched by his commitment to young people. In the early '20s, he was the first big-name conductor to give regular concerts for children under 12 years, who loved his easy manner and good humor. When he presented Saint-Saëns' "Carnival of the Animals," he had live animals onstage, including some baby elephants. For Prokofiev's "Peter and the Wolf," he substituted a huge dog for a wolf.

For a long time, Leopold had dreamed of forming an orchestra of highly talented young American players. In 1940, a few years after he left the Philadelphia Orchestra, his dream became reality with the establishment of the All-American Youth Orchestra. He traveled throughout the country to audition players and finally selected 100 of them, 15 to 25 years old, who soon were performing with resounding success. More important than the applause was the fact that the young musicians had an opportunity to play great music professionally.

Years later, in the '60s, Leopold organized (and helped finance out of his own pocket) the American Symphony Orchestra—again to give young people, and especially women and blacks, an opportunity to play. To this day, wherever I conduct I often find graduates from the American Symphony— some of the finest musicians in the world.

Through the years, Leopold at various times also conducted the NBC Symphony, the Hollywood Bowl Symphony, the New York Philharmonic, the New York City Center Orchestra and the Houston Symphony. It is hard to believe that he conducted music—gloriously—for more than 60 years, in over 7000 concerts.

That long musical trail began in London in 1882, where Leopold was born to a Polish father and Irish mother, neither of whom were professional musicians. A child prodigy, Stokowski played the violin, piano and organ (and somehow also acquired the curious European accent which so annoyed his detractors in later years). His first major job was as organist at St. James's Church in Piccadilly, and in 1905 he was invited to serve as organist and choir director at New York City's prestigious St. Bartholomew's Church. In 1909, when he was 27, Leopold became music director of the Cincinnati Symphony Orchestra, moving on to Philadelphia after three years.

Leopold Stokowski: The Glamour Boy Conductor 225

From the beginning, Leopold experimented with the placement of his orchestra to get a better sound. Although it was traditional for first violins to be at the conductor's left and second violins to the right, Stokowski placed all the violins on the left, violas in the middle and cellos on the right—the arrangement of most orchestras today. He dispensed with uniform bowing of the strings, knowing that the strength of each player's wrist varies and, to achieve the richest string tone, each player should have maximum elasticity. Leopold also encouraged his wind players to breathe as they wished. He didn't care, he said, how they made music—as long as it was beautiful.

Stokowski was the first to appreciate fully how broadcasting could increase the audience for serious music. In 1929, the Philadelphia Orchestra, with Stokowski conducting, became the first classical orchestra ever to be heard on commercial radio. He worked with experts at the Bell Laboratories and soon became an expert himself on radio and phonographic recordings as well as hall acoustics. I remember years ago when Philharmonic Hall (now Avery Fisher Hall) in New York City had just been built and many important conductors were asked to come and try it out. Leopold chose Beethoven's "Eroica" for his test. He conducted the opening chords, looked up and said, "They asked me too late." He then walked out, knowing the hall would have to be rebuilt. (In 1976 it was—at a cost of between $6 and $7 million—and now has excellent acoustics.)

Stokowski was also the first great conductor to plunge into the movies. His most famous was Walt Disney's "Fantasia," in which he shook hands with Mickey Mouse—and brought some of the greatest music of Bach, Beethoven, Mussorgsky, Schubert, Tchaikovsky and Stravinsky to millions. In the process, he used 18 separate sound channels—a forerunner of stereo.

"Fantasia" created a furor when first released, partly because Stokowski had made changes in the scores. In fact, he was frequently criticized by purists for such tinkering. I once asked him about an ending he had changed. His reply: "I'm sure if the composer had heard it this way, he would have preferred it."

In Philadelphia, his audiences lionized him. Sometimes, though, he encountered difficulties with the ladies who flocked to his Friday afternoon concerts and were given to knitting, talking and general restlessness during pieces they didn't like. He was always quick to criticize their bad manners, and once simply stopped conducting and walked away. But applause never displeased him, even at supposedly wrong moments. I was present on one occasion when, after a rousing opening movement, some of the audience began clapping. When others shushed them, Leopold turned around and said, "No, you people who shush are wrong. If someone likes something, it's only right he should show his approval. We performers *like* applause."

Indeed, whenever people talk about Leopold Stokowski, they invariably bring up his ego and his penchant for the spotlight. Everything he did was news, including marriage. His first wife, Olga Samaroff, was an accomplished pianist; his second was heiress Evangeline Brewster Johnson. In 1945, when he was 63, he married 21-year-old Gloria Vanderbilt. In between marriages, he was romantically linked with many famous women, including Greta Garbo.

But it was his actions as a conductor that caused the most comment. People came to Stokowski's concerts not only to hear his music but to see what he might do. Once he conducted in near darkness, feeling that light was a distraction to the audience. The musicians—with only tiny lamps on the stands— could hardly see the music. A bright light, however, focused on Stokowski's hair and hands. Some felt this was to give the maestro more attention. But he explained later that the light was necessary so the musicians could see his hands and facial expressions.

For all the talk about Stokowski's showmanship and ego, though, he was the most considerate of men. Whenever he engaged a soloist for a concert, he first asked the guest to make five suggestions for the evening's concerto. Leopold would select one of these and only then build the rest of the program around it. When he auditioned young players for a position, he always understood that the player might be nervous. Many times he would interrupt, give some advice and then allow the player to start again.

In all our conversations, Leopold avoided talking of the past. Often he would say to me, "Don't ask me about what was, but what is to come." It was typical of my friend that when he died of a heart attack in September, 1977, at the age of 95 he was still making plans for the future. Shortly before, he had signed a contract with Columbia Records to make four records a year until 1982—when he would have been exactly 100.

The Three Lives
of Ethel Waters

by Allen Rankin

HIGH OVER the crowd-packed stadium at a Billy Graham Crusade, a familiar and jubilant voice was heard. Warm and mellow as a muted trumpet, it broke free from the staid cadences of the choir and took off on exuberant excursions of its own. The years was 1972, and at the age of 76, soloist-evangelist Ethel Waters was turning in the most fulfilling performance of her half-century of stardom. "I love getting up and showing that being a witness for the Lord is no hard, long-faced affair," she liked to explain, "but the easiest, gladdest thing that I or anybody ever did!"

Her ample, statuesque presence crowned by white hair, Miss Waters was a compelling figure in her later years. Because of a heart condition that was to kill her at the age of 80, she moved slowly, cautiously, easing along like a stately parade float. But her famous full-moon smile was brighter than ever, and when she sang or ad-libbed in her folksy way, coliseums became warm, intimate places. In the early 1970s, the Waters appeal was even stronger than it was in the 1920s and '30s, when she was in her prime and an all-time-great blues and torch singer, or in the '40s and '50s, when she was establishing herself as a first lady of the American theater and screen.

"Until about 15 years ago," she told me in our 1972 interview, "I was never really happy or sure of myself. I was always in some show or nightclub act. But this ain't no show, sugar, and it ain't no act. I'm a born-again Christian, doing what I was always intended to do!"

Almost apologetically, the maker of 259 notable recordings added: "I never had a big enough voice to be a shouting kind

The Three Lives of Ethel Waters

of singer, and what voice I did have is mostly gone. But like my grandmother used to say, 'You don't have to holler; God has big ears and can hear you if you whisper.' Like in the psalm, I guess you'd say I just get up and make a joyful noise."

A joyful noise it was, the one Ethel always made and millions, old and young, flocked to her Crusade performances or watched her other appearances on television. "When she walks out on the platform," said Billy Graham, "I've seen 75,000 people all rise at once. Ethel Waters is one of the most beloved, remarkable, and *electric* women of the century."

She was always as uninhibited and irrepressible as a hurricane. Her speech was a magical mixture of Bible quotations, slum and show-business slang, murdered grammar and pure eloquence. Even at her most serious moments a laugh was never far away. For example: "The Lord is Almighty," she was sermonizing to me, "but"—with a sudden impish grin—"don't forget the devil. He can be pretty powerful. I know, because I used to be one of *his* best customers, too! I mean he lost a good bet when he lost me!"

Thinking back, she reflected: "I used to be streamlined—the Twiggy of my day, when I was dancing the shimmy. Now look at me! I'm so big and fat it takes two guardian angels to watch over me!" Her throaty chuckle filled the room. Serious again, she quoted from her new book, *To Me It's Wonderful*: "The fact is that some of the worst of us make the happiest Christians. The further we've gone as sinners, the more enlightened believers we can become." Then the priceless observation: "Some folks are so heavenly minded they ain't any earthly good."

Born October 31, 1896, in a Chester, Pa., slum, Ethel Waters was the daughter of a 12½-year-old black girl who had been raped at knife-point. Along with her frightened, unmarried child-mother, she grew up in back-alley neighborhoods that her grandmother and other relatives temporarily called home. Ethel sprouted into an over-tall, over-tough little girl, pretty well able to fend for herself by the age of six. Often hungry, she shoplifted food in order to eat.

However, the tall, lanky girl with the big head and wide, sensitive eyes lacked something she couldn't steal—affection. At first she got attention by shocking adults with her profanity. But she was softened by three things: the influence of her valiant grandmother, Sally Anderson; the kindness of the sisters at the

Catholic day school she entered at eight; and a real spiritual awakening she experienced at 12 at a revival meeting.

Even so, she seemed trapped by her environment. A marriage at 13 to a man much older than she failed dismally. Later she was making $3.50 a week as scullion and substitute chambermaid at a Philadelphia hotel. But she could clean up a room fast enough to have a few moments left to pretend she was a great actress, singing and dancing before the mirror.

Then on the night of her 17th birthday, at Jack's Rathskeller, one of the competitors in a talent contest failed to appear and Ethel went on. A couple of vaudeville troupers in the audience liked her sweet, bell-like voice and signed her up at a salary of $10 a week.

In her first featured stage performance, Ethel wanted to sing a new number she had heard a female impersonator do. She wrote the copyright owners, Pace and Handy, in Memphis for permission. And so, in the shabby Lincoln Theater in Baltimore on a night in 1915, she became the first woman ever to sing professionally the classic "St. Louis Blues." In her brand-new soft-voiced and intimate style, she sang and acted out the song. A pandemonium of applause rose from the audience, and Ethel was on her way.

Traveling on the small-time vaudeville circuit, she was billed as "Sweet Mama Stringbean, direct from St. Louis." Then in the early 1920s she became one of the first entertainers to draw white crowds and their money to a Harlem nightclub. Her singing and dancing helped transform Edmund's Cellar "from a low-class dump to a high-class dump." Her wry, easy wit delighted newspapermen. Of her nightclub stints she later told Earl Wilson, "I worked from nine to unconscious." To the international society set, Ethel was an irresistible enigma. Here was a beautiful girl who drank nothing stronger than milk, who refused to hustle customers for drinks, who laughed and joked. Yet if sufficiently provoked she could—and once did—knock down a man with a single punch.

Soon she began to appear in the big glittering show houses, getting ovations with such greats as Al Jolson and Will Rogers. Behind the sassiness of the gutsy up-and-comer was a serious artist. Every song she agreed to plug had to *mean* something to her, and she had almost as much to do with creating many a lasting hit as did the composer. "Dinah," for example: she introduced it, and her recording made it an international hit.

The Three Lives of Ethel Waters

"Am I Blue?" was another. While appearing with Duke Ellington's orchestra in 1933, she was asked to introduce a new number which had a lot of stormy noise-making effects. She opined that the piece should have "more to do with human emotions" and less with the "rumblings and rattlings of old Mother Nature." A new arrangement was made and Ethel ushered in "Stormy Weather."

It was an apt theme song for her personal life. She was famous now, but her second marriage was falling apart. A lover of children, she was childless and would remain so.

Onstage, however, things were flawless. Theater critic Brooks Atkinson hailed her for "knowing how to make a song stand on tiptoe." She had few equals as mimic, parodist, dancer. By 1934, in the revue *As Thousands Cheer*, she was burning up Broadway with her high-temperature rendition of "Heat Wave," then dousing flames with the tearful dirge "Supper Time." For the show and nightclub dates, she was grossing $4000 a week.

Having gained the peak in one career, Ethel reached for a second as a dramatic actress. But could a show girl, a blues singer, play the lead in a tragedy? There were many skeptics in the Empire Theater at the opening of *Mamba's Daughters* on January 3, 1939. Ethel played Hagar, the lumbering, confused, tormented mother—who was, she felt, much like her own mother. She was determined to show the fine, white audience "what it is like to be a colored woman, dumb, ignorant, and feeling everything with such intenseness that she is half-crazy." She was giving vent to feelings dammed up inside her for years. In the final scene with the sporting man who had betrayed her daughter, she strangled him with such convincing fury that when the curtain fell there was stunned silence. Then the applause thundered out, and there were 17 curtain calls for Ethel alone.

As it turned out, her triumph was neither the pinnacle nor the happy ending. Her mother was now ill, a love affair was going on the rocks, and a rough stretch of road lay ahead. Yet she turned down initial offers to play a huge role—that of a life-seasoned, philosophical but bitter servant—in a Broadway dramatization of Carson McCullers' *The Member of the Wedding*. "I was looking for God in the book," she told the producers. "I didn't find Him."

Eventually, in 1949, the producers agreed to let her have a

freer hand in giving the part her own spiritual interpretation. Thus, Ethel Waters, directed by taste and uncompromising integrity, literally helped *create* her most beloved stage and movie role—that of Berenice Sadie Brown, the cook who gives counsel and solace to a little girl heartbroken because she can't go on her brother's honeymoon. It was Ethel who suggested the old folk hymn she sang at the close of the final act. A testament of simple faith, it was the hit of the play and became the title of her moving autobiography, *His Eye Is on the Sparrow*.

About this time Ethel's health began to collapse, and her weight soared to over 350 pounds. Her main trouble, she realized, had nothing to do with the ailments the doctors said she had. She was "lonesome for Jesus." She missed the comforting closeness she had felt with him as a child. Late at night, she kept hunting around her radio dial hoping to find "a real preachin' man."

Then, one May evening in 1957, she found herself at the opening of the Billy Graham Greater New York Crusade in Madison Square Garden. "As I walked in," she recalled, "the choir was singing 'This Is My Story,' one of the songs we used to sing in the little church in Chester. I didn't know a soul, but I never felt so much at home anywhere. And, when Billy began to preach, it seemed he was talking just to me. I felt that the Lord was calling me, His child, to come on back home."

Ethel returned the next night, and the next. Then, to get an even better reserved seat, she joined the choir, and continued to drink in the sermons. "And," she said, "the Lord gave me fresh answers to my problems. For one thing, I realized that, though I hadn't been displeasing Him too much, I hadn't been really *pleasing* Him either. And what a difference there is in those two!"

When the four-month Crusade was over, Ethel found that she couldn't return to theater work. Her old life and her new feelings didn't mix. "But how are you going to get along?" someone asked.

"Through the mercy and grace of God," Ethel answered, "everything is going to be all right. The Lord will take care of me."

And so it worked out. During her last two decades, as a full-time evangelist, she had the time of her life singing and witnessing at Graham Crusades and before such groups as Youth for Christ. Said Billy Graham, "I've thanked the Lord a thousand times that He allowed her path to cross ours."

Horowitz the Thunderer

by Hubert Saal

IN HIS LIFE as well as his art, Vladimir Horowitz is a glorious eccentric. When he goes out of town to play a concert, he embarks in 19th-century style—traveling with his wife (who is the daughter of Arturo Toscanini), a piano tuner, his tour manager, a water purifier, his own pots and pans. In an era of musical informality, he dresses for concerts as though he were playing for royalty—in bow tie, gray vest, striped trousers and cutaway.

His concerts always begin at four-thirty on Sunday afternoon. When he finishes his program, he is showered with adulation—and repeatedly money, enough to make him, per performance, the highest-paid classical artist in history. Nevertheless, his next public appearance is always a matter of doubt.

His most protracted encapsulation lasted 12 years, and when he returned to the concert stage in 1965, it was called the musical event of the decade. Its counterpart in the '70s was Horowitz's celebration of his American jubilee—the concert he gave in January, 1978, almost exactly 50 years after his American debut on January 12, 1928. His remarkable performance proved what has long been an open secret among Horowitz fans—that over the years Hercules has become Jupiter, able to hurl thunderbolts of sound with even more impact than he did over half a century ago when he earned himself the nickname of the Thunderer.

The occasion could not have been more dramatic. Horowitz had not played with an orchestra in 25 years. He decided to commemorate his anniversary with the New York Philharmonic in Carnegie Hall, the same orchestra and the same auditorium of his 1928 debut. His choice of music was equally momentous—Rachmaninoff's Third Piano Concerto, a fiendishly difficult, passionately Russian epic.

The work is made for Horowitz: it makes every kind of demand on a pianist's technique and allows the widest latitude in interpretation. It is probably the most challenging of all piano concertos, shifting moods from extreme tenderness to unbridled fury. Horowitz gave it everything that is uniquely his—the volcanic sonority of tone, the whispering pianissimo, the febrile energy, the thunderous runs of octaves resonating like sonic booms.

He took great liberties with the score, inverting dynamics, stretching time to extreme limits. Occasionally he slowed the breakneck pace almost to a halt to create moments of quivering tension in which the musical line threatened to break. But it never did; then he would be off again as if pursued by furies. The performance brought the audience to its feet. The cheers were like those for a man who has gone into a cage with a hungry lion and, instead of being eaten alive, has tamed it.

Only Horowitz, 73 at the time, could have given such a performance of the Rachmaninoff. Said his old friend violinist Nathan Milstein: "He's unique. Probably he is often wrong. But you can't say Niagara Falls is wrong." In his freewheeling style, Horowitz belongs to a tradition that goes back to Franz Liszt. "I am a 19th century romantic," he once said. "I am the last." Milstein added: "Other pianists are the perfume. But Horowitz is the essence from which they make the perfume."

Horowitz tampers with almost everything he plays, changing accents, bringing out inner voices to great prominence, imposing his strong personal and sometimes perverse views on the music as a partner of the composer—sometimes the senior partner. Not even the classic masters are safe from Horowitz's iconoclastic scrutiny. "You can improve on Beethoven and everybody," he says. "The score is not a Bible."

Horowitz calls his style the "grand manner." In part he means audacity. "I must tell you I take terrible risks. Because my playing is very clear, when I make a mistake you hear it. If you want me to play only the notes without any specific color dynamics, I will never make one mistake. Never be afraid to dare. And never imitate. Play without asking advice."

Horowitz has always been willing to take risks to achieve greatness. At the age of three, imitating his mother's keyboard technique, he strummed on the windowpanes so hard that he smashed them and covered himself with blood. He was born in 1904 in Kiev, Russia, youngest of four musical children whose father was a well-to-do engineer. His first cousin Natasha Saitzoff remembered him as a five-year-old seated at the piano, dressed in a sailor suit, explaining to his listeners as he played: "Now it's going to rain, now the sun is shining."

By the time Horowitz graduated from the Kiev Conservatory at 17, the Revolution had torn his family's life apart. "The communist motto," he says, "was 'Steal What Was Stolen.' So they stole everything. With my own eyes I saw them throw our piano through the window."

It was then that he first encountered Nathan Milstein, who describes him at 17: "He looked like a beautiful portrait, like a Pre-Raphaelite. A 17-year-old pianist has to be burning up—and he was. He broke the piano strings when he played."

Between 1922 and 1925, the young Horowitz's Russian career boomed. In Leningrad, his fans carried him from the concert hall to his hotel. "It was very uncomfortable," he says. By exchanging rubles for pounds on the black market, Horowitz was able to save the equivalent of $5000, which he stuffed in his shoe when he left Russia.

He performed with fire and passion throughout Europe. "I remember I was playing the Brahms B-flat Concerto in Dortmund, Germany," he says. "After the rehearsal, the concertmaster took me to the finest bordello in town. The madam showed us seven naked girls. But I thought I had better be good, with a concert the next day. So while the concertmaster took a girl, I sat down at the upright piano and practiced. Once I looked up to find myself surrounded by these naked girls. The next day at the concert when I went out onstage, there in the first box were the madam and seven girls."

In 1933, now world famous, Horowitz married Wanda Toscanini. "I fell in love with his pedaling," she says. "On the piano, not the bicycle." He says: "She made a man out of me—and her father made me a musician. He was uncompromising and I began to play more straight. My God, he was a warm man."

Then, at the peak of his fame, in 1953, Horowitz quit. "I couldn't take the traveling, five days a week, all those trains, all those towns, no sleep, bad food. I stopped like a car must stop or burn its motor out. When an artist gives gives gives, he gets emptier emptier emptier. I remember one of my last recitals in Paris. People were sitting on the stage. I played Chopin's A-flat Polonaise. Big crescendo. I was exhausted. I hear this man say to his wife, 'Just wait, he's only beginning.' I played my heart out and he says, 'This is nothing. Just wait. There's more, much more.' Well, there wasn't."

In the next years, Horowitz reveled in his peaceful life. "I thought I would never play in public again," he says. "But then, a young person I knew said to me, 'I hear you're a great pianist. Is that true?' And I realized that a whole generation didn't know me." His return caused a lasting sensation.

There is no sign in Horowitz's private life of the imperious, larger-than-life-size romantic.

"I am a soldier," says Horowitz about the simple, rigid routine that governs his life. He doesn't drink alcohol or coffee, eats sparingly, practices the piano every afternoon for an hour or two, then takes a brisk two-mile walk. "If I don't walk," he says, "my fingers don't run."

If you ask him whether he has suffered during his life, he answers, "I had appendicitis once." But no, he insists, there was no self-doubt or anguish. His wife says, "He draws an iron curtain around himself. He won't let unpleasantness touch him." He was, of course, deeply wounded by the death of their only daughter, Sonia, at the age of 40, in 1974.

An astute businessman, Horowitz knows his audiences and his value. Although he plays only about five to ten concerts a year, per performance he is reportedly the highest-paid pianist in history. That's because he commands top ticket prices, and 80 percent of the box-office gross. "Plus record royalties," he admonishes, leaning forward to wave a finger.

Though Horowitz has been a U.S. citizen since 1944, his heavily accented English was not always as fluent as it is now. In 1931, he played at the White House and after he was introduced to President Herbert Hoover, he volunteered: "I am delightful."

But he has earned his Yankee credentials. During World War II, he performed for war-bond sales. In Carnegie Hall one memorable afternoon in 1943, he shared a concert with his father-in-law that brought in $11 million. "I love this country," he says with great feeling. "I have been to all states, to large towns and small, to Kankakee, Albuquerque, Ann Arbor, Shreveport, Lincoln, Des Moines, Jacksonville, you name it.

Especially I love the Midwest. So open and simple and genuine the people. They even teach me to like pumpkin pie, which I detest."

"The American public and I, we have grown up together," he says of music-making. The affair between them is more outlandish than ever. He is invariably greeted by standing ovations. "Why not?" he asks. "I'm standing, too." He always comes out onstage smiling, bathed in a beatific aura. "Why not?" he asks. "Some stood in line all night, with children. Should I frown? No, I am grateful. If I have a fault, it is my need to be loved. I don't need people to tell me I play beautifully. I will know if I did or didn't. When I play in public, I invite the audience to love me. When I come out and smile, I'm happy. I'm just like you. The only difference is I don't pay for my seat. But the moment I sit down at the piano, I am different. I am a king."

Itzhak Perlman: "The Polio Didn't Affect My Hands"

by Annalyn Swan

A CONCERT VIOLINIST, Jascha Heifetz once said, must have "the nerves of a bullfighter, the vitality of a woman who runs a nightclub and the concentration of a Buddhist monk." Add to that the antic soul of a born ham, and you have Itzhak Perlman.

Minutes before a 1980 recital in St. Paul, Minn., Perlman is munching pizza and swigging soda. He is chubby, cherubic and curly-haired. "How many Californians does it take to change a light bulb?" he asks a stagehand. "One to screw in the bulb," Perlman says, breaking out in a huge grin, "and three to share the experience."

With that, Perlman, a childhood polio victim who wears leg braces and walks with crutches, maneuvers his way smartly onstage. He drops the crutches beside his chair, tucks his 1714 Stradivarius under his chin—and the clown vanishes. From the first arc of his bow, Perlman becomes the consummate virtuoso, simultaneously in command of the music and relaxed enough to let it sing. He seems at once lost in an intensely private world and as engagingly open as if he were entertaining friends in his living room.

One is astonished at the delicacy of Perlman's fingers and huge hands (they span 12 notes on the piano) one moment, and their dramatic power the next. The music seems not so much played as *felt*, spilled out in great rushes of warm, lyrical sound. By the time he finishes, the rapport between artist and audience is so strong that people are humming along and even shouting requests. Behind his formidable musicianship and technique,

Perlman communicates a love of playing that is, quite simply, irresistible.

Everything about Perlman is outsize: his talent, his love of living, his almost childlike enthusiasm and energy. Perlman's personal style—huge Chinese feasts, poker evenings with the boys, rah-rah support of the New York Yankees and Knicks—matches the exuberant way he plays.

One of the highest paid of classical artists, with fees ranging into five figures, he performs more than 100 concerts a year in the United States, Europe and the Far East. His recordings regularly top the classical charts. He appears on innumerable talk shows. As he says, "I've been on the 'Tonight,' 'Tomorrow,' 'Today,' 'Yesterday' and 'A Little Bit Later' shows."

Perlman loves to show off. Once, at an outdoor cookout in Aspen, Colo., he grabbed a fiddle from the evening's entertainers, a jug band, and played a raucous "Turkey in the Straw"—just this side of the speed of sound.

Wherever he goes, he attracts diehard fans. "We came all the way from Chicago to hear you," said one couple in Iowa City, spotting Perlman in a Chinese restaurant. He has what the late impresario Sol Hurok called "the ability to go right over the spotlights." "People only half listen to you when you play," Perlman says. "The other half is watching."

Since the early 1800s, when Niccolò Paganini established the violin as a virtuoso instrument, solo violinists have practiced the most dazzling—and dangerous—of arts. To begin with, there are the vagaries of the instrument itself. Like the human voice, the violin is sensitive to a fault. One of its four strings may go flat in the middle of a passage, forcing the performer to scramble desperately for new fingering. The weather may throw off its tone. There have even been reports of violins sounding seasick after crossing the English Channel.

The violin is also hellishly hard to play. Fine points like vibrato—how fast and widely the fingers vibrate on the fingerboard—can't be taught. "There are so many factors involved in playing," says Perlman. "You have to worry about whether to move the bow slowly or quickly. Is the bow absolutely straight? How hard do you want to press the bow against the strings? All of this involves just the right hand. Then there is the left hand.... Just to get a decent sound can take years. And only *then* do you start thinking of the music

Itzhak Perlman: "The Polio Didn't Affect My Hands" 241

and developing your distinctive style."

Audiences have always been dazzled by virtuosic playing. What's rare, as in the case of Perlman, is for other master violinists to be dazzled. "His talent is utterly limitless," says Isaac Stern, who became a mentor for Perlman. "Nobody comes anywhere near him in what he can physically do with the violin. He plays with incredible accuracy and dexterity." In all of his playing, one can hear the same ideal combination of romantic fire (the Russian fiddler-on-the-roof sound) and classical poise.

Most striking about Perlman is his profound simplicity: Every note seems perfectly placed, and the most hair-raising passages sound effortless. The tone is pure and singing. Yet, as one gradually realizes, it is also big and emphatic. The effect is like looking at a Titian painting: the surface has a beautiful sheen, but there's also a powerful bite to it.

Given Perlman's physical handicap, his achievement is almost incredible. Great violinists have always stood to play, thus putting the entire body behind the bow. "To overcome that fact—that he must play seated and still bring the music across—is a marvel," says his friend, violinist Pinchas Zukerman.

Equally marvelous is Perlman's courage in the face of endless airports, hotels and concert stages, those staples of a soloist's life that are all designed without a thought for the handicapped. On tour, he must constantly think ahead to the next hurdle. But few people have ever seen him frustrated or angry. "He has an easygoing, shining quality—and it comes out in his playing," says Zukerman.

There was never a time, Perlman recalls, when he wasn't fascinated with the violin. The only child of Polish émigrés to Israel, Perlman could sing back opera arias from the radio when he was 2½. At 3½, he asked for a violin, after falling in love with its sound on the radio. At 4, he caught polio. Shortly thereafter, he began to study the violin in earnest—partly because so many other things were denied him. ("I played soccer in the street, though," he recalls. "I was the goalie. With both my crutches and my legs, I could stop anything.") "My parents instinctively did things right," he says now. "They treated me in a natural way."

Perlman grew up practicing three hours a day. In 1958 he was chosen as a part of a group that represented Israel on "The

Ed Sullivan Show" and then toured the United States. He and his mother (now dead) traveled here for two months, winding up in Manhattan.

His first years in America were hard. He studied at home with tutors—both because of his handicap and because his parents wanted him to have maximum time to practice. He played for Jewish fund-raising dinners. "I would perform around midnight, after the fund-raising part, and I was up against the sound of waiters collecting the forks," he recalls. "It was terrific training. My debut at Carnegie Hall was a breeze in comparison."

Some musicians go on automatic pilot while performing. Not Perlman. "The most important part of any concert is to listen to myself *while* I'm playing," he says. "It is a great pleasure to accompany him," says Zubin Mehta, conductor of the New York Philharmonic. "He molds his own voice so closely to the orchestra's. The result is intensive music-making."

Perlman is the complete family man. On the road, he spends every available weekend with his wife, Toby, and four children at their country house in upstate New York. "If you're not careful," he says, "the children will grow up on you and you'll miss the most glorious part of life."

In the city, the ménage is housed high above the Hudson River, in an 11-room apartment that was once Babe Ruth's. On any given day, Perlman is likely to be in the kitchen fixing lunch while the children play noisily and the phone rings constantly. "In this business, you can tell what sort of person someone is by the old friends he keeps," says Perlman. "It's too easy to fall into the 'beautiful people' trap."

Over the years there has been a steady personal deepening. As his fame has grown, Perlman has used it to help the handicapped. He has campaigned to make airplanes less of a problem for the disabled. ("Try getting a wheelchair into the bathroom of an airplane," he says.) He is also on the board of two rehabilitation hospitals for severely handicapped children. On one visit to Blythedale Children's Hospital in Valhalla, N.Y., he took apart his bow to show the horsehair. ("Obviously from Secretariat. Ha-ha.") He made his violin moo and twitter. He had the children sing a song, any song, picked up the melody and accompanied them.

Then he asked for questions. "How long have you been playing?" asked one boy. "Well, I'm 34 and I started when I was 5, so that makes 29 years," answered Perlman. "Aren't you *tired* of playing?" the boy persisted. Amid the laughter, Perlman—also laughing—said that no, he wasn't tired of playing at all. As if to prove it, he picked up his bow. As his fingers flew, there came to mind the woman—also handicapped—who leaned over to him during a recent airplane flight and said, "It's so nice to see somebody who hasn't given up."

"The polio," he replied, "didn't affect my hands."

Weavers of Fantasy

My Heart Belongs to Peter Pan

by Mary Martin

OF ALL THE exciting shows I did, the marvelous moments I knew, the happy memories I have of a long, long life in the theater, *Peter Pan* looms largest in my mind. Partly because I love Peter so, partly because everyone else in the world loves Peter so. But mostly, I think, because Never-Never Land is the way I would like real life to be: timeless, free, mischievous, filled with gaiety, tenderness and magic.

I cannot even remember a day when I didn't want to be Peter. When I was a child growing up in Weatherford, Texas, I often dreamed I could fly. During my early days in Hollywood, I went to costume parties dressed as Peter Pan. I vowed that I would play the role somewhere, someday.

My chance came in 1954, when Edwin Lester, director of the Los Angeles and San Francisco Civic Light Opera companies, asked if my husband, Richard Halliday, and I would be interested in doing an entirely new, musical version of the play. Richard was to be co-producer. I was to be Peter.

Of course we agreed. I couldn't wait to take on a role that several generations of actresses had made memorable. I played Peter in San Francisco, Los Angeles and on Broadway in '55, '56 and '60. The last show was taped and has been reshown occasionally, most recently in 1973. All told, I played Peter about 250 times.

From the beginning my "flying" instructor was a young Englishman named Peter Foy. One single English family had "flown" all the London-stage Peter Pans for 50 years, and Peter Foy had learned his trade from that family. As a rule, Peter Pans had never flown far—just in through the window of the stage set, over to the mantelpiece, around the room and back out the window. I was determined to fly all over the place, and I wanted a flying ballet with Peter and the children all sailing around together. Peter Foy sort of gulped, but he agreed to try.

I was hooked to piano wires attached to a padded harness that went around my waist, over my shoulders, through my legs. Peter Foy and an assistant held control ropes in the wings. When they pulled, I was hoisted up by the harness, and away I went. They became so expert that they could swing me back and forth, up and down, and drop me wherever they wanted me onstage as lightly as a trout fisherman drops a fly on water.

But mishaps occurred. The most serious one happened during rehearsals for the last time I played Peter Pan on television. Peter Foy was still there to fly us, but he had a new assistant. The first day of rehearsal, I went up on the wire to show the new cast of children how to move and turn. Suddenly I knew something was wrong. I was going faster and faster, in the pendulum swing, toward the brick wall of the theater. There was a sound like a rifle shot when I hit the wall. Thank fortune, I didn't faint or scream or do anything to scare the children. I had broken a bone in my arm, but I went right back out and flew again. I had to. The children would have been terrified if I hadn't. They might never have flown again—and maybe neither would I!

Later, after a doctor had set the arm, we found out what had happened. Peter Foy's new assistant had thought I was really flying and he had dropped his rope. It wasn't his fault, really. He just "believed," and that is what *Peter Pan* is all about.

And how the children loved the show! When the performances ended, they didn't want to go home, ever. As long as I live, I will hear the sound of the children's voices at *Peter Pan*. All that energy sitting in the audience—well, not exactly sitting. They stood on their seats, ran down the aisles, tried to reach Peter. When Captain Hook came onstage, they would shout, "Look out, Peter!" or "He's right behind you, Peter!" I loved it. They were *in* the show.

One child actually stole the show during a performance in San Francisco. A darling little girl got away from her parents in box seats and suddenly appeared onstage. She was about three feet tall, dressed all in white, with a straw hat on and

My Heart Belongs to Peter Pan

clutching a bouquet of flowers wrapped in lace.

I must have been onstage alone at that moment and I started toward her. She looked absolutely terrified, so I stopped. Everything stopped. There was such a silence, the quietest moment I've heard in a theater. I got down on my hands and knees and crawled across the stage toward her. She backed away, so I backed off and she came toward me. It became like a ballet, back and forth, back and forth. It was clear that she longed, yearned, to touch Peter, but she didn't dare. Finally she came close enough to hold out the flowers. Her tiny hand came out. I said, "Thank you, little one. May I pick you up?" She didn't say a word. I carried her back to her mother and father. They asked to come backstage after the show, and I said yes.

In my dressing room, the little girl put her arms around my neck and kissed me. When I asked her name, she didn't reply. She was a deaf-mute; and when she climbed out of that box and walked onto the stage, it was the first thing she had ever done all by herself, with no direction. Such is the magic of *Peter Pan*.

My favorite Peter Pan story took place soon after the 1960 television show when my husband and I were in Brazil. Richard and I and two male friends put on jungle clothes, packed some sandwiches and a chocolate cake I had baked, piled into a Jeep station wagon and went off to visit an American who had once been ambassador to Brazil. We started at 4:30 a.m. and, just before dark, arrived at a marvelous house by a huge river. But the house was closed, doors shut, windows shuttered. Richard and our two friends got out and knocked, loud. No answer. Then they tramped around the house looking for a sign of life.

I was sitting in the Jeep and I thought I saw a shutter open just a little, and behind it a small white figure. I shouted, "Look, there's somebody in there!" and at that instant the shutter closed.

I climbed out, in my jungle pants and boots and short hair, and went over to knock lightly on the closed shutter. It opened again, very slowly. Behind it was a lady's face. The lady looked at me for a moment and then said, "Peter! You've come to my window."

I replied, "Yes, I have."

Then she said, "Peter, I didn't think you would ever come. Come in."

I stepped right through the open shutter, and there we were, face to face. She was very tiny, frail and old. She said, "I have prayed for this, but I didn't think it would ever happen." Then she looked out at the Jeep and asked, "Have you friends with you?"

Solemnly I replied, "Yes. I have a few Lost Boys out there."

When she let us in, we learned that she was the 80-some-year-old sister of the former ambassador. Her brother was away on a trip, so she was alone in the house with only a Brazilian girl to help. She had recently been in Washington, D.C., and the last television show she had seen was *Peter Pan*. She had then gone straight to the jungle house. The first human being she had seen, except for the housekeeper, was me, standing outside her window in boy's clothing.

As I was washing up for dinner, she came to my room. "Peter, I have a surprise for you which you won't believe," she said. She led me to her bathroom, and in her bathtub was a crocodile! It wasn't very big, and she apologized because it didn't have an alarm clock in its stomach. But she said, "Peter, there's your friend."

The Brazilian girl cooked us all a marvelous dinner. After we had eaten, I decided it was time to produce my chocolate cake. "Now I have a surprise for you," I said, and brought it out. That darling lady burst into tears. "How did you know?" she asked. "How on earth did you know that it was my birthday?"

The Lost Boys and I were in shock by this time, so all I could think of to reply was, "In Never-Never Land, you just know."

Next morning we left. The last time I saw her, she was waving and calling out, "You'll come back next spring, Peter?" She was echoing a line from the play.

I have been back each spring, in spirit and in my heart. I will go back that way forever, each springtime.

Walt Kelly's
Furred and Feathered Friends

by Joseph P. Mastrangelo

IN 1948, I was working as an apprentice artist on a new afternoon paper, the New York *Star*, when Walt Kelly took over as art director and comic-strip editor, and brought little Pogo, his cartoon opossum, with him. Getting to know Kelly was one of the good things that have happened in my life.

Kelly, then 35, had grown up in Bridgeport, Conn., where his father was a factory worker. After a short stint at a New York art school, and a spell as a newspaper reporter, he began drawing a weekly comic strip on the life of P.T. Barnum, the circus king, for the Bridgeport *Post & Telegram*. Tiring of this, he went to work as a welfare investigator. When that paled, he headed for Hollywood, where he landed a job with Walt Disney. He spent six years learning from Disney before coming back East in 1941 to try his hand at comic books.

Kelly wasn't happy about the "Sock!" "Bop!" type of book the industry was turning out. He came up with the idea of a strip about a young boy named Bumbazine, who lived deep in the Okefenokee Swamp of Georgia with his "furred and feathered" friends. The dialogue that Kelly used in his balloons was a mixture of Georgia "cracker talk," old English fairy-tale dialect, and just plain having fun with words. Before long, Kelly retired Bumbazine, and Pogo, a minor character in the strip, took his place—"because Bumbazine, being human, was not as believable as the animals."

More than 150 characters were to appear over the years. Uncle Antler, for example, a moose who came into the swamp in 1923 to attend an Elks convention and never left. And Howland Owl, who is scientific and pretends to know it all. (He once said, "Nuclear physics ain't so new, and it ain't so clear.") And Beauregard Bugleboy Frontenac, a hound dog who says, "I, Sir, am man's best friend—the noble dog." Beauregard wandered into the swamp one day looking for someone who was lost; it turned out to be him.

In 1946, the comic-book company folded and, after a stint as a commercial artist, Kelly and Pogo came to the *Star*. The *Star* was a happy paper to work on with Kelly running your shop. He wasn't a boss; he was a teacher. No idea you might have was so farfetched that he wouldn't consider it seriously.

But the happy times didn't last. One night, Kelly came in with a long look on his face and sent us to a staff meeting in the city room. There the publisher told us we had just published the last edition. The city room ended up standing three deep at a bar. Kelly came up behind a few of his ex-staff and told the bartender to give us anything we wanted. We all switched from beer to Scotch, and it was the first dollar cigar I ever smoked.

After the *Star* folded, Kelly again turned to Pogo and, four months later, managed to get the Post-Hall Syndicate to distribute it. The strip quickly picked up momentum. By 1951, Pogo was in 100 papers, and Kelly was making about $50,000 a year.

Things picked up a little for me, too. I went back to school on the GI Bill, and made wedding plans. Kelly had once said, "If you ever need anything, call me." So I did, and borrowed $100. I promised to pay it back when my situation improved, but he brushed it aside. "Joe, getting married to the right person is too important a step to put off for any reason. Don't worry about the money. If things get tough, give me a chance to help." Knowing you had Walt in your corner made New York City seem a little easier to live in.

A few months later, a letter arrived from Kelly. It was a total surprise: "Dear Joe: Your letter and contents arrived. Thanks. I figure I've loaned out $1600 since 1945, and you're the first bird to pay me back." When I asked some questions around the house, I found that my wife had been saving money each month and had sent Walt the $100, and I was getting the credit.

Kelly's charities were mostly of his own making. If a fellow cartoonist or writer was down and out, he might suddenly find his rent paid for the next two months—by Kelly. The morning

Walt Kelly's Furred and Feathered Friends

after the papers reported a policeman shot in the line of duty, Kelly would make out a generous check for the widow. A priest running a mission on the Lower East Side in Manhattan was another beneficiary. A Jewish friend received a monthly Kelly check for a group that was hunting ex-Nazis.

By 1960, Pogo was in 142 papers, and Kelly was becoming wealthy. Not so with me. My newspaper was being hit by strikes, and that meant unemployment. Along about the second major strike, Kelly, knowing I was out of work, called me and said that he was behind in production of Pogo books—could I help him? Soon this became routine. Some union disagreement would shut down the papers, and Kelly would call me, "desperate" for help.

By this time, Kelly was working out of a big studio on Madison Avenue and employed six people. When you worked with Kelly, there was play time and deadline time. On any day of the week, he would invite the whole staff out to lunch. We would go to one of the best restaurants. He would order cocktails for everybody, thick slabs of roast beef, wine, dessert, brandy, cigars. About five o'clock a weary waiter would smile when he got a big tip. Then next day, when someone would look up from his drawing board and ask, "Anyone for lunch?" Kelly would say, "Those lunch hours you guys take last too long."

When Kelly worked, he liked to sit in a big chair, a beat-up soft hat on his head, a thick unlighted cigar in his mouth. He worked with his drawing board propped up on a big old-fashioned desk, which had letters stuffed into every pigeonhole. Pinned along the edges of his drawing board were dozens of notes.

He received about 150 letters a week—from children, whom he loved, as well as from adults. The children never complained; but certain adults did, usually because Walt had given some politician the Kelly treatment in his strip.

"Politicians are wheeler-dealers, and they're all ripe for lampooning," he used to say. He sent his swamp characters into every major political situation. In 1952, he had a character called Tammananny Tiger, who teamed up with Albert the Alligator to run Pogo for President. But Pogo couldn't make up his mind whether to run or not. Readers began to write, accusing him of sounding too much like Adlai Stevenson, the "reluctant candidate."

A pig came into the swamp one day dressed as a pirate, with a bandanna wrapped around his head, an earring dangling from an ear, a cockatoo perched on his arm. A lot of readers thought the pig-pirate was Khrushchev, and that the cockatoo resembled Bulganin. The thought became stronger when a pair of cowbirds showed up calling themselves "home-grown communists," who were completely confused by the pig who kept changing policy. Every time the pig spoke, the cockatoo would say, "You said it." When readers complained, Kelly answered, "Communism is a part of the passing comedy."

Pogo got deep into politics during the Sen. Joseph McCarthy period with a character called Simple J. Malarkey. Simple was depicted as a wildcat, sometimes called Wiley Catt, who bullied his way around the swamp waving a shotgun that would go off every once in a while. When an editor in Providence had his artist alter a cartoon involving Wiley Catt, Kelly answered by having Wiley Catt put a pillowcase over his head, saying, "Nobody from Providence should see me." The paper soon apologized.

In later years, there was a hyena dressed in the uniform that showed up briefly on the White House guards. He threw his weight around, complaining about the media. His pal, who was ready to indict them all, was a pipe-smoking bird. To some readers they looked like Spiro Agnew and John Mitchell.

When I moved away from New York to Washington, D.C., to take a job with the Washington *Post*, I missed seeing Kelly standing at the bar in Tim Costello's on Third Avenue, making everyone around him feel good. But I kept up with the strip, reading it every day. I saw the little inside messages that he got across to his friends. Kelly had a way of saying "hello" to people by using their faces on the lesser animals and lettering their names on the side of the old swamp boat that Pogo and his pals sat in while drifting through Okefenokee Swamp. One day, the name of some friend's child who was recuperating from an illness would appear. Another time, that of a fellow cartoonist.

In 1973, I learned that Kelly was ailing. When I called to say hello, he said, "When you get up to New York, call me and we'll go out and tie one on."

I never did see him again. But, a few weeks later, I picked up the paper and turned to Pogo, and there was my name lettered along the side of the boat. I knew that Kelly was saying, "Hello. I'm thinking about you."

Pogo was 24 years old when Walt Kelly died in October. He now appeared in over 300 papers in the United States and Canada. He was also known in Australia, France, New Zealand, Greece, Portugal, Italy, Lebanon, South Africa, Spain, Sweden, Thailand and South America. Kelly's books had sold close to three million copies.

Selby Kelly, Walt's widow, and his son, Steven, continued the script, aided occasionally by some of his old-time assistants.

While Kelly lived, his swamp folk always approached Christmas with great glee. For weeks leading up to the day, they would spend panel after panel getting the choral group together to practice a few carols. Kelly liked to mix the lyrics of their carols in a mild protest against "the people who worship the buck rather than the reindeer."

On Christmas day, 1973, there was not great merriment among the swamp citizens. The strip appeared in two separate wide panels. The first panel showed Porkypine partially hidden by one of those unknown swamp trees. Miz Beaver was sitting in the boat, and Pogo was pushing it away from shore. The boat bore the initials W.K. on its side and a pair of hearts entwined on the stern. Owl was saying, "Kinda Christmas you feels more quiet and thoughtful than jumpin' and singin'." Pogo said, "Ummm.... We lost so much this year." Miz Beaver said, "We didn't lose so much.... We jes' gave it back after borrowing it for a while."

In the second panel, the boat was drifting out into the swamp, with Miz Beaver saying, "He allus said, don't take life too serious.... it ain't nohow permanent."

Happily Ever After With the Brothers Grimm

by George Kent

ONCE UPON a time there lived in Germany two devoted brothers who wrote a little book. They were so modest and they expected so little of the book's sales that they were willing to take no money for it.

To their astonishment, it was a great success. And over the years it has continued to please until today it is, second only to the Bible, the world's most famous book—the most widely read, the most generally remembered. It has sold close to a billion copies in no fewer than 20,000 editions. It has been translated into more than 50 languages in some 40 countries. It is still in print after 171 years, and still has a magical impact on our ways of writing, thinking and looking at life.

The title of the little book was *Tales for Children and the Hearth*. We know it better as *Grimm's Fairy Tales*, after the brothers who wrote it—Jakob and Wilhelm Grimm. Its story is an extraordinary chapter in the annals of publishing.

It began when one of the brothers' college professors aroused in them an interest in historical research. As they explored the past, both brothers became fascinated with children's stories— but not because of the tales' interest for children. The Grimms were scholars, and to them the old stories were important in the way fragments of pottery are important to an archeologist— for the light they shed on man's history.

The stories were part of a great oral tradition, in existence long before men knew how to write. Some had been collected and published, but many others had never been written down, and only a few aged peasants here and there remembered them. When they died, the tales, some of them dating back thousands of years, would die with them. It was urgent to record them before their tellers should all vanish from the earth.

So, when Jakob was 22 years old and Wilhelm 21, the brothers Grimm began looking for people with good memories. It was not easy. Those who knew the fairy tales decided that the brothers must be a little crazy. What possible interest could grown men have in witches and talking stones and gingerbread houses? Still, they were pleasant, persuasive young men....

A shepherd was happy to spend an afternoon spinning the old yarns for a bottle of wine. An old cavalry sergeant come upon hard times told a few more in return for a patched-up pair of pants. One old woman, living in a home for the aged, hesitated to talk. If she was heard telling her stories to anyone but children, she might be locked up as a madwoman, she said. So Wilhelm Grimm got a friend to take along his children as an audience for her, and she began with alacrity, "Once upon a time—" The friend wrote down her stories while Wilhelm listened, hidden behind a curtain.

The Grimms' best source turned out to be a tailor's wife. Not only did she tell her stories well, but she told them each time in exactly the same words. If she went too fast and was asked to repeat, she would retell them slowly, without a change.

After five years, the brothers had 86 stories. Being scholars primarily, and unconcerned with the matter of entertainment value, they put the manuscripts on a shelf "for future reference." There they might have remained if a friend, Achim von Arnim, had not come to town and read several. "What a marvelous collection!" he exclaimed. The stories must be published, he insisted. Von Arnim personally made the necessary arrangements with a printer in Berlin.

A few days before Christmas, 1812, the first edition of *Tales for Children and the Hearth* went on sale. It came in two versions: one poorly printed, another on quality paper. Because the stories were put down as they had come from the mouths of the old people, simply and without moralizing, the result was a book that children could read without difficulty. It was enormously popular.

This first collection included many of the stories that have become part of our language: "Hansel and Gretel," "Snow

White," "The Frog Prince," "Cinderella," "Rapunzel" and "Tom Thumb," among others. Two more volumes followed, and the total of the Grimm collection now came to 210 tales.

Many of these tales date back to a time when myth and reality were almost indistinguishable. The long slumber of Briar Rose or "Sleeping Beauty" may represent winter, her awakening the kiss of spring. Cinderella's triumph may stand for the bright sun of morning after a troubled night. Of all the stories, incidentally, "Cinderella" is the most told. More than 345 versions have been identified; it is known in every country of the world.

Some of the magical stories are "simpleton tales," told by mothers to their less bright children to build up their self-confidence. In these, the poor, weak, often stupid hero wins happiness and wealth, not so much by his own efforts as by the aid of divine grace in the shape of a bird, a kindly old man or a warmhearted witch. Ill-doers are punished, often horribly.

Soon, in translations, the tales were being read or listened to by the little ones of every civilized nation. The stories were published even in Swahili, Tajik, Bengali and other languages of Africa and Asia. As they entered the jungle, the old tales changed. "Cinderella" in one version goes to the ball in a canoe. In Africa, the witch's house in "Hansel and Gretel" is made not of cake but of salt, a greater delicacy there. Since snow is unknown on the equator, Snow White's name becomes Flower White.

More than 200 plays for the stage and marionette theater are based on stories told by the Grimm brothers. More than 40 have become operas, of which the most celebrated is Humperdinck's *Hänsel und Gretel*. "Sleeping Beauty" is the favorite with composers, especially ballet makers. In addition, a vast number of choral works, novels and movies have been drawn from the Grimms' tales.

The brothers who gave the world such a bountiful storehouse were the two oldest sons of a family of six children born to a lawyer in Hanau, Germany. It was a strict but cheerful household, and there was always great affection between the two brothers. They went to the same school, and at college both studied law in obedience to their father's deathbed wish. They wrote books together. Yet the two men were very different.

Jakob was small and neat, with sharp, light-blue eyes. A

serious individual with a superb intellect, he did not smoke, drank little and had little use for society. He died a bachelor. Wilhelm, one year younger, was taller than his brother, a handsome, smiling man with dreamy, poetic eyes. And he loved people. He delighted in spending an evening with friends shouting out the old folk songs. Both brothers cajoled people into telling them stories, but it was Wilhelm—a born storyteller—who wrote the final versions in the form we know. Though he always had an eye for the girls, he did not marry until he was 40.

When he did (the bride was a druggist's daughter who had helped him in his hunt for fairy tales), he insisted that Jakob live with him and his wife. A great-hearted man for all his austerity, Jakob became part of the household. Wilhelm's three children were as dear to him as if they had been his own. It was a noisy, happy home, and the young ones had the run of the house, except for Jakob's large workroom. This was off-limits to the rioters. At bedtime, Wilhelm would start them on the way to sleep with a Grimm fairy tale.

The brothers devoted 50 years of their lives to the study of antiquity. Huddled over old parchments, they found the material for a long list of books with such forbidding titles as *Legal Antiquities* and *German Heroic Sagas*. They learned to read in a dozen languages and translated the myths of Norway, Denmark, Scotland and Ireland. They became fascinated with linguistics and helped to transform the study of words into an exact science. Jakob, who did most of this work, is often described as the "father of philology."

Though the brothers were triumphant as scholars, economically they never quite got their heads above water. Having written the most fabulous best-seller of all time, they were paid next to nothing for it. At no time during their careers as librarians and professors did they have a year's income equivalent to more than $5000. When recognition came to them, neither of the brothers was impressed. They lived for their work, not for rewards.

The brothers spent their last years working on a colossal dictionary which was to be their masterpiece. Unfortunately, it ended with the letter F. Jakob was writing the word *Frucht* (fruit) one September day in 1863, when he fell ill at his work. He died a week later, aged 78. Wilhelm, always sickly, suffering from asthma and heart trouble, had died five years earlier. In 1960, the dictionary brilliantly begun by the brothers was finally published—in 32 volumes. It is a fitting monument. But it is the little book of children's tales that is destined to live happily ever after.

Dr. Seuss:
Fanciful Sage of Childhood

by James Stewart-Gordon

IF KIDS who are less than ten years old ever get the vote, Dr. Theofrastus Seuss, the man who writes books about delightfully crazy creatures like Sneetches, Drum-Tummied Snumms, Cats in Hats and elephants who live in trees, is a shoo-in for the Presidency. For the Doc, who is not really a doctor at all and whose real name is Theodor Seuss Geisel, is the most popular children's author and illustrator in history. His 44 books—which have sold more than 90 million copies—have taught millions of children (and their teachers) that learning can be fun.

Light years removed from schoolbooks about moppets named Dick and Jane and dogs named Spot, Dr. Seuss' creations feature a marvelous menagerie of wild, weird, far-out animals with soup-plate-size eyes, prodigious whiskers and implausible bodies who have the most astounding adventures and are drawn with a dash that makes Picasso look like a realist. Necks are so long that they wind and twist on each other like discarded Christmas ribbons; smiles are so wide that they have to be tied behind heads to hold them in place. Asked why he draws so bizarrely, the Doc says modestly, "Because I don't know how to draw at all!" But he points out that it is all done with logical insanity: "If I draw a character with two heads, I always make sure that he has two toothbrushes."

Regardless of this tendency to freewheel and fantasize, the sagas of Dr. Seuss remain monuments to old-fashioned morality. In the strange and wondrous tale of *Horton Hatches the Egg*, Horton, the kindly elephant, sits in a tree for 51 weeks foster-mothering a bird's egg. He had been conned into this uncomfortable position by a persuasive fowl and, as Horton points out, "I meant what I said and I said what I meant. An elephant's faithful one hundred percent." And when the Grinch tries to steal Christmas by absconding with everyone's presents, he discovers that the Christmas spirit is more important than just gifts.

In the process of making good triumphant, the Doctor has enriched our vocabulary with such words as Grinch, StarBelly Sneetch, Thneed and Three-Muffed Apfel Moose. He explains, "When I can't find the word I want, I think one up." (Since there are often no adequate words to describe his whimsies, he has become a word coiner extraordinary.) A Grinch, for example, is a creature who can't bear the sight of anyone enjoying himself without getting so mad it bites itself. A StarBelly Sneetch is an ordinary Sneetch with a star on its belly that makes it think it is better than plain-belly Sneetches.

While no Dr. Seuss book is very thick, it takes him an average of a year to write such seemingly simple classics as *Fox in Sox*. "You can't write down to kids," he says. "You have to interest them by telling a story and yet remember that they can't read more than a few hundred words. They like nonsensical repetition and rhyme because it fixes sounds and meanings in their minds. (*Fox in Sox*, for instance, contains such tongue twisters as: "Knox in box. Fox in socks. Knox on fox in socks in box.") He polishes each line he writes and each drawing he creates innumerable times before he is satisfied that he has used the right number of words conveying exactly the right shade of meaning and that each drawing fits each portion of the text exactly. He estimates that he writes and draws more than 1000 pages for each 64-page book he completes.

According to the Doctor, some books write themselves and some spring from happy accidents. In the case of *How the Grinch Stole Christmas*, he found himself faced with a deadline and no book. Never having missed a deadline in his life, he sat down and in one week completed the Grinch. However, he adds, "I had been thinking over the idea of just what Christmas means for about 12 years before I was able to put all the pieces together."

One June morning the Doc was standing at his drawing board searching for an idea when a gust of wind wafted the picture of an earnest-looking, flop-eared elephant onto the top

Dr. Seuss: Fanciful Sage of Childhood 263

of a drawing of a discouraged-looking tree. Geisel picked up the two pictures, studied them for a moment and *Horton Hatches the Egg* was born. ("I have been leaving windows open ever since," says Dr. Seuss. "And all that happens is that I catch colds.") On another occasion, he was lying by a swimming pool in East Africa when he looked up and saw that three elephants had suddenly appeared. As he watched them, the story of the Lorax (winner of a Keep America Beautiful award), his plea for saving the world's forests and fields, was born.

Called the "only authentic genius I have ever published" by the late Bennett Cerf, the Doctor always has at least four projects going at once. His volcanic creativity has erupted in many directions. A wartime lieutenant colonel, he was awarded the Legion of Merit for his work with the Army Training Film unit headed by director Frank Capra. After he became a civilian, three of his films won Academy Awards (*Gerald McBoing-Boing*, the whimsical tale of a little boy who spoke only in sound effects, is rated as one of the ten greatest short films of all time). And his television special, *How the Grinch Stole Christmas*, narrated by the late Boris Karloff, has become a Yuletide classic.

On a personal level, the Doctor is six feet tall, weighs 167 pounds, parts his hair in the middle and lives on top of a mountain in La Jolla, Calif., surrounded by his wife and two stepdaughters, his rock garden and a couple of stone dinosaur tracks that he got by mail order. He was born on March 2, 1904, in Springfield, Mass., with a natural inability to see or draw like anyone else. At the end of his first high-school art class, his teacher called him aside and said, not unkindly, "You will never learn to draw, Theodor. Why don't you just skip this class for the rest of the term?" Crushed, Theodor soothed his battered ego by sending in unillustrated jokes to the high-school paper.

He went to Dartmouth College, where as editor of the humor magazine he managed to get his drawings and stories in every issue. Thinking that he wanted to teach English, he had stints at Oxford University and at the Sorbonne in Paris. Thoughts of teaching died at the latter institution, after he was told by the world's leading authority on Jonathan Swift: "We know everything about Swift except what he wrote between the time he was 16½ and 17. Find out what that was and your future is made." Instead, he quit that afternoon and tried to write a book, failed, and returned to the United States to begin a career as a cartoonist.

Trying to make a living by making people laugh, he soon discovered, was a precarious business. His principal market was *Judge*, a weekly that bought his cartoons and stories but paid him off in merchandise bartered by advertisers for space. It was one of his cartoons—a knight in armor confronted by an enormous Seussian dragon, with the caption: "Oh darn it, just when I sprayed the whole castle with Flit"—in *Judge* that eventually introduced him to prosperity. The wife of an advertising executive who handled the Flit account saw the cartoon, was amused by it and told her husband. The Doc got a contract to do a series of advertisements in which various horrendous flying objects attacked a citizen, who bawled in terror, "Quick, Henry, the Flit!"

With the financial stability this contract afforded, Dr. Seuss (the name he used on all his cartoons, in anticipation of one day writing a serious novel under his real name) decided to try his hand at children's books. His first published effort, *And to Think That I Saw It on Mulberry Street*, was turned down 28 times by publishers who were confused by his fantasy of a little boy walking down a street transforming ordinary objects into strange and wonderful variations. Finally, a friend at Vanguard Press decided to take a chance on it; it has now sold over a million copies.

For seven years after the war's end, the Doc worked in Hollywood, fiercely trying to retain his sense of identity while making Oscar-winning films. Then he decided to give up movies, advertising and anything else that involved duels with vice presidents, committees and all the paraphernalia of big business.

"But what *will* you do?" his agent asked. "Well," mused Geisel, "I might write books. Do you think I could work up to royalties of $5000 a year?" After being assured that this was in the realm of possibility, the Doctor promptly rapped out books like *Horton Hears a Who* and *If I Ran the Circus*, and launched himself as a millionaire.

In 1954, author John Hersey, disturbed about the inability of many children to learn to read, became convinced that the reason was the kind of books they were getting in classrooms. In an article in *Life*, Hersey suggested that imaginative writers,

Dr. Seuss: Fanciful Sage of Childhood

such as Dr. Seuss, be asked to write some books that would be helpful. The ground rules devised by education experts were that the prototype book must have a vocabulary of about 200 words, a simple and logical story line and, above all, the power to make children want to read it from start to finish.

The Cat in the Hat took over a year to produce, but it was an instant blockbuster, one of the all-time phenomena of the classroom world. Everything Dr. Seuss put into the story was absolutely essential, and its progression was so logical and smooth that it reminded critics of an animated cartoon. It has grossed over $4 million for its creator and his publishers, made educators take a second look at what really can be used to interest children and launched an industry called Beginner Books (a division of Random House) of which Dr. Seuss is president, that has now produced 150 books, every one a hit.

I journeyed to La Jolla to visit the sage of childhood. The sun bounced off the top of Soledad Mountain, the Doctor's home peak, and inside his house, highlighting the subtle grace notes of Seussiana abounding there. Chippendale chairs had Seuss characters carved on their backs and the heads of Snumms and Grinches mounted like trophies smiled benignly down on us.

In a closet off the studio are the 500 thinking caps that play important roles in the creativity of Dr. Seuss. If he fails to hit the right note at his typewriter or drawing board, he will take out one of these hats—it may be anything from a shako made of rock-wallaby fur to an Ecuadorian fireman's helmet—and put it on. Suddenly, there is magic: verses tumble from his typewriter; Sneetches and Snumms take shape on the drawing board; the world begins to rock with wonder.

As we said good-by I mentioned the possibility that the nine-and-under vote might one day sweep him into the Presidency. His smile prompted me to add, "Come to think of it, Doctor, if you ever decide to make the race, some of us ten-year-olds might vote for you, too."

The Magical Muppets

by John Culhane

A LIFELESS KERMIT THE FROG lay on the table at the Muppets' Manhattan workshop. Then, with a hand, a voice and a brain, his creator, Jim Henson, revitalized him, and Kermit began to give off the kind of vibes that have made him one of the most engaging puppets in history.

"Hey, look! I can cross my legs!" he said, in that sassy-but-charming voice. "Taa-dahhh!"

But the marvel wasn't that Kermit could cross his long green limbs. That was just a small advance in the technology of puppeteering made by one of the puppet-builders at Henson Associates (letterhead: ha!). The marvel was the pleasure that Kermit seemed to be getting out of being able to cross his legs. That was a matter of magic—the imbuing of an inanimate object with a personality all its own.

The appealing personality of Kermit the Frog is just one reason why the Muppets have become the most popular puppets in the world. Indeed, the success of television's "The Muppet Show," which began its first season in 1976, is such that the program has lined up 162 American stations with a total expected viewing audience of 40 million. Abroad, 200 million people see the show in 100 countries.

On "The Muppet Show," hosted by Kermit the Frog, stars of flesh and blood (Edgar Bergen, Bernadette Peters, Elton John, to name a few) perform with stars of voice and construction materials. And for the first time since two dummies named Charlie McCarthy and Mortimer Snerd made Candice Bergen's father, Edgar, a star of stage, screen and radio, the inanimate

The Magical Muppets

are rivaling the animate in the affection of viewers—especially adults. During its first season in England, for example, when "The Muppet Show" was moved to a viewing time suitable for children but not adults, the 75-percent-adult audience protested so lustily that the show had to be moved back.

What are Muppets? Henson himself coined the term to describe his own individual combination of marionette and puppet. The heads of many of the Muppets are basically hand puppets, but the hands and other parts of many of their torsos may be operated by strings and rods and other controls, like marionettes.

Anyone who has watched hand puppets or string puppets for any length of time knows that unless a puppet becomes a personality, it cannot be believed. And if it cannot be believed, it won't be remembered. Yet Henson and his associates have created at least 600 Muppets that are distinct caricatures of human-personality types and attitudes—from an optimist like Kermit to a pessimist like Oscar the Grouch on "Sesame Street," and from an introvert like the "Sesame Street" Big Bird to an extrovert like Miss Piggy, who pokes her snout into everything.

How can puppets express so many personalities so well? To understand, one has to start with the personality of the mastermind of the Muppets, Jim Henson.

A tall, thin, brown-bearded man, Henson was born in Greenville, Miss., in 1936. "My dad was doing research with the Department of Agriculture—pasture crops like bird's-foot trefoil," he recalls. "I have memorialized that crop in a Muppet named Herbert Bird's Foot—a very dry lecturer." (Sooner or later, most experiences in Henson's life seem to turn into a Muppet's personality.)

Henson's infatuation with puppets began in 1949, after the family had moved to a Maryland suburb of Washington, D.C. They had just bought a television set, and Burr Tillstrom's memorable "Kukla, Fran and Ollie," starring a very human Fran Allison conversing with puppets Kukla and Ollie the Dragon, was then on the air. So, too, was Bil and Cora Baird's work with marionettes, and both made a big impression on Henson.

Henson became involved in a high-school puppet club and, between graduating from high school and entering college, auditioned for a local television show in Washington, D.C., with puppets he had built himself. It folded after three weeks, but Henson's work had been noticed. While he was learning acting, staging and scenic design at the University of Maryland, he appeared on other local shows. And he was also being noticed by a fellow student named Jane Nebel. In 1955, Henson was offered a late night five-minute television show of his own called "Sam and Friends." Jim asked Jane to join him in operating the puppets. (In 1959 they would become partners in marriage as well.)

A series of successful commercials that the Henson and Nebel team developed in the Washington area was eventually noticed by network executives in New York. In 1957, the Muppets made their network debut on Steve Allen's "Tonight!" show with a year-old frog character named Kermit. Kermit wore a blond wig and sang "I've Grown Accustomed to Your Face" to a purple monster operated by Jane. The monster promptly ate its own face, then tried to eat Kermit. Audiences were enchanted.

The whole nation noticed the variety of Muppet personalities in 1969, with the debut of "Sesame Street," the public-television program that continues to entertain preschoolers as it teaches them to count and read. In 1974 and 1976, "The Muppets of Sesame Street" won television's Emmy Award for "Outstanding Achievement in the Field of Children's Programming."

But as great a success as the Muppets became on "Sesame Street," the success was also a setback to Henson's original conception of the Muppets as entertainment for everybody—not just children. Henson tried strenuously to interest the three major U.S. networks in a weekly Muppet variety series for viewing by the entire family—but the TV executives couldn't see it. So when England's Lord Grade invited him to London to produce "The Muppet Show" for world distribution by ITC Entertainment, Inc., it was a dream come true. The response to the first season of "The Muppet Show" went a long way toward proving Henson's contention that the Muppets are for everybody. And it helped when the American Guild of Variety Artists gave the Muppets a 1976 "Entertainer of the Year" award as "Special Attraction of the Year"—not "special children's attraction," just "special attraction."

There are now over 120 people employed by Henson Associates. At his workshop there are a dozen puppeteers, and some 15 artisans. "Basically," Henson told me, "it all starts with sketches of characters based on a personality type or an attitude. Then we begin building—often altering as we go along."

When a Muppet starts to show a personality in an expression, a puppeteer begins working on it to see what its potential is for expressing that personality in voice and movements. Explains Henson: "You have to learn what works with puppets, and you have to learn what works with puppets on television, specifically. With puppets, we're dealing with a very limited form. While an actor has an enormous range of expressions on his face, most of the Muppets can only open their mouths. Thus, the angle that the head is held, how it's moved, or where the puppet is looking creates the expression. Five degrees of tilt can convey a different emotion."

As for the mechanics, the puppeteer is usually beneath the stage. For a Muppet like Kermit, who cannot grasp things with his hands, the arms are moved with thin rods, painted to match the background so they are hard to see. A Muppet who can hold things takes two people to operate. One puppeteer will do the puppet's mouth and one hand with his two hands, and a second puppeteer will do the puppet's other hand; both will be studying television monitors to see what the audience is seeing. It usually takes a couple of years to train one of Henson's puppeteers.

In the spring of 1977, Kermit the Frog was feted on his 21st birthday by a special, hour-long celebration on the Dinah Shore show. Miss Piggy confided to Dinah that she was desperately in love with Kermit. "Please, Miss Shore, help me get my frog," said the puppet pig. But Kermit was more interested in singing "There's No Business Like Show Business" with Ethel Merman. "When she sings," said Kermit, "I get a people in my throat."

The highlight of the party came when Jane Henson joined her husband to re-create their debut on "Tonight!" 20 years before. Once again, Kermit sang "I've Grown Accustomed to Your Face" to a purple monster that ate its own face and then tried to eat Kermit.

One measure of how high the Muppets have risen since that debut was the debut of a giant Kermit balloon in the 1977 Macy's Thanksgiving Day Parade in New York City. Kermit's inclusion with balloons of such famous animated-cartoon personalities as Mickey Mouse, Popeye and Bullwinkle reminds us that puppetry on television has come of age through the larger-than-life personalities of the Muppets.

Walt Disney's Impractical Dreams

by Roy Disney

NOT LONG AGO, at our Burbank, Calif., studio, a group of animators and writers were holding a story conference on a new Disney cartoon feature. They were having a tough time agreeing on a story line, and the atmosphere was as stormy as the weather outside. Suddenly, lightning scribbled a jagged streak over the San Fernando Valley and there was a rolling clap of thunder. "Don't worry, Walt," one of the animators quipped, glancing heavenward. "We'll get it yet."

As I write this, in early 1969, my brother Walt has been gone for more than two years, yet his influence lingers like a living presence over the studio where he turned out the cartoons, nature films and feature movies that made him known and loved around the world. Even now, as I walk around the studio lot, I half expect to encounter that gangly, country-boy figure, head bowed in thought about some new project. Walt was so much the driving force behind all we did, from making movies to building Disneyland, that people constantly mention his name as if he were still alive. Every time we show a new picture, or open a new feature at Disneyland, someone is bound to say, "I wonder how Walt would like it?" And when this happens, I usually realize that it was something he himself had planned. For my imaginative, industrious brother left enough projects in progress to keep the rest of us busy for another 20 years.

Walt was a complex man. To the writers, producers and animators who worked with him, he was a genius who had an uncanny ability to add an extra fillip of imagination to any story or idea. To the millions of people who watched his TV show, he was a warm, kindly personality, bringing fun and pleasure into their homes. To the bankers who financed us, I'm sure he seemed like a wild man, hell-bent for bankruptcy. To me, he was my amazing kid brother, full of impractical dreams that he made come true.

In the late 1960s, his family and mine—wives, children and grandchildren—went back to our old hometown of Marceline, Mo., for ceremonies celebrating the issuance of the Walt Disney commemorative stamp. As the gleaming Santa Fe train rolled across the green midwestern prairie, memories of the pleasant years that Walt and I spent there inevitably flooded back.

The apple orchard and weeping willows stand green and beautiful at our old farm, where Walt sketched his first animals. I recall how Walt and I would snuggle together in bed and hear the haunting whistle of a locomotive passing in the night. Our Uncle Mike was an engineer, and he'd blow his whistle—one long and two shorts—just for us. Walt never lost his love of trains. Years later, an old-fashioned train was one of the first attractions at Disneyland.

As far back as I can remember, Walt was drawing. The first money he ever made was a nickel for a sketch of a neighbor's horse. He studied cartooning in Chicago, and then started a little animated-cartoon company in Kansas City that flopped. I was in Los Angeles when Walt, just 21, decided to try his luck in Hollywood. I met him at the station. He was carrying a cheap suitcase that contained all of his belongings.

We borrowed $500 from an uncle, and Walt started a cartoon series called *Alice in Cartoonland*. It was tough going. Walt did all the animation, and I cranked the old-fashioned camera. The Alice cartoons didn't make much of a splash, so Walt started a new series called *Oswald the Rabbit*. Oswald did better, but when Walt went to our New York distributor for more money he ran into trouble.

"What kind of a deal did you make, kid?" I asked.

"We haven't got a deal," Walt admitted. "The distributor copyrighted Oswald and he's taking over the series himself." Strangely, Walt did not seem downhearted. "We're going to start a new series," he enthused. "It's about a mouse. And this time *we'll* own the mouse."

The rest is history. Walt's mouse, Mickey, celebrated his 40th birthday in 1968, and a happy 40th it was. A quarter of a billion people saw a Disney movie in '68, 100 million watched

Walt Disney's Impractical Dreams

a Disney TV show, nearly a billion read a Disney book or magazine and almost ten million visited Disneyland. And Mickey, as Walt used to say, started it all.

Mickey was only the first successful product of Walt's matchless imagination and ability to make his dreams become reality. It was an ability he could turn on for any occasion, large or small. Once, when my son Roy Edward had the measles, Walt came and told him the story of *Pinocchio*, which he was making at the time. When Walt told a story, it was a virtuoso performance. His eyes riveted his listener, his mustache twitched expressively, his eyebrows rose and fell, and his hands moved with the grace of a musical conductor. Young Roy was so wide-eyed at Walt's graphic telling of the fairy tale that he forgot all about his measles. Later, when he saw the finished picture, he was strangely disappointed. "It didn't seem as exciting as when Uncle Walt told it," he said.

Like many people who work to create humor, Walt took it very seriously. He would often sit glumly through the funniest cartoon, concentrating on some way to improve it. Walt valued the opinions of those working with him, but the final judgment was always unquestionably his. Once, after viewing a new cartoon with evident displeasure, Walt called for comments from a group of our people. One after another they spoke up, all echoing Walt's criticism. "I can get rubber stamps that say, 'Yes, Walt,'" he snapped. Then he wheeled and asked the projectionist what he thought. The man sensed that dissent was in order. "I think you're *all* wrong," he declared. Walt just grinned. "*You* stick to your projector," he suggested.

Bankers, bookkeepers and lawyers frequently tried to put the brakes on his free-wheeling imagination and were the bane of Walt's existence. As his business manager, I was no exception. "When I see you happy, that's when I get nervous," he used to say. Since Walt would spare no expense to make his pictures better, we used to have our battles. But he was always quick to shake hands and make up.

Walt thrived on adversity, which is fortunate because we had it in spades. Even with Mickey a hit, we were constantly in hock to the banks. When he made his first real financial bonanza, with *Snow White*, he could scarcely believe it.

Sure enough, the good fortune was too good to last. *Snow White* made several million dollars when it came out. But Walt soon spent that and then some by plunging into a series of full-length cartoon features and building our present studio.

To keep the studio afloat we sold stock to the public—and it sank immediately from $25 a share to $3. Troubles piled up. The studio was hit by a strike. Then World War II cut off our European market. More than once I would have given up had it not been for Walt's ornery faith that we would eventually succeed.

He drove himself harder than anyone else at the studio. His two daughters, Diane and Sharon, learned to ride bikes on the deserted studio lot on weekends—while Walt worked.

Walt involved himself in *everything*. During one story conference on the Mickey Mouse Club TV Show, the story man, pointer in hand, was outlining a sequence called "How to Ride a Bicycle." "Now when you get on your bicycle . . . ," he began. Walt stopped him. "Change *your* bicycle to *a* bicycle," he said. "Remember, every kid isn't fortunate enough to have a bike of his own."

Very little escaped Walt's perceptive eye. Animators often found their crumpled drawings retrieved from the wastebasket with a notation from Walt: "Let's not throw away the *good* stuff." And that, I think, was his greatest genius: he knew instinctively what "good stuff" was. After others had worked on a story plot for months, Walt would often come in, juggle things around a bit, add a gag or two—and suddenly the whole thing came to life.

Walt demanded a lot of people, but he gave a lot, too. When the Depression hit, and it looked as though we might have to close the studio, Walt gave everyone a raise. Some thought him crazy, but it gave morale a big boost. He hated to fire anyone, and if someone didn't work out in one job Walt would try to find a niche where he was better suited. Once, when we were faced with having to drop some animators, Walt found places for them at WED (for Walt E. Disney) Enterprises in nearby Glendale, where he was secretly developing plans for what eventually became Disneyland.

The story of Disneyland, perhaps better than anything else, illustrates Walt's vision and his stubborn determination to realize an idea he believed in. For years, Walt had quietly nursed the dream of a new kind of amusement park. It would be a potpourri of all the ideas conjured up by his fertile imagination. But the idea of sinking millions of dollars into an amusement park, even Walt's kind of amusement park, seemed so pre-

Walt Disney's Impractical Dreams

posterous that he wouldn't mention it to anyone. He just quietly began planning.

As usual, though, he infused all of us with his own enthusiasm when he finally told us about the project. Predictably, we had trouble raising money, but Disneyland did open, in July 1955. Since that first day, millions of people, including eight kings and eight Presidents, have flocked to see the unique creation of Walt's imagination. Like a kid with a new toy—the biggest, shiniest toy in the world—Walt used to wander through the park, gawking as happily as any tourist.

The overwhelming success of Walt's "crazy idea" triggered a dramatic about-face in the Disney fortunes. Yet success never changed Walt. He remained the simplest of men. He hated parties, and his idea of a night out was a hamburger and chili at some little restaurant. His only extravagance was a miniature railroad that ran around the grounds of his home.

"What do you do with all your money?" a friend once asked him. Pointing at the studio, Walt said, "I fertilize that field with it." And it's true that Walt plowed money back into the company almost as fast as it came in. When Disneyland opened, it had 22 attractions and cost 17 million dollars. Today it has 57 attractions, and the total investment is 217 million dollars!

Typical is what happened one day when Walt and Admiral Joe Fowler, Disneyland construction supervisor, were looking over the park's Rivers of America attraction. It was the scene of feverish activity. The paddle-wheeler *Mark Twain* was puffing around a bend. Two rafts crowded with children were crossing to Tom Sawyer's island. Several canoes, manned by real Indians, were racing. It looked as though the whole flotilla was about to converge in one huge collision.

"Gosh, isn't that great!" Walt exclaimed. "Do you know what we need now?"

"Yeah," grunted Fowler. "A port director."

"No," said Walt. "Another *big* boat!" And he got one, the *Columbia*, a full-scale replica of the first American square-rigger to sail around the globe.

Being solvent for the first time since he started in business gave Walt a chance to develop other ideas. These included the California Institute of the Arts (Cal Arts), for which he donated the land and over 30 million dollars; and most ambitious of all, the Walt Disney World complex located on a 28,000-acre site near Orlando, Florida.

Tragically, in the midst of all this activity, Walt was stricken with his fatal illness. I heard him refer to this cruel blow only once. "Whatever it is I've got," he told me, "don't get it."

I visited him in the hospital the night before he died. Although desperately ill, he was as full of plans for the future as he had been all his life.

Walt used to say that Disneyland would never be finished, and it never will. I like to think, too, that Walt Disney's influence will never be finished; that through his creations, future generations will continue to celebrate what he once described as "that precious, ageless something in every human being which makes us play with children's toys and laugh at silly things and sing in the bathtub and dream."

POSTSCRIPT: Roy Disney died in December, 1971, but his brother's dreams continue to enrich the lives of millions of people around the globe. Mickey Mouse celebrated his 54th birthday in 1982. Walt Disney World now represents an investment of 800 million dollars. On October 1, 1982, Epcot Center, a one billion dollar project, opened its doors. Walt Disney World is expected to host 20 million people during the first year of Epcot Center's operation. And in April of 1983, Tokyo Disneyland will open its doors in Japan.

The Heart of an Artist

Presenting Liv Ullmann

by Liv Ullmann

I WAS BORN in a small hospital in Tokyo. Mamma says she remembers two things: A mouse running across the floor, which she took as a sign of good luck. A nurse bending down and whispering apologetically: "I'm afraid it's a girl. Would you prefer to inform your husband yourself?"

My first year at school, in Norway, I remember as long hours of sitting with apprehension in my stomach, waiting for recess. Sometimes there were team games, but other breaks were endless minutes of lonely desperation during which I pretended to be busy with something I preferred to do alone.

Snowball fights in winter. The fear when the big boys forced my head down into the snow.

I was small and thin and wild. But I was the only one in the school who could do a handstand on the handlebars of a bicycle.

The movies on allowance day. Queues winding round corners, making the feast inside even more fantastic because access to it was so difficult.

The pictures, the flight from reality, the world of dreams: experiences and people I believed would become part of my everyday life in the future. Tragedies so great that there was still a lump in the throat many hours later. Wonders so great that my feet did not touch the ground all the way home.

And love.

I yearned to experience it as it happened on the screen: stand close up against a man with a white shirt and a white smile who looked down at me tenderly and whispered the same words the Hero was whispering to the Heroine.

Hear violins when he kissed me.

Dancing school. Thirteen years old. Skinny and ungainly, with close-cropped hair. The tunes of those days still fill me with aversion. A memory of boys in white shirts storming across the floor when the mistress clapped her hands and said, "Take partners."

Always the same little group who pretended to be thinking of something else when they sat down and the dance began without them. Who never realized that they shared the fate of thousands of women, small and grown-up all over the world. Thirteen-year-olds convinced they would remain wallflowers for the rest of their lives. For each, an experience that seemed unique.

When I was 22, Peter Palitzsch, one of Germany's leading directors, came to our theater in Oslo. He taught me that everything we portray on the stage ought to be shown from two sides. Be illustrated in both black and white. When I smile, I must also show the grimace behind it.

I learned to work more consciously. I remember the opening scene of *The Caucasian Chalk Circle*. At the first reading I thought I was to play a woman in a heroic situation. Her name was Grusha. Revolution had come to the village. While she was running away she found an infant abandoned by its mother. My interpretation was to sit down and look tenderly and softly at the baby. Sing to it, pick it up, and then take it with me.

"Think a bit deeper," the director said. "Show her doubts—surely she must have had some? Her cowardice: don't you feel it? The audience will recognize you as acting in a way they themselves might have acted. No spontaneous nobility. Not necessarily symbolizing goodness all the time."

My interpretation became this: The woman puts the baby down as she realizes what a hindrance it will be on her flight. She stands up and walks away. Stops. Doubt. Turns back. Reluctantly sits down again. Looks away. Then, finally, she picks it up with a gesture of resignation and runs on.

Only when no situation or character is obviously good or evil is it truly interesting to act.

* * *

The first summer was pure happiness. We were making the movie *Persona* on the island.

It was hot. I was experiencing another human being. He was experiencing me. And we didn't need to talk about it. I was barefoot in sand so fine it felt as if it breathed beneath my feet. We went for walks along the shore and never spoke, made no demands, were not afraid.

Once we wandered far from the others, discovered a small ridge of gray stones with barren, unfertile earth beyond. We sat and looked at the sea, which for once lay completely still in the sunlight.

He took my hand in his and said: "I had a dream last night. That you and I are painfully connected."

On the spot where we were sitting he built his house. And that changed his life. And mine.

A little child grew up with us on the island. I stood in the hospital corridor the night after she was born. Through a window I could see all the small, crying, newborn infants, and somewhere among them slept the one who was mine. I stood there for hours, filled with happiness, until a night nurse sent me to bed.

There are many pictures of Linn from that time. She is chubby and happy; her eyes look as if they already appraise everything that happens around her. Eyes full of humor.

I know I can never make amends for the wrongs I have done her. All the choices I made that were not to her advantage. I want to take her in my lap today and tell her how much I love her and how I miss the warmth and the absolute trust. The moments of belonging when we walked in the woods and picked strawberries. When it thundered so terribly one night, and we all three lay close together in bed and laughed.

Linn's voice on the telephone. There is distance and reserve. I assure her of my love. "Little one, I care more for you than anyone else."

"No, you don't." The child's voice cuts deep.

I am in the tour bus jolting along toward another out-of-the-way part of Norway. Almost always on the way somewhere. Seldom home. And I see the nurses and neighbors holding my daughter, doing what my arms and my hands should be doing.

* * *

I think of my sudden breakthrough as a star in America. Unexpected and for me still inexplicable. I don't know if it has made me happier.

A few months ago I was in California and they spoiled me, as if I were a princess in one of Linn's fairy tales—or myself in one of my childhood dreams. I was surrounded with kindness and helpfulness.

I don't altogether trust that life. I know that today it is still possible to invest in my talent and my personality. But what's going to happen when I become too old? When I am no longer a desirable commodity? When it becomes quiet around me?

"What is your strongest happiness?" I say to a man for whom I care. We are in the new summer cottage. Rain is pouring down from a sky that is drearily gray.

"My happiness?" he replies. "I think it is when I have worked in the sweat of my body a whole day on something hard and physical. When I've had to use my entire body, when I've become exhausted and my limbs are aching—and then finally I finish and relax in the joy of a job well done."

He does not ask what my happiness is. But the next day I know. We have had a sumptuous lunch. He praises my cooking and takes several helpings. And we lie on the bed and are close, without any fears or questions between us.

When I awake and it is still light outside, he is gone, and I go with bare feet into the living room, still warm and happy from him, and see that he has lighted the fire. In the kitchen I find coffee he has put on the hot plate for me, with a cup beside it.

I have not a thread on my body as I go out into the garden. It is still raining and toes slide into earth that is wet and fragrant. And then I see him down by the garage splitting wood so that I shall have enough for the winter. He looks so happy and brown and alive. Suddenly I remember that he is in the middle of his happiness.

And I go in again and feel *my* happiness flowing through my whole body.

I am expecting an important visitor. Henry Kissinger is to escort me to a big ball.

He has inquired in Los Angeles who would be the most

Presenting Liv Ullmann

suitable date for him on this "event of the year" in Hollywood. Someone came up with me.

It is the year of his glory, and everybody wants to meet him.

A girl friend from Norway is to pose as my private secretary. Since Mr. Kissinger is the first blind date of my life, I was confused on the telephone and forgot to ask when he would fetch me. Consequently both the "secretary" and I have been dressed up for the last three hours.

From some official department in Norway has come a letter about oil. It is obvious they want me to inform Mr. Kissinger about something, but it's not clear to me what. My suite has been searched—so whoever recommended me was not convincing enough: I might still be a secret agent or have bombs under my bed.

The "secretary" and I go through the program again: how she is to serve wine, perhaps mention something about oil in a passing remark, bumble about a little, tidy up some papers—and then keep quiet.

A knock at the door. We both make a rush for it, stumbling over each other. I open it myself. He is smiling and much smaller than I. I know I picked the wrong shoes.

We shake hands while he waves reassuringly to some grave-faced men in the corridor.

She who is to pour wine lets most of it spill on his trousers. Feverishly all three of us try to remove the stain, and in the end one can hardly see it.

It is only in the elevator that I realize that the cleaner's tag is still attached to my dress, and I tug and tug, and tug off a little bit of the dress as well. (The "secretary" remarks on my return that this was clearly visible on television.)

I swish into a car with bulletproof windows, followed by men with little microphones into which they speak all the time. I think that I am very far from Trondheim.

I play film star with my child and jump with her fully dressed into the swimming pool, because we've read they do this here.

It is a short love story that resembles so many others.

It lasted five years.

She was no longer blind to his faults and weaknesses, as she had been at the beginning. But her understanding and respect for him grew. The adoration disappeared. She noticed that his hair was gray; he was much older than she; he was wise and stimulating; he was vain and egotistical. And she discovered to her surprise that this was love.

With sadness she realized that it would soon be over, that she had come to him when he was already on his way somewhere else. She looked at their child and realized that she would soon have that responsibility alone.

She tried to recall who she had been when she came to the island five years before. Something had been crushed in her, and something was more alive. She had undergone a change. And when bitterness and hate and despair were gone, she was sure she had experienced love and been enriched.

She had seen into another person and was full of tenderness for what she had found. For a period of time they had taken each other's hands and been painfully connected. But only when it was all over did they become true friends.

I left the island and my roots were never allowed to take hold in the earth, but they are forever planted in the experiences the island gave me. Many of my dreams were never to be fulfilled, but I had found what I had never dreamed of: reality can be magnificent, even when life is not.

Destiny's Child

by Eleanor Ruggles

LATE in the 1840s a middle-aged man and a boy, the one obviously in the care of the other, could occasionally be seen weaving through the streets of New York, Philadelphia and other eastern cities. Although led by the boy, the lurching, grizzled man still carried himself imperiously and had a look of being *somebody*. This, combined with the exceptional beauty of the dark-haired, anxious-eyed child, made passers-by ask one another: "Who's that?"

"It's Mr. Booth, the actor. Junius Brutus Booth. He's drunk again."

"And the boy?"

"His son Edwin."

For years the name MR. BOOTH on a playbill could fill any theater in America. In the 1820s the actor (one of whose sons, John Wilkes Booth, years later was to bring infamy to the family name as Abraham Lincoln's assassin) had come from England to enthrall the drama-hungry audiences in this country. He was often paid $100 a night, a fabulous salary at the time. As the years wore on, however, the elder Booth became a man against himself. When he was young, fame was his spur. When he had achieved fame, the spur was wanting.

He took to reviving himself after the play with brandy. From there it was only a step to drinking beforehand to brace himself. Then he began to act when drunk, though this was nothing singular at the time. All too frequently an actor, wholly fuddled, fell plunk to the floor and was hauled off by the elbows and heels.

But Junius Booth's drinking was only one symptom of something more alarming. He began to show signs of derangement. Once, for no reason, he played Cassius in *Julius Caesar* walking on tiptoe, and Pierre in *Venice Preserved* speaking in a whisper. Often he bolted from his dressing room and disappeared before the curtain rose. He was a favorite, so the audience usually stayed seated while a gentleman or two from the boxes hurried out to find him. During *The Merchant of Venice* in New York they discovered him, dressed as Shylock, slaving at the pumps to put out a fire many blocks away.

"Father's calamity" was what Booth's children called his spells of madness. They learned from their mother to treat him during these periods with tact and patience mingled with reverence. The public was not so forbearing, and Booth was often blamed for being drunk when he was really ill. Eventually, as his drinking became more determined and his outbreaks more dangerous, he could no longer be trusted to travel unattended.

From Edwin's 13th year it was he alone of the children who seemed able to manage Booth during his outbreaks. Once it had been the father's powerful voice that dispelled the horrors of the night from a little son's imagination; now it was this son's quiet voice that soothed the father when Booth was lost in drink or madness.

Everywhere Booth was announced, the company soon learned to expect Edwin with him. The older actresses' hearts warmed to the boy; he wore his black hair long and usually was wrapped in a Spanish cape. Joseph Jefferson never forgot his first sight of Edwin at 16. Edwin looked tired and uncared-for; his face was strained. But Jefferson recognized the swan in the unkempt fledgling, whom he thought the handsomest lad he had ever come across.

Edwin walked with his father to and from the theater. He ate with him at the long tables of theatrical boardinghouses. He slept beside him as Booth rolled and tossed through the night. And if Booth couldn't sleep, neither should his son. While his father prowled the room, Edwin dragged out his banjo and perched on the edge of the crumpled bed, chanting soft melodies.

Usually, while Booth was behind the footlights, Edwin stayed in the dressing room. He could hear the voices from onstage ring along the corridors. The ovation that welcomed the star would thunder down to him. He would crouch by the door, shivering in anticipation of the opening clarion lines. Edwin drank it all in. This was the theater, the motive and excuse for an actor's being.

When the final applause had died down and Booth had surged into the dressing room, ripping off his costume, Edwin would spring up, instantly apprehensive. His own night's work was just beginning. It was to his son's vigilance that the father committed himself. But, having done so, he tried to escape this vigilance with all a drunkard's and madman's cunning. Often late at night Edwin hunted for his father through deserted streets, to discover him at last on the waterfront or in the mean outskirts of town, throned in some firelit tavern like a prince of vagabonds amid a court of weaving revelers. Once, locked into his hotel room from the outside, Booth bribed a passing bellboy to bring him mint juleps, which he sucked through the keyhole with a straw.

One September night in 1849 Edwin played Cassio to his father's Iago in *Othello*. He began to be billed variously, in type only a little smaller than that used for his father's name, as MASTER EDWIN BOOTH; MR. E. BOOTH (first appearance of); MR. BOOTH, JR. In New York the pair stopped on Broadway to greet an old actor, who asked Booth solemnly: "Upon which of your sons do you intend to confer your mantle?" Without speaking, Booth laid his hand on Edwin's head.

In April, 1851, they were playing at the National in New York when Booth announced one afternoon that he "didn't feel like acting." The play for that night was *Richard III*. Edwin reminded his father how vigorously he had rehearsed that day. Mr. Booth only smiled slyly.

"What will they do without you, Father?" cried Edwin.

"Go act it yourself," said Booth.

The first person Edwin met at the theater was John R. Scott, the manager. "No matter," Scott answered coolly after Edwin had breathlessly told his news. "You play Richard. Or we'll have to close the house."

Huddled willy-nilly into his father's tunic and cloak, which were much too wide, while one of the company holding the promptbook heard him repeat Richard's first soliloquy, Edwin was led into the wing like a lamb to the sacrifice. No explanation had been given the audience, and as he stepped onstage he was greeted with the usual clapping. The applause hadn't wholly died down when an inquiring buzz filled the house, and there was a general turning of the playbill to the light to see the name printed there. Then silence fell, and striking out into it Edwin forced his light voice into an approximation of his father's measured, chesty tones:

> "And all the clouds that lowered
> upon our house
> In the deep boōsom of the o-ce-an
> buried."

Mr. Booth always gave the word "ocean" three syllables, painting the rise, the swoop forward and sliding crash of massy waves, and on the word "buried" his deep, hollow tone dropped a plummet to the sea bottom. Edwin did this too. The receptive audience caught the picture from his voice, and when he limped forward, twisting his features into his father's expression of bitter malignancy, he felt the house warm to his earnestness. He was launched.

As the scenes flashed past, a wave of friendliness swept toward him across the footlights and from the wings, where all the actors not on stage were crowded three deep. It was all over surprisingly soon, and then, like music, came the longed-for ovation.

Scott hugged Edwin, then drew him before the curtain with a mingling of triumph and tenderness. "You see before you," shouted Scott, "the worthy scion of a noble stock!"—and to Edwin out of the side of his mouth, "I'll bet they don't know what *that* means."

The applause, which seemed to be produced by one pair of hands, blazed up again, making the stage tingle and vibrate. It was this night's applause that Edwin heard for the rest of his life. Until this night he might have been happier as a lawyer, his father's dream for him. Now it was too late. Retreat where he might, the compulsion of this applause faintly roaring in his memory's ear would draw him back again.

"Well," his father demanded coldly when Edwin arrived back at their dingy quarters, "how did it go?"

Booth was still precisely as Edwin had left him. Yet Edwin always suspected his father had gone out, had been in the theater and, moving fast, had got home just ahead of him.

Thus a capricious destiny unfitted Edwin Booth for any life

but that of the theater. And in time he was to eclipse his father and be hailed as one of the greatest geniuses the American stage has ever known.

Alan Alda:
Madcap Doctor From
"M*A*S*H"

by George Vecsey

THE HELICOPTER clatters onto the medical-base landing pad. A wounded soldier is lifted onto a stretcher. He looks around him and sees: a male medic dressed as a woman; a Teddy Bear of a colonel barking orders; a nervous young corporal who can barely carry his end of the stretcher; a beautiful female officer-nurse; and finally, a tall, dark-haired man in a maroon dressing gown, carrying a martini glass, who keeps insisting: "I'm a doctor. Really. No kidding."

What's going on? Is the soldier hallucinating, or is this really the hospital base where his life will be decided? Not for many bizarre days will he know how to react to Mobile Army Surgical Hospital No. 4077—abbreviated as M*A*S*H.

Television viewers know how they feel about "M*A*S*H." Since 1973, this Columbia Broadcasting System program about a medical base in war-torn Korea has been winning awards and gaining millions of fans who follow the antics of Klinger (the male medic in the dress), Colonel Potter (the snappish commanding officer), Radar (the young corporal), Major Hot-Lips Houlihan (the head nurse) and Capt. Hawkeye Pierce (the debonair, sarcastic, martini-swilling surgeon in the maroon dressing gown).

Ironically, what makes these characters so appealing—and the show so popular—is that, unlike most TV characters, the ones on "M*A*S*H" are quite capable of being cruel to one another, of taking advantage, even of making mistakes with their patients. They are so bitingly *human* that they stand above almost everything else on the tube.

The most caustic character of all—Hawkeye Pierce—is also

Alan Alda: Madcap Doctor from "M*A*S*H"

the most popular. At first glimpse, Hawkeye, who is trying to operate with a nurse when he should be operating on a patient, seems like a cad or maybe even a quack. But every fan knows that when the doc finally rolls up his sleeves, he is the best surgeon on the Korean peninsula.

As played by Alan Alda, Hawkeye comes across as funny, decent and intelligent. One of the strengths of the show—and one of Alda's strengths in real life—is that he is not afraid to portray his character, warts and all. "'M*A*S*H' is about real people," Alda says.

Klinger dresses up like a woman so the brass will think he is crazy and send him home; Colonel Potter becomes angry with himself if he forgets to telephone his wife, 6000 miles away, on their anniversary; Radar tries to help everybody; Hawkeye and his sidekick B. J. (a straight-arrow surgeon) are trained to put people together and do not appreciate being in a war in which both sides try to blow people apart.

In one of the shows Alda likes best, Hawkeye connives to send the innocent Radar to Japan for a little "R & R"—rest and recreation on an adult level. As Radar leaves for his unexpected vacation, he is hit by an enemy bullet, not seriously, but enough to make Hawkeye feel guilty for endangering his young friend. "Hawkeye feels so bad he gets drunk," Alda recalls. "And when he tries to operate, he has to leave the room before he gets sick. He realizes that drinking just made things worse, and he feels twice as bad. It shows Hawkeye can be as foolish as anybody. We're all human."

Alan Alda is also human, even though one of his neighbors insists that he is "a saint." Indeed, in his years in show business, Alda has never been the subject of one rumor about his personal life. Although he and his family try to avoid publicity, the fans have learned a few things about him. They know he used to rush from California to his New Jersey home to be with his family every weekend; they know he avoids the glitter of show business while remaining one of its busiest actors, writers and directors. "Dull, isn't it?" he asks in his quick, scalpel-voiced way.

In October, 1978, Alda and I were chatting on the "M*A*S*H" set, in a canyon near Malibu, Calif. He had a lot of time between takes and, as we talked, the strongest impression I got was that of an adult living at the peak of his ability, with great discipline, doing exactly what he wants: working with "M*A*S*H," writing and starring in his own movie, *The Seduction of Joe Tynan*, lobbying for the feminist movement, loafing with his wife on a Caribbean island, watching his three daughters grow up, and generally moving full tilt through life. Yet despite the fast pace and the blazing fame, there is a considerate, unpretentious manner about him. I was lugging a heavy tape recorder for our interview and he insisted upon carrying both our lunch trays and pushing open doors on our way to his air-conditioned trailer.

How did Alan Alda become this serious grownup, living several careers at once? His roots are in show business. His father, Robert Alda (born Alfonso D'Abbruzzo), is an actor and singer best known for his film portrayal of George Gershwin in *Rhapsody in Blue*. He also created the role of Sky Masterson in the original Broadway production of *Guys and Dolls*. Alan, born in 1936, was an only child. At age seven, he became ill and his mother, recognizing the symptoms of polio, rushed him to the hospital for treatment. "If she had waited any longer, I would have been crippled," Alda says. "When I came home from the hospital, she had to put hot packs on me every couple of hours for eight or nine months.

"I owe my life to women," he continues. "First to my mother, for recognizing the polio symptoms, then to the Australian nurse, Sister Kenny, who developed the treatment for it. I didn't become a feminist because it was 'this year's cause.' I became one because of the incredible waste of half the talent in the world."

Alda moved to New York in his teens, attended Fordham University and played summer stock. In his junior year he went to Europe to study and act with his father. After he returned home he met Arlene Weiss, a clarinetist with the Houston Symphony Orchestra. They fell in love and were married a few months later.

Arlene Alda gave up her job in Houston in order to teach school in the New York area while Alan looked for jobs in the Broadway theater. After several lean years working wherever there was a role, Alda earned his first Broadway recognition in *Purlie Victorious*. His first movie role was in *Gone Are the Days* (1963). In 1966 he was nominated for Broadway's highest honor, a Tony award, for his work opposite Barbara Harris in *The Apple Tree*. In 1978 he made three movies: *California*

Alan Alda: Madcap Doctor from "M*A*S*H"   293

Suite; Same Time, Next Year and *The Seduction of Joe Tynan*. In 1981 Alda made his debut as a film director in the highly successful *The Four Seasons*. He has won five Emmy awards, three for acting in "M*A*S*H," one for writing it, and the other for directing it. He was also voted television's most popular actor in 1974, 1975 and 1981.

Alan Alda is proud of learning the skills of the characters he portrays. In the supernatural thriller *The Mephisto Waltz*, for instance, he had to play five minutes of classical piano, which took six hours of practice every day for six weeks. "It was awful," he says. "My brain hurt like a sore muscle, but I could play those five minutes. Three weeks after the movie was finished I forgot everything."

The biggest challenge, however, came when "M*A*S*H" arrived in 1972-73, a TV series fashioned after a popular movie. "When I saw the movie, I remember thinking that it would be fun to bring my own interpretation to the Hawkeye character," Alda says. "I wanted to portray him a little differently. Let's just say the TV Hawkeye is a combination of the film and of me."

Even when he realized the show would survive a second year, Alda resisted moving to California—he didn't like the idea of uprooting his family. So his children continued to attend public schools in New Jersey, and Alan has maintained his exhausting coast-to-coast commute.

His first screenplay, *The Seduction of Joe Tynan*, is about a politician who loses touch with himself under the strain of his work. "It's a movie about how success puts pressure on a family," Alda explains. "We say we value our families and our integrity. On the other hand, we say success is the most important thing. People make compromises. They use their families."

There must be something positive in a film for Alda to appear in it. "I won't do a conventional war movie in which the excitement of war is the main adventure. In 'M*A*S*H' we show the effects of the war, not the fighting itself." Alda once turned down a commercial for cigarettes when he was $50,000 in debt and the money would have covered the whole thing. "I'm not going to ask somebody to get lung cancer so I can make $50,000."

Alda says his philosophy is reflected in a passage in *The Teachings of Don Juan*, a book by Carlos Castaneda. In it Don

Juan says, "Never take a path that has no heart in it." Alda adds: "You can't lose if your heart is in your work, but you can't win if your heart is not in it."

Sometimes that doesn't totally work out, however, as Alda discovered in 1975 when he tried writing another television series, "We'll Get By," about a middle-class New Jersey family. He felt he gave the series a more realistic dimension than most shows about family life, but it was dropped after a season—one of the few setbacks in his career. Some of the ideas were drawn from his own family life.

Though Alda devotes much of his time to acting, writing and directing for the movies, he is still heavily involved in "M*A*S*H" and writes many of the show's scripts. Larry Balmagia, another "M*A*S*H" scriptwriter, says: "I don't want to make him sound like God, because he's not, but the fact is Alan does the work of five people. I'm supposed to be the writer, but he writes twice as fast as I do."

On the set, Alda seems most comfortable hanging around with Mike Farrell, the actor who plays B. J. The two men joke easily together on the darkened indoor set at 20th Century Fox, where they spend hundreds of hours a year performing endless takes for the camera. As both actors wait for a scene to be shot, Farrell spots a unicycle leaning against a wall, and his long legs wobble as he attempts a ten-second spin. Alda, meanwhile, has gone on camera and is fluffing one of his lines. Each time he messes it up, he responds with his loud-pitched cackle, causing the other actors to laugh. Just when it looks as if the scene will never finish, Alda shouts, "That's all right. I don't want anybody to know I'm in this scene anyway."

Now in its 11th year, one of the most popular shows ever to hit television is shooting its final season. Several months ago, Alda speculated about how "M*A*S*H" might end when the series is discontinued. "Maybe we'll have the war ending," he muses, "everybody going home and talking about their hopes for the future. It's getting harder to think of new stories, and I'd like to be proud of the program all the time."

No doubt Alan Alda will be.

Ray Bolger: Leprechaun of the Light Fantastic

by Andrew Jones

DURING an evening concert in May, 1976, Arthur Fiedler, the white-maned maestro of the Boston Pops Symphony Orchestra, suddenly put down his baton, walked to the stage wings, and came back with his arm around a skinny, S-shaped man with rubbery legs, bug eyes, a round, puckered mouth, and a nose that looks like a beer-can opener. Taking advantage of the audience's surprise, the then 72-year-old Ray Bolger signaled the orchestra for background music, donned a floppy felt hat and launched upon his scarecrow routine from *The Wizard of Oz*, beginning with the knee-cracking sequence in which Dorothy takes him down off his pole.

Now, he exchanged the felt hat for a jaunty straw, and the orchestra drifted into the song that has long been Ray Bolger's musical mark of identity—"Once in Love With Amy"—from his smash-hit show *Where's Charley?* At first, there was only the loose-jointed, soft-shoe shuffle. Then, as he sang, the TV cameras panned across the audience: a chaos of people cheering, hugging each other and dancing in the aisles. In that instant, viewers across the country had an electrifying example of this man's ability to reach out and quicken others with his own exuberance and joy of living.

When you ask him how he achieves it, Ray's long face turns serious, the expressive eyes go grave. "I get it from the people out front," he says quietly. "I work with love for my audience and I get it back from them. Some people call it magic, and maybe that's what it is. But I call it love."

Raymond Wallace Bolger was born in Boston in 1904 to an Irish painter father and a culture-minded mother who took him to the opera and ballet. He was a bright student and a good athlete, who amused his hockey teammates by doing twirls, splits and high kicks on the ice. His interest in dancing crystallized during an embarrassing experience at a high-school prom—he only knew how to waltz, and when the orchestra played a fox trot or a one step, he had to keep on waltzing. The next day, he stopped in at a dancing school to pick up some other steps. And soon he was trying to learn all there was to know about dancing, through a succession of jobs (he was fired from one with an insurance firm for practicing dance steps in the hallways). His most important move was striking a deal with a local ballet-school operator to manage the school's books in exchange for ballet lessons.

Ray's first actual stage work was as second lead in a traveling repertory company that did seven different shows a week. He sold vacuum cleaners to buy his costumes—a trunk full of Palm Beach suits. The suits went with him when he teamed up with Ralph Sanford, a comedy straight man, and joined the vaudeville circuit. When Sanford left him, Ray was good enough to put his own act together and play four or five shows every day.

What Ray considers the most important event of his eventful life occurred one morning when he walked into Los Angeles' Orpheum Theater and came face to face with a 15-year-old stage-struck schoolgirl from Montana who was clutching a sheaf of songs she was trying to peddle. Little Gwen Rickard, in her gray suit with her long blond hair, never had a chance. Ray swept over to her and, in his fanciest continental manner (à la Maurice Chevalier), crooned, "Is zere something I can do for yoooo, mamzelle? Can we go across zee street and have zee ice-cream sooooodah?" Ray and Gwen were married three years later, in 1929, and for a honeymoon they went to London where he had an act booked.

Back in the United States, Ray played a season in *George White's Scandals*, then starred the following year in *Earl Carroll's Vanities*. It was the Depression, and the show went on the road, playing five performances a day at 40 cents a ticket. In the mid-'30s, Ray also began making movies—his first was *The Great Ziegfeld*, in which he did a couple of dances. Audience response to these was such that MGM boss Louis B. Mayer, realizing he had a new star on his hands, told his people, "Get Bolger under contract."

Ray Bolger: Leprechaun of the Light Fantastic

MGM had just announced plans to produce a movie of *The Wizard of Oz*, and would soon start casting for it. Ray and Gwen had been brought up on the Oz books, and Ray thought he'd like to play the scarecrow. Gwen jumped at the idea and insisted to MGM that the part be stipulated in his contract. The rest is theatrical history. Generations have thrilled year after year to the adventures of Dorothy, her dog, Toto, and her three stalwart companions in the Land of Oz.

Ray's first in a long string of Broadway musical comedies was *Life Begins at 8:40*, which opened in 1934. Two years later, he starred again, in *On Your Toes*, which included the most famous and demanding dance number of the entire Bolger repertoire—the frenzied ballet "Slaughter on Tenth Avenue." He had to dance for a solid 15 minutes around the body of a girl shot down in the street, finally falling across her. On opening night, he did fall, but he did not hear the thunderous applause that stopped the show and held the curtain up for one of the longest ovations in the annals of Broadway. He had fainted.

During World War II, Ray and pianist Little Jack Little teamed up to tour the South Pacific, doing a two-man gig for troops stationed on war-front jungle islands. It was, Ray recalls, much like the old vaudeville days, too little sleep, always in a hurry, but somehow oddly satisfying—a time of hilarity and heartbreak.

One night on Guadalcanal, Ray came upon a young Marine in a forward-area foxhole who was obviously in need of a little cheering up. Washing-Machine Charley (the nightly Japanese air raid) was due any minute, and the kid was scared stiff. Ray yelled at him, "Hey, Marine! Throw me that piece!" The boy tossed him his rifle, and Ray went on to ad-lib a Sad Sack manual-of-arms routine on the spot. He jammed his finger in the breech and whacked himself on the ear, bringing the weapon to his shoulder. His nose got in the way of his present-arms position and, bringing the piece to order arms, he managed to slam the butt smartly down on his right instep.

The young Marine and everyone nearby were hugging their sides with laughter. The youngster then produced a small piece of metal, part of a Japanese airplane, and asked Ray to scratch his name on it. A year later, a Marine lieutenant came up to Ray in a New York restaurant. "You remember that kid on the 'Canal, Mr. Bolger?" he said. "I was his platoon sergeant. He was killed in our next landing. He always carried that piece of airplane metal you signed for him, so we buried it with his body on Guam."

Ray's capacity for instant, precise satire comes, at least in part, from his habit of constantly watching for the small intricacies of human activity. Every morning, he and Gene Garf, his musical director for over 20 years, work on their routines, changing steps, polishing dance patterns, introducing new material. For instance, Ray will have recently followed a man down the street, watching him walk. Crossing Wilshire Boulevard, the man will be apprehensive, taking small steps, looking for oncoming cars. On the sidewalk he strides along, the big shot, making people step around him. In his hotel lobby, he becomes curious, glancing to see who's there, hands in pockets, walking back on his heels. With Gene improvising at the piano, Ray imitates the fellow's moods, exaggerating his facial expression and gestures. It may work into one of the acts or become the basis for a new one.

Within the greasepaint fraternity, Ray is today a living legend. In the early 1960s, during a rehearsal for a "Bell Telephone Hour Show," a young pianist named Marvin Hamlisch was impressed by Ray's enormous energy, his involvement not only in the music and staging but in such technical aspects as lighting and sound effects. In 1975, when by now world-famous songwriter-producer Hamlisch was casting *The Entertainer*, he thought of Ray again. Thus did the onetime vaudeville hoofer, in his first straight dramatic role as a onetime vaudeville hoofer, turn in a performance that earned him an Emmy Award nomination. "To say he's an old pro is not enough," Hamlisch declares. "He is the *original* old pro. He can do anything."

Can Ray really do all the things he once could? "I don't leap as high as I used to," he says. "And I no longer get the feeling of being suspended for just that fraction of a moment when I jump." But it's obvious that the will is still there; the essentials remain intact.

Besides his bread-and-butter shows (mostly one-man musical performances), Ray today gives regular benefit performances for United Way, the American Cancer Society, and a number of hospitals and institutions. He has narrated and appeared in an hour-long film, *Senior Citizen Shuffle*, produced by the Columbia Television Stations and depicting the problems of the aged in modern American society. He also worked with

Ray Bolger: Leprechaun of the Light Fantastic

the Center for Instructional Media and Technology at the University of Connecticut on a film called *A Time for Living*, dealing with the terror millions feel when confronted with retirement.

These projects are, perhaps, a kind of ultimate expression of what Ray Bolger is all about. To him, age is indeed a relative thing, for all the labors of his lifetime derive from a single ambition—to make "the people out in front" feel good about themselves.

He recalls that, on the opening night of his first play on Broadway, he received from his former boss at a Boston bank a terse reminder of his earlier days—a photocopy of the report filed by the personnel manager the day he was hired. It read simply: "Raymond Bolger. Very young. Very bright. Very fresh. Will probably outgrow it."

Grinning broadly, Ray says, "I wonder if I ever will."

"Charlie"

by Helen Hayes with Lewis Funke

> 'Twas on a Monday morning,
> Right early in the year,
> That Charlie came to our town,
> The young Chevalier.
>
> —ROBERT BURNS

CHARLIE MACARTHUR strolled into town at the peak of the roaring '20s. Almost immediately, he was adopted by New York's wits and hunted by the town's Dianas. This young chevalier had come well armed for conquest. He had wit, a dark, sloe-eyed kind of beauty, and he wove Homeric tales about the two great wars of the time, World War I and the war in Chicago's gangland. Not only had he fought his way through ever major engagement in which American doughboys participated, he had been a Chicago newspaper reporter. He was elusive and bore himself with a bland indifference. The crowning glory of my life was that somehow I saw below the surface to the real Charlie and recognized him for my own true love.

The first time I met Charlie was at a late-afternoon studio party given by the illustrator Neysa McMein. Although I was already a star in the theater, I was leading a most secluded life for an actress. I hardly knew a soul at the party. I sat in a corner going through the usual pantomime of listening and cocking my head at what was being said.

And then a beautiful young man came up to me with a bag of peanuts in his hand and said, "Want a peanut?" I was startled but answered, "Yes, thank you." He poured several peanuts into my hand, smiled at me and said, "I wish they were emeralds."

Years later, to my regret, I told this story to an interviewer in Hollywood. It was repeated over and over again until it nearly drove Charlie out of his mind. And so, when he came home one year from a long trip abroad, he did bring me a bag of emeralds. And he said, "I wish they were peanuts."

When I met Charlie, I was living in a three-room apartment with my mother and a friend. Charlie and I spent much of our courtship looking for places where we could be alone. We spent a great deal of time riding ferries to Staten Island and trains to Nyack, where we took long walks along the Hudson. Charlie had grown up in Nyack when his father was a minister there, and he loved the town.

We had a rather long courtship. Also, it was a troubled one. Someone said that the community always tries its best to pull lovers apart before, and keep them together after, marriage. In our case, the sides were sharply drawn between my protectors, who feared that I would be run over and squashed, and Charlie's admirers, who thought he would be bored to death. It took all of Charlie's wisdom to pilot us through their nonsensical interference.

I had scored a great success in *Coquette*, and Charlie made up his mind that he wasn't going to marry me until he had a triumph equal to mine. So the 1928 opening of *The Front Page*, which he and Ben Hecht had written, was the most important of my life. I went to the premiere in a state of terrible tension and sat alone up in the balcony near a fire exit. I wanted to be able to get out fast after each act in order to report to Charlie and Ben, who had elected to sit it out on the fire escape.

The curtain went up, and it wasn't long before the audience began warming to that rowdy play about the gentlemen of the press. At the end of the act, I raced out. The heroes of the night were huddled on the iron steps, all pinched and white in the half-light. Reaching Charlie's arms in two bounds, I babbled wildly about the audience's reaction—Charlie Chaplin in stitches, Heywood Broun slapping his knees and roaring, Alexander Woollcott puffing up like a blowfish, "and you should have seen—" Charlie silenced me by holding me tight against his chest. Then he pushed me off and said, "Helen, will you marry me?" And I said, "You took the words right out of my mouth."

During all the years of our marriage, Charlie was a gallant lover. He knew how to lift a woman's heart. In World War II he served as assistant to the Chief of Chemical Warfare Service. Shortly after D-Day I was looking out the window of our house in Nyack when suddenly I saw him coming up the walk. My excitement, indescribable, was increased by something at once ludicrous and marvelously romantic. There Charlie was, in full uniform, battle ribbons across his chest, silver lieutenant colonel's oak leaves on his shoulders—carrying a somewhat beat-up rose in his hand. He had plucked that rose in a garden in Normandy and kept it in a container of water all the way home on the plane!

His letters were ardent. I think this one, written in Washington, D.C., in 1943, speaks for itself:

Angel,

It's 5:30 a.m., and I've given up the idea of sleep, so I might as well be writing you a letter. I've been remembering so many things, from our buggy ride to Fraunces Tavern on down the years—all my boobish love antics return to entertain me. I run upstairs in East 40th Street with you in my arms (I believe I could do it still without getting too much out of breath)... The first time I ever kissed you in a cab, and how you lied ever after when you said you didn't lean toward me first. And sitting up with you in Childs and the swing at Syosset and the open fire at Otto Kahn's.

And the Victrola I bought you for your birthday and the way your stomach felt at the Santa Barbara Biltmore when the embryo Mary was only a few weeks old, and how I rubbed your stomach later with cocoa butter and got my face slapped for further familiarities. The bed at 15 Park we were never going to sell. And my horror the first time I went back and saw you in a bustle after a performance of Victoria....

Don't worry about me, I hope I always have this particular form of insomnia. Thank you for a very pleasant night, my dearest, only love.

All this is so little of my happiness,

Charlie

He understood human beings. Old friends—F. Scott Fitzgerald was one, and Bob Benchley another—would come to see Charlie in troubled moments. These friends knew that Charlie was never going to be righteous with them. They could talk and unburden themselves without hurt or embarrassment.

I do not mean to imply that Charlie was a saint. He wasn't. He was full of mischief and laughter, and there are those who can still spend nights on end regaling listeners with stories of their adventures with him. It also is true that from time to time he had a few more drinks than were good for him. I witnessed one bout that continues to astound me whenever I recall it. John Barrymore came visiting, and the two of them downed goodness knows how much Scotch. They polished off a great deal of wine at dinner, and after dinner they were at it again, finishing every bottle in the house. I just watched in awe.

At one point I was dispatched to Charlie's study to get a copy of Whitman's *Leaves of Grass*, which contains a poem Charlie wanted John to read to him. John put on a pair of nickel-rimmed glasses—I hadn't seen anyone for years wearing those things. He turned the pages until he came to "Song of the Open Road." Awash in alcohol, he started. He read with such beauty, with never a hesitation over a word or an emphasis. It was like a concert. Charlie reveled in it—and I did, too.

Sometime the next afternoon Charlie and Jack wobbled down to our swimming pool for a cold, cold dip; but the water seemed tepid to them. So Charlie called the local ice company and ordered its entire supply, two truckloads of ice. The trucks were backed up to the pool, and out shot the great blocks. Jack, lolling on his ice floe, was most appreciative and said he felt like a fly in a highball.

Charlie always had a clear picture of himself and his place in the world. "He was born," Ben Hecht said, "without the illusion of permanence." As for Charlie's success in the theater, he was constantly aware of how fleeting it could be. Even when I first met him—when he was on the way up, and people like H.L. Mencken and George Jean Nathan had great regard for his potential—he was preparing himself for the way down.

When Charlie's productive force slackened, there was much that he still wanted to say, yet somehow he was unable to say it in a manner that pleased him. I was miserable for him because

I knew how troubled he was. One night, especially blue, he disappeared into his room and I was alone with F. Scott Fitzgerald, who had come on a visit. I talked with Scott, a man who knew his own despairs, his own loss of productive force. He said something I never forgot and which consoled me: "There are some people who have to *do* in order to make their mark. They have to perform, to contribute. And there are some people who only have to *be*. Charlie is one who just has to *be*."

And this was true.

As Ben Hecht said in a eulogy, "He seemed never interested in attracting anyone, yet people scampered toward him as if pulled by a magnet. Alex Woollcott, who loved him, once said, 'What a perfect world this would be if it were peopled by MacArthurs.'"

No Business Like Show Business

Ethel Merman Knocks 'em Dead

by Landt Dennis

WITH MERMAN, you know you've got a hit," said producer David Merrick, whose *Hello, Dolly!* was one of the longest-running musical comedies in Broadway history. "Twelve times I asked her to do Dolly, and she turned me down every time—even though Jerry Herman wrote the show with her in mind. When she finally said yes, it was probably the greatest surprise of my life. It takes courage, you know, to step in after six famous stars have played a part."

When she opened on March 28, 1970, as the indomitable Dolly Levi—long auburn hair piled high beneath a monumental hat of white dove feathers, size-14 figure snugly fitted into a high-waisted, ankle-length Victorian dress—she waited calmly in the wings. When her cue came, she made the same explosive entrance that she has given audiences for 40 years: "One, two, three—go!" The moment ticket holders recognized her wide-angle smile and saucer-plate eyes, what British critic Kenneth Tynan calls her "strutting incarnation of style," they were on their feet shouting and cheering.

"Without Ethel," Merrick reported, "we might never have broken *My Fair Lady's* record. But people would pay to hear Merman sing the telephone book. She is the most thoroughly professional star I've ever done business with. She's out there every single performance, dedicated, making a show really work." "There's no one else like her," Irving Berlin said of her. He called Merman "a songwriter's dream. If she trusts you she'll do your material exactly as it's written. She's as good the last night of a run as she is the first." And she's deadly with a spoken line, too—such perfect comic timing and facial animation that both Bob Hope and Jimmy Durante ranked her as one of the country's finest comediennes.

In the course of her 14-Broadway-hits career, Ethel appeared in more than 6000 performances, a figure few performers can beat. From the night of October 14, 1930, when she opened in George Gershwin's *Girl Crazy*, she never had cause to doubt her ability to hold a Broadway audience. Early in the first act, after belting out "Sam and Delilah," she doubled time, modulated key and swung into "I Got Rhythm." "For 16 breathless bars at the end," one theater-goer put it, "she held a penetrating C as the orchestra laid into the melody." Suddenly, all hell broke loose, or from the audience's point of view, all heaven. Merman had become a star.

It didn't seem to her as if she had done anything unusual that night. She'd always been singing that way. *Time* magazine described it: "She aims at a point slightly above the entrails, and knocks you out every time." After numerous encores, the young Merman hurried backstage, so that the show's real star, Ginger Rogers, could have the footlights again. Gershwin grabbed her. "Ethel," he said, "don't ever let anyone give you a singing lesson. It'll ruin you!"

It is advice she has followed to this day. Confident in her skill, she never vocalizes before a performance, nor does she bother to keep in training between shows. To her, to sing, or "to let her blow" in her words, is as normal as to live. She never stops. "If you write for Merman," Irving Berlin said, "the lyrics better be good—because everyone's going to hear them."

The girl who was born Ethel Zimmermann has been acknowledged "the greatest" by the most discerning men in the business, including Gershwin, Berlin and Cole Porter. She estabished her credentials as an entertainer before she was six years old, with appearances at the Astoria, N.Y., Episcopal Church, her father's Masonic lodge and the local Women's Republican Club. "I can never remember being afraid of an audience," she wrote in her autobiography. "If the audience could do better, they'd be up here onstage and I'd be out there

Ethel Merman Knocks 'em Dead

watching them," was the way she said it later. During her run in *Call Me Madam*, she was asked one night if she was nervous. "At $9.90 a ticket, they're the ones who should be nervous, not me," Ethel said.

In high school she took bookkeeping, shorthand and typing. Her first jobs were secretarial for small Long Island firms. But at nights and on weekends she sang in clubs and vaudeville theaters. "It was a double life that taught me the necessity of efficiency and excellence in whatever I do," she said. "Why, even today, I never employ a secretary, never." Business and thank-you letters Merman types herself, at 60 words a minute.

She never hesitated about her theatrical goals. "I knew what I wanted to do. I shied away from chorus-girl parts," she said, a touch of New Yorkese in her warm, friendly voice. "I couldn't dance to begin with; I wanted to sing. And if I didn't make it in *Girl Crazy*, I thought, I can always go back to taking shorthand, ya know."

Merman loves to tell about a meeting she once had with several theater people. Names, deals, possible roles were flying around the room, and Ethel unobtrusively took everything down in shorthand. When the meeting broke she walked over to a typewriter and banged out several transcripts. "Better read this over," she said, handing out the copies. "We don't want trouble later." It is this no-nonsense Scots-German efficiency that caused Merrick to say, "Ethel always keeps her word and you'd better damned well keep yours, too. She remembers everything you've said."

This efficiency and a sometimes brusque public manner tend to make Merman seem hard-boiled and brassy. Her co-workers insist the image is not true. Jack Klugman, Ethel's co-star in *Gypsy*, told about the time he was auditioning for the part of Merman's suitor in the musical: "I told them I couldn't sing, and I kept stumbling through. Finally, I just didn't think I could continue, so I told them to find another leading man. That was when Ethel turned to me and, with the most wonderful warmth and affection I've ever seen in the theater, she said, 'Come on, Jack. You can do it.'

"In front of the critical eyes of all those casting people, she began to sing our duet, 'Small World,' with such love for me and such conviction that I could make it, that I did. I started to sing in a way I'd never sung before. When it was over, the part was mine because she'd made it mine. The two years I played with her I grew more as an actor than I ever had before."

Merman's concern for others is a characteristic Irving Berlin knew well. During the Boston tryout of *Annie Get Your Gun*, he decided that the words to "Doin' What Comes Naturally" were wrong. So he rewrote them. Handed the new lyrics on Tuesday, Merman sang them letter-perfect on Wednesday (she is a legend for her speed in memorizing a part). Audience reaction was poor, and Berlin decided to change back to the original lyrics. "Ethel never said a word to me," he said years later, still in awe of her tact and courtesy.

Offstage, Merman is an extremely reserved, almost shy woman, especially among strangers. She lives by herself quietly in a three-room New York hotel apartment. Married and divorced four times, Ethel has had two children, Robert and Ethel. In 1967, Ethel died, leaving two children. The succession of husbands and the death of her daughter have left their scars. But self-pity is not part of her personality. "When Ethel died," she told me, "I thought at first: 'What am I going to do without her?' Then I realized that I would have to adjust my life. And I realized that I still have my career, my son, my grandchildren, and a wonderful bunch of friends. Now I can talk about her."

Merman loves her work, and is willing to sacrifice everything for it. Anyone who doesn't feel the same way, Merman believes, should get out of the theater, or at least out of the play *she* is in. Punctual as a Cape Kennedy blast-off, she follows one rule on stage: "Stick to the book, to what's written."

One of the very few times Merman allowed herself the luxury of an ad lib was in *Gypsy*. She was playing the role of burlesque star Gypsy Rose Lee's mother, a determined woman with tenderness hidden beneath her impenetrable breastplate of ambition for her child. "It was a part Ethel could perform beautifully since she understood it so well," co-star Klugman insisted. "The last night, when the house was packed, she sang 'Together Wherever We Go' with such radiance and emotion that the audience was overwhelmed. Suddenly, to my astonishment, Ethel held up her hand to quiet the shouts for encores and said, 'Do you really want more?' You could have heard the explosion in China. 'Okay, boys, let's take it from the top,' she said, and that's exactly what she did. She's a great, great lady."

Ethel Merman Knocks 'em Dead 311

Merman's work is now confined to concerts with symphonic orchestras. She makes occasional TV appearances, but she insists that she'll never return to Broadway.

The Great and Only P. T. Barnum

by W. Bruce Bell

ONE QUIET summer afternoon in 1835, the young proprietor of a side-street grocery in Little Old New York was reading the "Business Opportunities" section of the *Sun* when a friend walked in. "Phineas," he said, "you're always looking for a golden opportunity. I think I've found one."

"No physical labor involved, I trust," the storekeeper replied.

The man pulled out a clipping from the *Pennsylvania Inquirer* and read aloud: "The citizens of Philadelphia have an opportunity of witnessing one of the greatest natural curiosities ever witnessed, viz. Joice Heth, a Negress aged 161 years, who formerly belonged to the father of General Washington."

This living relic was on exhibition in Philadelphia, but her owner lacked ability as a showman and was seeking a buyer. Next morning the young storekeeper caught the stagecoach for Philadelphia. He went immediately to the Masonic Hall and was ushered into the presence of a blind, toothless black woman, partially paralyzed but mentally alert. She spoke lovingly of "dear little George," croaked an ancient hymn, and then lit a corncob pipe—a habit she admitted to having for more than 120 years.

Enchanted but still skeptical, Phineas asked for proof and was shown a bill of sale dated February 5, 1727, from Augustine Washington to his sister-in-law for "One Negro woman named Joice Heth, aged 54 years, for and in consideration of the sum of £33 lawful money of Virginia."

The Great and Only P. T. Barnum

The asking price for this ancient curiosity was $3000, a formidable sum for the indigent young grocer, who haggled it down to $1000. He returned to New York, sold his grocery interest, wheedled $500 from a friend, and suddenly—for better or worse—P.T. Barnum was in show business.

New York in the early 1830s was in the grip of blue laws, and any entertainment more dramatic than a travel lecture was shunned as immoral. In the handbills, pamphlets and broadsides with which Barnum flooded the city, he revealed his talent for plucking the right strings:

"Joice Heth," the advertising claimed, "was the first person who put clothes on the infant George Washington. She is a Baptist and takes great pleasure in conversing with ministers and religious persons."

For several months Barnum's show grossed $1500 a week; when interest began to wane, "Aunt Joice" was trundled off on a successful tour of New England.

Not until she died the following winter did an autopsy reveal to Barnum and the rest of the world that Aunt Joice had been a delightful fraud. Only then did the red-faced public ask, "Who is this P.T. Barnum?" It was a good question.

Phineas Taylor Barnum was a Connecticut Yankee who, before turning impresario at age 25, had been a jack-of-all-trades and a fizzle at most of them. He came into the world on July 5, 1810, in Bethel, a strait-laced community where the price of a cuss word, if overheard by a church official, was 40 lashes.

In this puritanical atmosphere an odd form of amusement came into flower—the practical joke. Putting one over on your neighbor was a pastime that everyone could enjoy without fear of damnation. By exploiting this type of entertainment—and charging admission for it—P.T. Barnum built a fabulous career and amassed a fortune of $4 million. In the process he became a champion of free speech and free conduct, having rebelled from his teens against the forces of religion and government that stifled the enjoyment of life. He wrote passionate "letters to the editor," and when they were pigeonholed as too inflammatory, he bought a printing press and turned out his own four-page *Herald of Freedom*. The paper exposed what Barnum called "religious bigots," "temperance liquor-dealers," "underhanded deacons"—and it named names.

Above all, P.T. Barnum was a born showman. Legend has it that he boasted, "There's a sucker born every minute." No evidence of this boast has ever been found, but for half a century Barnum stood the public on its head and made it turn cartwheels.

By the time Joice Heth had been laid to rest, Barnum was already peddling his second attraction, an Italian juggler billed as Vivalla. With this mediocre act Barnum served his apprenticeship in the field of entertainment on which his greatest fame would rest—the circus.

The first circus to play in America under full canvas was a four-wagon troupe of acrobats and performing horses owned by a British ex-shoemaker named Aaron Turner. Barnum offered Turner Vivalla's juggling act and his own services as ticket seller and bookkeeper for $30 a month, plus one-fifth of the profits.

In 1841, after several seasons on the road, Barnum heard that Scudder's American Museum on Broadway was for sale. The total price was $15,000. "I'm going to buy it," he announced.

"What with?" a friend asked.

"Brass," Barnum replied, and with this plentiful currency he persuaded the building's owner to buy the museum collection for cash and sell it and the building to him on credit.

In a few weeks the drab old marble hulk was transformed. Floodlights on the roof drew night customers like moths. On the third-floor balcony overlooking Broadway Barnum installed a large band of trombone and trumpet players, more to create discord than harmony, and thus drive the crowds into the museum. He introduced educated dogs, a flea circus, ventriloquists, tightrope walkers, giants, dwarfs, fat boys, gypsies, the first Punch and Judy show in America, and even tribes of "savage" Indians. The sideshow was born not in a tent, but in Barnum's American Museum.

The practical joker in him was always ready to come to the fore. One day, Barnum noticed that great numbers of people were bringing their lunches to the museum, which also housed a great collection of relics and curiosities, and using it as an all-day picnic ground while crowds of potential customers outside were being turned away. To solve the problem he had a door cut in the rear wall, and over it hung a large, impressive

The Great and Only P. T. Barnum

sign: TO THE EGRESS. "What's an egress?" the patrons asked one another. "Never heard of it—let's have a look."

When they did they found themselves outside in the alley.

On his stage Barnum held one of the first showings of *Uncle Tom's Cabin*. Citizens who wouldn't have been caught dead in a theater flocked to the lecture room to boo Simon Legree and weep with joy as Eliza ascended into Heaven. Whatever else Barnum may have done for Americans, he made theatergoing respectable.

In the quarter-century of its existence, the American Museum became the best-known landmark in New York City. Barnum and his agents scoured the globe for the new and the spectacular—such oddities as the Feejee Mermaid, the Siamese Twins, Jumbo the Elephant, and Madame Clofullia, the first of many bearded ladies. And always he managed to have a headliner whose authenticity could be doubted. While the public was arguing "Is it or isn't it?" Barnum was adding fuel to the flame of controversy—and unprecedented receipts to his box office—by advertising the freak as genuine and secretly planting rumors that it was a fake.

But Barnum found his stepping stone to international fame in the person of a midget christened Charles Sherwood Stratton. When Barnum discovered him as a precocious child of four in Bridgeport, Conn., he was 25 inches tall and could have been weighed on a postal scale. Barnum hired him and billed him as General Tom Thumb.

Tom Thumb was a smash hit wherever he appeared. Barnum raised his salary to $50 a week, and took the child star on a three-year grand tour of Europe. The miniature general did three command performances for Queen Victoria. A critic in 1844 thus described a typical Tom Thumb audience: "They push, they fight, they scream, they faint. I would not have believed it of the English people."

Tom's success in Paris was even greater. Said Barnum: "I was compelled to take a cab to carry my bag of silver home at night."

During breakfast in his Connecticut home one morning in 1868, Barnum picked up a newspaper and read: BARNUM'S MUSEUM BURNS. It was a total loss and now, at 57, he thought of retiring.

For two years he traveled, lectured and pursued hobbies

such as cultivating his garden. Then a former roustabout named William Cameron Coup and an ex-clown named Dan Castello conceived the idea of borrowing Barnum's money, fame and talent to create a mammoth circus. Barnum listened to their proposition and shot out of retirement like a thunderbolt.

The great enterprise of Barnum, Coup and Costello opened in Brooklyn in 1871 under three acres of canvas. As Barnum's Great Traveling World's Fair, it grossed $400,000 that summer, and in the second season made almost a million dollars. Finally Barnum bought out his partners.

Perhaps no private profit-making enterprise has ever enjoyed such wholehearted civic support as did Barnum's company. Wherever they played, it was Barnum Day and a local holiday. In the flickering gaslights President Garfield, delighted by Mademoiselle Zazel, the Human Cannonball, the Tattooed Greek, the tumbling clowns and the troupe of dancing stallions, exclaimed, "P.T. Barnum is the Kris Kringle of America!"

It was now that Barnum met his match in showmanship: short, thin, intense, 33-year-old James Anthony Bailey. When Barnum first heard of him, Bailey had just conducted the Allied Shows Circus on a successful two-year trip around the world. Allied Shows made national headlines when Hebe, one of its elephants, gave birth to the first Indian baby elephant born in captivity in the United States. Coveting the attraction, Barnum wired Bailey an offer of $100,000 for the mother and child.

Bailey wired an instant refusal. "If you can't lick 'em, join 'em," said Barnum, and he put out the first feeler that soon was to lead to a successful merger.

Barnum and his new associate first presented their combined talents to an audience of 9000 in Madison Square Garden on March 18, 1881. On the marquee, banners carried the slogan that was to become a universal byword: BARNUM AND BAILEY— THE GREATEST SHOW ON EARTH.

It was an overpowering spectacle. For the first time three rings were used, and the whole performance glittered under the new electric lights. There were 338 horses, 14 camels, 20 elephants, 370 costumed performers, 4 brass bands, and the 41-year-old Tom Thumb and his midget wife, Lavinia.

In the fall of 1890 Barnum suffered a stroke. All his life he had been the subject of controversy, and now that the end was near he was curious to know just how posterity would judge him. Learning of this, the editor of the New York *Evening Sun* obtained permission to publish Barnum's obituary in advance. On March 24, 1891, two weeks before he actually died at age 80, he read and enjoyed his four-column obituary, headlined: THE GREAT AND ONLY BARNUM.

Mickey Rooney Takes a New Bow

by James Stewart-Gordon

BROADWAY ADDED to the legend that there's no business like show business when the curtain went up shortly after eight o'clock at the Mark Hellinger Theater on the night of April 18, 1980. As Mickey Rooney came onstage, wearing a derby hat, red-flannel underwear and a grin as wide as the Los Angeles Freeway, the audience rose en masse and sent cheer after cheer rocketing to the rafters. Mickey stood there, his eyes glistening, saying, "Thank you, thank you." Not until 8:24 did the cheering finally stop. Rooney started to say something, choked and recovered. Then he smiled, cocked his derby over one eye, hollered, "Let's get on with the show," and proceeded to tear up the turf in *Sugar Babies*—singing, dancing, mugging, and ogling the very ogleable legs of co-star Ann Miller—while the audience jumped for joy.

Mickey Rooney, in show business for 58 of his 60 years, had just returned from the Hollywood Academy Awards presentation, which he had attended as a nominee for his role in *The Black Stallion*. He hadn't won, but the audience at *Sugar Babies* was handing him its own award—the ovation of a lifetime.

After the show, Rooney said, "Sure, I'd love one more Oscar. But tonight that bunch out front gave me something more—their affection—and isn't that what it's all about anyway?"

The much-married Mickey Rooney, whose off-screen life and on-screen career have been a roller-coaster ride of ups and downs, made his first stage appearance at 15 months as a midget smoking a rubber cigar. Since then he has made 139 feature

Mickey Rooney Takes a New Bow

films, been nominated for Oscars four times and won his own special Oscar.

Part of Rooney's ironlike durability stems from his super-versatility. Mickey has done everything from low comedy to Shakespeare, from melodrama to musical comedy. When Max Reinhardt arrived in Hollywood in 1934 to direct *A Midsummer-Night's Dream*, he picked 13-year-old Mickey to play that mischievous, blithe spirit, Puck. The part fitted Mickey amazingly well, and at 60 he explained, "I always identified with Puck."

Mickey was a smash success at 17, turning out eight or nine pictures a year and making an annual $250,000 in prewar cash by the time he was 21. Those were the days when MGM bosses put in overtime counting the millions of dollars that Mickey produced for them. The backbone of the bonanza was the Andy Hardy series, 17 pictures throughout which Mickey, who is only five feet, three inches tall, looked an eternal 17 for nine years.

To the World War II generation, Rooney as Andy Hardy typified what life in a small town should be like. His father, wise, white-haired Judge Hardy (Lionel Barrymore first, then Lewis Stone for the rest of the series), was always on hand to set Andy on the right road. His confidant was Judy Garland, a pigtailed kid with freckles and wide eyes who shared his irrepressible optimism. ("We've got talent. We've got a barn," he told her in *Babes in Arms*. "Let's do a show!")

And his steady girl, Polly Benedict, played by Ann Rutherford, was as curvy as a country road and as wholesome as a Hershey bar. The parade of girls who temporarily diverted Andy from Polly was a covey of young quail named Lana Turner, Esther Williams, Kathryn Grayson and Donna Reed. All grew up and became sex symbols, while Mickey as Andy continued to worry about whom to take to the junior prom.

In addition to the Hardy series, Mickey starred with Judy Garland in such memorable musicals as *Babes on Broadway*, *Girl Crazy* and *Strike Up the Band*. A polished actor, he co-starred with Spencer Tracy in *Captains Courageous*, taught Elizabeth Taylor how to ride a horse in *National Velvet*, and created an unforgettable Huck in *The Adventures of Huckleberry Finn*. In 1938, 1939 and 1940, Mickey topped Clark Gable, Gary Cooper and Spencer Tracy at the box office. For

Mickey, this was his summertime. The living was easy and seemed likely to go on forever.

Mickey Rooney had begun life as plain Joe Yule, Jr., born September 23, 1920, in Brooklyn, N.Y. His parents, Joe Yule, Sr., a Scottish-born comedian, and Nell Carter, a dancer, had a small-time vaudeville act. In 1924 they separated. Nell took her son home to her parents in Kansas City, but the smell of greasepaint was strong. A few months later she picked up Mickey, then still known as Junior, and headed for Hollywood. There, she hustled Mickey from studio to studio, and occasionally they got work as extras. Mickey's break came in 1926, when Fox Studios needed a midget. Nell dressed the six-year-old in a tuxedo and was about to lead him out the door when she noticed that Mickey, just cutting his permanent teeth, lacked two in front.

"Here," she said, sticking that old rubber cigar in his mouth. "Keep that there and no one will notice."

When production of some two-reel comedies based on the popular newspaper cartoon "Toonerville Folks" was planned, the studio needed someone to play Mickey (Himself) McGuire, a tough tot in a battered derby. Junior got the part—and eventually became Mickey Rooney. After some 28 Mickey McGuire episodes, Mickey began making feature films for MGM.

MGM needed low-budget films to fill double bills for its theaters. One of these, *A Family Affair*, dealt with a small-town boy named Andy Hardy. Mickey was cast as Andy, and audience enthusiasm was so high that the next year he made three more Hardy films. He bought his mother a large home in the San Fernando Valley with 12 acres of grounds.

"It's like a movie, Ma," said Mickey, the first night in their new house.

"It *is* a movie," his mother replied. "And it's got a happy ending."

In 1939, 18-year-old Mickey and his on- and off-screen friend Judy Garland won special Oscars for their artistry. Sundays, Mickey liked to visit Judy and sing songs from their movies, or go to the Santa Monica amusement park, try the rides and eat popcorn. Why didn't he ever suggest marriage to Judy? "It would have been like marrying my sister," he says.

Mickey's screen success rolled on, but his off-screen life began to change. He took an occasional drink, went out with

Mickey Rooney Takes a New Bow

more than an occasional girl. His short stature perhaps made him assume an aggressive posture. Mickey was young, rich and famous, and girls fell all over him. MGM czar Louis B. Mayer was appalled when he heard that his symbol of clean-living, teen-age youth planned to marry smoldering starlet Ava Gardner. But Mickey was as tenacious as a summer cold, and he and Ava were married in January, 1942. From the beginning, the marriage was a bomb. Mickey drank, gambled, stayed out late. In May, 1943, they were divorced.

Mickey's professional life peaked in 1944, then began a long downhill slide. First there was a hiatus: in 1944 Rooney was inducted into the Army. As a GI, he was assigned to a combat entertainment unit that played before front-line troops. His "jeep show" covered 100,000 miles, playing to some two million GIs before the war ended.

Mickey was discharged in 1946 and returned to Hollywood, having been assured that his career would pick up where it had left off. The studios, however, nervous about the prospect of competition from television and the breakup of their big theater chains, were cutting costs, terminating contract players. Mickey quarreled with Mayer, and his contract was not renewed. So Mickey formed his own production company.

At 30, he found studio gates locked. His superb talent was still there, but nature had played a trick on him: he was too short to play romantic leads. As Mickey recalls: "One day I woke up and realized that I was never going to play a love scene with Ingrid Bergman. I knew it, the studios knew it, and we both knew there was no way to get around it."

What he couldn't play on the screen, he tried to play in his private life. After Ava Gardner, Mickey raced to the altar seven more times, and fathered ten children. (He is now married to Jan Chamberlin, a country-and-western singer.)

In 1962 Mickey's company filed for bankruptcy. But he kept on trying. He wrote movie scripts, worked as a featured player, played nightclubs and once, when his luck was at its lowest, was hired to be a guest at a cocktail party by someone who wanted to impress his friends. The unkindest cut of all came when Rooney was asked not to attend the Academy Awards dinner.

In 1963 there came a moment when the past seemed to lift and summertime return. Judy Garland, another star-crossed legend, had been making a comeback and had signed to do a TV series. She asked Mickey to appear on her first show. They met in a studio. Both had aged. Mickey had put on weight; Judy was as thin as a dime. They threw themselves into a rib-crushing hug—and the years fell away. For the six days of rehearsal and taping, like two kids on the MGM lot, they sang and danced their way through their routines.

But while Judy's career went into a decline, Mickey's, by sheer force of will, was slowly regaining ground. He played summer stock and got some movie roles.

Then, in the spring of 1979, Francis Ford Coppola decided to film Walter Farley's children's classic *The Black Stallion* and cast Mickey as the old trainer who teaches a young boy to ride. In the movie, Mickey wasn't just good, he was great. Meanwhile, Broadway producer Harry Rigby was planning to do an old-time burlesque show, with producer Terry Allen Kramer, and needed two principals, a top banana and a dancer. Unerringly, he picked Mickey and Ann Miller. The show opened in San Francisco and was such an explosive hit that Rigby had to negotiate for a bigger house before bringing it to New York in October, 1979. Mickey had never played the Great White Way, but he knocked 'em dead, garnering a nomination for Broadway's Tony Award.

One of the highlights of *Sugar Babies* is the grand finale. On a stage set that looks like the flight deck of the *USS Saratoga*, Mickey appears in a naval uniform and a plumed hat sprinkled with stars—possibly a creation of the Mad King of Bavaria. Surrounding him is an armed guard of chorines in star-spangled hot pants; on a stairway above, Ann Miller. While the band blares a patriotic tune, Mickey waves the American flag, parades the stage, the chorines perform the manual of arms, and Ann, veteran of countless MGM musicals and the world's fastest tap-dancer, comes down the steps, her flickering feet sounding like a rifle-shot fusillade. Mickey and Ann link arms, march off with Old Glory waving, the chorines in formation and the audience shouting itself hoarse.

On January 29, 1981, nine days after their release from Iran, 22 of the hostages and their families were ushered into the Mark Hellinger Theater, which was festooned with yellow ribbons, bunting and flowers. Mickey, Ann and the cast sang, clowned and danced out their hearts. At the end of the show, just after the curtain had been rung down, Mickey, still in his "admiral's" costume, appeared at the footlights.

"Ladies and gentlemen," he said, "in honor of our returned heroes, let us sing 'God Bless America.'" The audience rose, the orchestra struck up the music and, led by the unsinkable Mickey, a wave of emotion-charged sound rolled over the theater. There wasn't a dry eye in the house, or on the stage, that night. It was, for everyone, the performance of a lifetime.

The Human Cyclone Called Carol

by James Stewart-Gordon

I SAT in the Hollywood office of Carol Burnett, bemusedly watching her nibble on a pre-performance carrot. "I think," I found myself saying, "that you are the funniest woman I have ever met in my life."

She tilted back her dark glasses and smiled—not one of her great big toothy on-camera smiles, but just a wonderful, warm smile—and I couldn't help adding, "And maybe one of the most genuinely beautiful, too."

That's the effect Carol has on people: superlatives tumble out. Onstage and off, she has more facets than the Koh-i-noor diamond—and twice the sparkle. She appears at first blush to be tall, bumbling and awkward, with incredibly loose-jointed arms and legs—the prototype of the perpetually over-eager girl next door whose life is a succession of disasters. In reality, she has a ballerina's grace and a life-style of rollicking success, attained by a fusion of tremendous talent, great imagination, incredible discipline—and more gag routines than the four Marx Brothers combined.

Her form-free art is showcased on her syndicated television show, before an audience of untold millions. The acknowledged Queen of the Zanies, during the past twenty years she has won, among scores of other awards, four TV Emmys for her matchless comic performances.

Aiding Carol's marvelously mobile face, with its hazel eyes that can narrow to Oriental slits or explode into fiery coronas, are the props that she loves to use: fright wigs, outsize false eyelashes and eyeglasses, strange sweaters that look like Salvation Army rejects. Thus dressed for action, she may turn up

The Human Cyclone Called Carol

as a frumpy charwoman, deposed empress, betrayed housewife in a spoof of detergent drama ("As the Stomach Turns"), sultry superstar of old movies, or Mermanesque belter of ballads.

No actress ever put more physical effort into earning her daily bread. When the script calls for Carol to take a nose dive, she throws the resilient Burnett body into it with the determination of a kamikaze pilot. If she has to do a somersault, she turns into a pinwheel. "When she is supposed to look like a horse," summed up Jack Gilford, an actor who has worked with her a number of times, "she doesn't just look like a horse, she looks like the start of the first race at Santa Anita."

As a result of such enthusiasm, Carol has at various times smashed a cartilage in her foot, sprained an ankle (six times in one season), sprained her back, acquired a permanent bruise on her left thigh, and experienced a chill that nearly turned into pneumonia. The latter was the result of being doused with cold water during a slapstick skit, at a time of relative (for Carol) inactivity: she was starring in a Broadway show, was a regular on the Garry Moore program, was keeping house for her sister, and doing volunteer work at a hospital for handicapped children.

Like the material in some of her skits, Carol Burnett's actual life story has elements of pure soap opera. The daughter of talented, but alcoholic parents (her father was a theater manager, her mother a writer), Carol was born in San Antonio in the Depression. She was taken to Los Angeles at the age of eight to be raised by her grandmother, Mrs. Mae White, the former belle of Belleville, Ark., who, when not fighting off admirers, found time to take Carol to a minimum of six movies a week.

An athletic and editorial-writing success but somewhat of a social failure at Hollywood High School—she had reached her present height of 5-foot-7 by the time she was 11—Carol worked part-time at various Hollywood Boulevard theaters. As a cashier at one which broadcast the dialogue of the daily film fare to passers-by via loudspeaker, she heard but did not see *Ivanhoe* 107 times, and to this day can repeat verbatim long passages from the screenplay.

Graduating from high school, Carol entered U.C.L.A. and majored in theater arts. The jolt that started her in show business came in her junior year, when she and fellow student Don Saroyan were asked if they would entertain at a society party. After hearing Carol sing a parody of melodies from *Annie Get Your Gun*, one of the guests said, "Kids, you were great. I'll give you the money to get to Broadway." Laughing skeptically, Carol thanked the man and took the business card he pressed into her hand.

Two days later, Carol and Don went down to his office—and were astounded when he handed each of them a check for $1000. "Use it to get started," their benefactor said. "I came to this country as a penniless immigrant, and now I want to show my appreciation to America by helping others. Pay me back in five years, if you make it, and someday do the same for someone else."

Telling her nonplused grandmother, "I'm going to be a star," Carol spent $300 getting her teeth straightened, quit school and said good-by to her friends. Then she flew to New York with prospects of fame and fortune dancing in her head—along with the plots of old Ruby Keeler movies about Broadway. Taking a job as a hat-check girl, she set out to conquer the big city.

For month after discouraging month, she made the rounds of agents in search of a stage job, but the turndown routine never varied: "Sorry, can't use you until you get some experience." Carol finally landed a summer-theater job in the Catskills, where, at summer's end, she realized that she needed vocal training. Voice coach Ken Welch, impressed with her raw talent, told her that she could owe him his fees until she got a job in the theater. Carol agreed only after he let her sign promissory notes, which she made good with a hail of quarters from her hat-checking tips.

By the close of the following hat-check season, Carol and Don Saroyan had married—and were wondering how to keep their careers alive when Welch lined them up at a summer theater in the Poconos. Helped by this summer's experience, Carol auditioned for Garry Moore and was given a chance to do sketches and sing an occasional song on his morning TV program. While she was appearing on the Moore show, a New York nightclub specializing in fresh talent gave her a trial. Ken Welch wrote a comedy act for her, and she began appearing nightly. Later that season, he wrote her a song with the unlikely title "I Made a Fool of Myself Over John Foster Dulles," an ode to the unrequited affection of a young girl for the austere Secretary of State.

The combination of the incongruity of the song and Carol's inspired delivery was blockbusting. Immediately, there was an offer for her to appear on "The Jack Paar Show" to chant her Dulles love call. The following Sunday, she repeated the song on "The Ed Sullivan Show," watched at home by Dulles himself. Questioned later on "Meet the Press" about his reaction to the ballad, Dulles drew himself up and said coldly, "I never discuss problems of the heart." Then he winked.

With Carol's career at last beginning to take wing, she got the part of the tomboy Princess Winifred in the off-Broadway musical *Once Upon a Mattress*. Her performance won ecstatic comment, but six weeks later closing notices were posted. Firm in her belief that the show was too good to shut down, Carol persuaded the cast to picket the theater to urge the management to keep it running. They were joined on the picket line by a group of neighborhood children with whom Carol had made friends at a nearby candy store. One newspaperman, convinced that the picketing was just a publicity stunt—with Carol paying the kids to participate—journeyed downtown, met Carol, talked to the kids and wrote in his column, "I apologize. Carol Burnett *is* the best-loved girl on Second Avenue." Helped by the publicity, the show moved to a new theater, this time *on* Broadway, and stayed open for over a year.

Meanwhile, Garry Moore's daytime show had moved to a nighttime spot. Martha Raye, scheduled to appear as a guest one evening, took sick, and the show's producer asked Carol if she would pinch-hit. Right after the show, Martha Raye phoned Moore. "I knew you were going to have to get someone good to replace me," she said, "but did you have to get someone *that* good?" Then she sent Carol a dozen roses. By year's end, Carol was a regular on the Moore show, playing everything from a barking seal to Scarlett O'Hara.

While professional success had arrived, Carol's personal life was being subjected to a number of strains, including a divorce. Although she tried to submerge her life in her work, she worried that material success might make her egocentric. She applied to the New York University Medical Center's Institute of Physical Medicine and Rehabilitation to see if, by any chance, someone was needed to read fairy stories to the sick children. "We don't need a reader," she was told, "but we do need someone to work with badly handicapped children. I have to warn you, though, that some of these patients are terribly deformed."

Carol asked to see the ward. At first it was all she could do to avoid fainting. Then one child, almost entirely without arms or legs, grinned at her. "Hey," he said, "are you that nut on TV?"

"Yeah," said Carol, her fears dissolving in the kid's grin. "I'm that nut on TV. But do you mind calling me Carol?"

From that moment on, until she remarried and left for Hollywood four years later, she worked once or twice a week as a volunteer at the center. And today, as star of television and movies, Carol is just about as she always was: unspoiled, fiercely loyal, anxious to repay every past kindness. She has never forgotten the conditions of the loan which enabled her to come to New York, and has endowed drama scholarships at U.C.L.A. and Emerson College in Boston.

Longtime friend Ken Welch summed up the attitude of everyone who has ever worked with her: "Some people can give 100 percent. Carol never gives less than 200 percent—and then she wonders if it is enough!"

The Great Schnozzola

by Frank Capra

THE WORLD was sunk in economic depression during the late 1930s, so it was easy to understand the grim mien of the passengers on a memorable flight I took across America. Suddenly, one man leaped to his feet and began strutting up and down the aisle like a demented penguin, flapping his arms and hollering in a voice like a jailbreak in Brooklyn: "What holds it up? What holds it up!"

We looked at that merry-eyed man with the Punchinello nose and the hands that kept trying to strangle his battered fedora, and we burst out laughing. And when we laughed, we forgot our worries.

By the end of the flight we were all friends, exchanging confidences. I have forgotten many of the people I met that night, of course; but I will never forget the one whose antics brought us all together—"Schnozzola," the unforgettable Jimmy Durante. It was his first flight on an airplane, and he did what he did everywhere he went—he made people laugh.

Jimmy was a compassionate clown: he let you know he was bothered by the same things you were, but that if you couldn't change them, you might as well laugh at them. As he often said, "Dem's da conditions dat pervail."

I really came to know Jimmy as a result of a film idea—"The Jimmy Durante Story"—proposed by Frank Sinatra. The film never materialized, but I spent many hours of reminiscence with Jimmy, hovering between laughter and tears as he told me the story of his life.

According to Jimmy, who claimed to remember the event

vividly, a distraught midwife attending his birth on February 10, 1893, protested, "Dis ain't da baby—it's da stork!" Jimmy always joked about it, but his world-famous nose was a secret sorrow to him all his life. Maybe the reason that his comedy was so good-natured, so free from malice, was that, from his childhood days on New York's Lower East Side, Jimmy knew what it felt like to be laughed at.

"Every time I went down the street I'd hear, 'Look at da big-nosed kid!'" he said. "And if they said nothin', nothin' at all, I'd shrivel up and think they was sayin', 'What an ugly kid!' Even when I am makin' a fortune on account of the big beak, and while I am out there on stage, laughin' and kiddin' about the nose, at no time was I ever happy about it."

At the age of 10, Durante enjoyed the distinction of having the loudest newsboy's voice ever heard in Lower Manhattan. But he already had his heart set on another job. "I'm passin' the joints on Fourteenth Street between Tird and Fort' avenoos," he remembered. "I peeps under da swingin' doors and keeps thinkin' that the swellest job in da world is da guy what bangs on the pianna. I want to be him!"

Bartolomeo Durante, Jimmy's understanding father, was struggling to raise a family of four children in the three-room apartment behind his barbershop. When Jimmy was 16, his father celebrated the occasion by giving his son his first shave. And when he learned that Jimmy had musical ambitions, he bought his boy a "pianna" and engaged a music "perfesser." Both Bartolomeo and Jimmy's mother, Rosa Lentino, loved classical music. But soon Jimmy had a confession to make. "Papa," he said regretfully, shyly, "I can't play classical like you want me to play. I just can't. I don't feel it. I'd rather go to Coney Island and play ragtime."

"Coney Island? No, no, my son. Carnegie Hall."

"Papa. Imagine what dey'd do if I came out in Carnegie Hall and dey see dis nose. Dey'd laugh at me, Papa—no matter how good I played."

After a pause, Bartolomeo said, "God works in inscrutable ways. He'll take care of you. Go ahead to Coney Island."

So Jimmy went to Coney Island, where he played at a place called Diamond Tony's for $25 a week. The hours were "eight in the evening until unconscious." After Diamond Tony's there were other saloons and dance halls. Ragtime Jimmy, as he

The Great Schnozzola

called himself, played the piano in the honky-tonk style of the day—a steady beat in the bass contrasted by a syncopated melody.

Strictly as a piano player—no singing yet, no clowning—Durante made it to the Club Alamo in Harlem. He even got to book some of the acts. He hired a singer and dancer named Eddie Jackson who didn't read music. Jimmy accompanied him, picked out his songs, taught him the melodies, gave him confidence. "When you go on the floor with that man," said a grateful Jackson, "you're in."

One day a young singer from the Midwest named Jeanne Olson came to the Alamo. Durante heard her sing and hired her on the spot. Three years later they were married.

Jeanne believed in Jimmy's talent, as did Frank Nolan, a headwaiter at a high-class Broadway café, who convinced Durante that they could "make a million" with their own place. Nolan rented a 20-by-100-foot loft above a garage on 58th Street, just east of Broadway, and there the *Club Durante* opened in January 1923. Jimmy insisted that Eddie Jackson be made a partner.

Jimmy loved people—especially those in trouble. When he met former vaudeville headliner Lou Clayton in 1923, Clayton was just off a three-night tilt at a floating crap game that had left him flat broke. A friend took him to the *Club Durante* to cheer him up. Jimmy was playing the piano, and Clayton was persuaded to sing a song called "Willie the Weeper." He went on singing song after song during the night and, around 6:30 the next morning, Durante said, "Lou, why don't you come in with us?"

The comedy team of Clayton, Jackson and Durante became the toast of the town. The columnists raved about them. "A good part of the fun of watching Durante," wrote an admirer, "is in the way we're with him and love him, the way we spot him for a good and happy guy." Clayton said it best: "You can warm your hands on this man."

Now their jokes were getting a reputation. It was Clayton who called Jimmy's proboscis his schnozz and dubbed him The Great Schnozzola—a *nom de guerre* listed in *Who's Who in America*.

One of the funniest bits that I remember was when Jimmy told of a hot, muggy day at the beach. Flies landed all over him. He suffered them without complaint until one walked on his nose. "Just for dat," said Jimmy, "you all get off."

That was Jimmy, always understanding the other guy—to a point.

Another gag had to do with a blind date. "I walked over to the telephone—pickin' up the receiver, I said '*Hel*-lo!' She sez, '*Hel-lo*, come right over. When I got dere, she took one look at my nose and said, 'You sure musta hurried. You forgot to hang up da phone!'"

The act was funny, and Hollywood noticed; so did Broadway. The trio's Broadway debut was in 1929 in Ziegfeld's *Show Girl*, and their movie debut in Paramount's *Roadhouse Nights* (1930). Then Jimmy got a long-term Hollywood contract, and the team broke up. Clayton became Jimmy's business manager, and there followed over 20 films in 10 years, and several more Broadway musicals.

Bad times came to Jimmy in the early 1940s. His career had waned so badly that the only part he could get was in a Gene Autry western called *Melody Ranch*. "I'd never rode a horse, and the horse had never been rode," said Jimmy, "so we started on even terms. It was a catastastroke."

Then Jeanne had an abdominal operation and the doctors discovered cancer. Jimmy took her home, and Jeanne wrote friends that "we are happier than we have ever been." But, professionally, Durante had reached what he later called "a lowest pernt."

After Christmas 1942, manager Clayton had a serious talk with Jimmy. "Let's face it," he said, "you are slipping in the public mind. Get a nurse for Jeanne; then go out and make some money."

Clayton got Durante two weeks of radio and nightclub bookings in New York, but Jimmy didn't want to leave Jeanne. She insisted. After the first radio show, he anxiously telephoned her across the continent. "I liked the program, Jimmy," she said. "It was very good." That night Durante slept soundly for the first time in weeks. But in the morning a call came from Jeanne's mother telling him his wife of 22 years was dead.

After the funeral, Jimmy returned to New York to open at the Copacabana. His fans hadn't forgotten him; he packed them in. And Clayton and Jackson rejoined him in the old act. Night after night the drums rolled, the horns blared the opening notes of "Inka Dinka Do," and Durante, center stage, gargled, "Lemme hear dat band!"

Jimmy entertained to forget his grief; watching him, the war-weary crowds forgot theirs. It was a time of terrible casualty lists: the whole country needed to take its mind off its troubles, and at age 50 Durante found himself making a sensational comeback. Before 1943 was over, he had a network radio show.

Radio was the perfect medium to capture what critic Gilbert Seldes called "Durante's inspired, headlong rush at a word—let the consonants fall where they may." His writers were under strict instructions to write the real words in the scripts—and let Jimmy bollix them up naturally. Durante could be counted on to turn "corpuscles" into "corpsuckles," "non-fiction" into "non-friction," "cataclysmic" into "casamyclysmic." For Durante, sight reading was a constant catastastroke—and a joy forever.

His jokes always had the common touch. Durante's foil on radio was Garry Moore. In one memorable sketch, they described returning to college:

Durante: Ya know, Junior, dis year college is a serious ting wid me. I get to the classroom every morning at four o'clock.

Moore: Four o'clock in the morning! What do you take?

Durante: Oh, the usual tings—a pail and a mop.

But at the end of each program he changed from his clowning manner to an attitude of utter seriousness, and said tenderly, "Good-night, Mrs. Calabash—wherever you are."

The identity of Mrs. Calabash became what the New York *Times* called "a national mystery"—but Durante never told. Even clowns have their secrets.

Those who were down on their luck continued to find Jimmy the softest of touches. Manager Clayton had to put him on an allowance, and he usually gave most of that away. When he was teased about the large amounts of money he gave to panhandlers, Jimmy answered, "Maybe we ain't born equal, but it's a cinch we all die equal."

In 1950 Lou Clayton died of cancer. Clasping Durante's hand, he murmured his last words, "My Jimmy, my Jimmy."

In the years to come, Jimmy Durante raised millions of dollars, clowning at benefits for the Damon Runyon Foundation for Cancer Research, to fight the disease that had killed his wife and his best friend. Typically, he fought everything, even death, with laughter.

Radio and the stage had launched Jimmy's comeback, but it was on television that we could all see his unforgettable facial expressions and body language. He wrote songs to fit his unique personality: "I Ups Ta Him, And He Ups Ta Me"; "I'm Jimmy That Well-Dressed Man"; "I Know Darn Well I Can Do Without Broadway (Can Broadway Do Without Me?)"; and "Did You Ever Have the Feelin' That You Wanted to Go, Still You Have the Feelin' That You Wanted to Stay?"

Jimmy had been right when he talked with his father about his choice of a career—practically any juxtaposition of Jimmy Durante and classical music struck audiences as hilarious. In his hit movies and radio shows of the '40s, in the television series and specials of the '50s and '60s, he clowned with concert-hall greats—the Metropolitan Opera's Lauritz Melchior and Helen Traubel; the concert pianist José Iturbi. And when he declared in a song called "Toscanini, Tchaikovsky, and Me" that "We are definitely da Big Three!" it brought down the house.

In those days in the fall of 1959, when I was listening to Jimmy tell me the story of his life, he was a happy man. He had ended his regular Saturday night, half-hour television show at the height of his popularity. He still appeared on TV once or twice a year as a guest on variety or comedy shows or in specials. He was so well fixed financially, he said, that his house had two swimming pools—"one for swimmin' and one for rinsin' off."

Seventeen years after Jeanne Durante's death, Jimmy married Marjorie Little. He was 67; she was 39. On Christmas Day in 1961, they adopted an infant daughter, Cecilia Alicia. The little girl was nicknamed CeCe, and Jimmy cherished her. She was his only child. When Jimmy died, in January 1980, Margie and CeCe Durante, then 18, wept together over a casket topped with a battered fedora.

Maybe it was for the best that a film was never made of Durante's life. He had a wonderful life, it was a wonderful story—but what actor could really do justice to The Great Schnozzola? He was unique. Just the other day he turned up on television on "The Best of Ed Sullivan." There he was singing, in that voice with a frog in it as big as a lily pad,

The Great Schnozzola

"You can laugh when your dreams fall apart at the seams...."
Better than most, he knew how to do that.

> ... And if you should survive
> To a hundred and five
> Look at all you derive
> Outta bein' alive.
> Now here is the best part—
> You have a head start—
> If you are amongst
> The very young—at—heart.*

Good-night, Mrs. Calabash—and Jimmy—wherever you are.

---

*"Young at Heart," words and music: Carolyn Leigh & Johnny Richards, © 1954 Cherio Corp. International, copyright secured. All rights reserved. Used by permission.

*More Exciting Books from America's
Most Popular and Most
Trusted Magazine*
READER'S DIGEST

___ **ORGANIZE YOURSELF** 06580-4/$2.95
How to get the most out of your time, your money and your daily life.

___ **WORD POWER** 06549-9/$2.95
is a fascinating anthology of tests from "It Pays to Enrich Your Word Power," with articles by such language experts as Clifton Fadiman, Edwin Newman and Vance Packard.

___ **LAUGHTER, THE BEST MEDICINE** 05155-2/$2.75
Quick relief for life's aches and pains!

___ **SUPER WORD POWER** 06819-6/$2.95
More entertaining ways to enrich your language skills.

Berkley/Reader's Digest Books

Available at your local bookstore or return this form to:

BERKLEY
Book Mailing Service
P.O. Box 690, Rockville Centre, NY 11571

Please send me the titles checked above. I enclose _____ Include 75¢ for postage and handling if one book is ordered; 25¢ per book for two or more not to exceed $1.75. California, Illinois, New York and Tennessee residents please add sales tax.

NAME_____
ADDRESS_____
CITY_____STATE/ZIP_____

(allow six weeks for delivery.)

Glittering lives of famous people!
Bestsellers from Berkley

✯✯✯✯✯✯✯✯✯✯✯✯✯✯✯✯✯✯✯✯

___ JANE FONDA: HEROINE FOR OUR TIME Thomas Kiernan	06164-7—$3.50
___ BRANDO FOR BREAKFAST Anna Kashfi Brando and E.P. Stein	04698-2—$2.75
___ CONVERSATIONS WITH JOAN CRAWFORD Roy Newquist	05046-7—$2.50
___ THE JEAN SEBERG STORY: PLAYED OUT David Richards	06314-3—$3.95
___ LADD: A HOLLYWOOD TRAGEDY Beverly Linet	05731-3—$2.95
___ MISS TALLULAH BANKHEAD Lee Israel	04574-9—$2.75
___ MOMMIE DEAREST Christina Crawford	06302-X—$3.95
___ MOTHER GODDAM Whitney Stine with Bette Davis	06454-9—$3.50
___ MY WICKED, WICKED WAYS Errol Flynn	06479-4—$2.95
___ NO BED OF ROSES Joan Fontaine	05028-9—$2.75
___ RICHARD BURTON Paul Ferris	05711-9—$2.95
___ RITA HAYWORTH: THE TIME, THE PLACE AND THE WOMAN John Kobal	05634-1—$2.95
___ SELF-PORTRAIT Gene Tierney, with Mickey Herskowitz	04485-8—$2.75
___ SHADOWLAND: FRANCES FARMER William Arnold	05481-0—$2.75
___ SUSAN HAYWARD: PORTRAIT OF A SURVIVOR Beverly Linet	06425-5—$3.50
___ TYRONE POWER: THE LAST IDOL Fred Lawrence Guiles	04619-2—$2.75
___ EDDIE MY LIFE, MY LOVES Eddie Fisher	06755-6—$3.50

Available at your local bookstore or return this form to:

BERKLEY
Book Mailing Service
P.O. Box 690, Rockville Centre, NY 11571

Please send me the titles checked above. I enclose _____. Include 75¢ for postage and handling if one book is ordered; 25¢ per book for two or more not to exceed $1.75. California, Illinois, New York and Tennessee residents please add sales tax.

NAME_____

ADDRESS_____

CITY_____STATE/ZIP_____

(allow six weeks for delivery)

6a

From the stage, screen and TV—
Celebrities you want to read about!

✮ ✮

__**P.S. I LOVE YOU** Michael Sellers   06052-7—$2.95

__**A DREADFUL MAN: THE STORY OF**   04715-6—$2.75
GEORGE SANDERS Brian Aherne

__**ELVIS: THE FINAL YEARS** Jerry Hopkins   06461-1—$3.50

__**GARY COLEMAN: A GIFT OF LIFE**   05595-7—$2.95
The Coleman Family and Bill Davidson

__**HITCH: THE LIFE AND TIMES OF ALFRED**   05099-8—$2.95
HITCHCOCK John Russell Taylor

__**HOLLYWOOD IN A SUITCASE** Sammy Davis Jr.   05091-2—$2.95

__**JUNE ALLYSON**   06251-1—$3.50
June Allyson and Frances Spatz Leighton

__**MERMAN: AN AUTOBIOGRAPHY**   04261-8—$2.50
Ethel Merman with George Eells

__**THE PLAYBOY INTERVIEWS WITH**   05989-8—$3.50
JOHN LENNON AND YOKO ONO
David Sheff and G. Barry Golson

__**SHOW PEOPLE** Kenneth Tynan   04750-4—$2.95

__**STAR BABIES** Raymond Strait   04930-2—$2.75

__**STARMAKER: THE AUTOBIOGRAPHY**   05141-2—$2.95
OF HAL WALLIS Hal Wallis and Charles Highman
with forward by Katharine Hepburn

__**STRAIGHT SHOOTING**   04757-1—$2.75
Robert Stack with Mark Evans

__**THE CONFESSIONS OF PHOEBE TYLER**   05202-8—$2.95
Ruth Warrick with Don Preston

__**THIS FOR REMEMBRANCE**   05968-5—$2.95
Rosemary Clooney with Raymond Strait

Available at your local bookstore or return this form to:

BERKLEY
Book Mailing Service
P.O. Box 690, Rockville Centre, NY 11571

Please send me the titles checked above. I enclose _____. Include 75¢ for postage and handling if one book is ordered; 25¢ per book for two or more not to exceed $1.75. California, Illinois, New York and Tennessee residents please add sales tax.

NAME_____

ADDRESS_____

CITY_____STATE/ZIP_____

(allow six weeks for delivery)   6b

*THE RUNAWAY BESTSELLER!
NOW IN PAPERBACK*

The One Minute Manager

**Kenneth Blanchard, Ph.D.
Spencer Johnson, M.D.**

It works—for everybody! That's the revolutionary message of this amazing new theory that is sweeping the country by storm. Whether top-level executive, busy homemaker, educator, student, secretary, or parent, THE ONE MINUTE MANAGER has the answers that will change your life.

BUY IT. READ IT. USE IT.

IT WORKS FOR EVERYBODY

___ 06265-1—$6.95

Available at your local bookstore or return this form to:

BERKLEY
*Book Mailing Service
P.O. Box 690, Rockville Centre, NY 11571*

Please send me the titles checked above. I enclose _____ Include 75¢ for postage and handling if one book is ordered; 25¢ per book for two or more not to exceed $1.75. California, Illinois, New York and Tennessee residents please add sales tax.

NAME_____

ADDRESS_____

CITY_____STATE/ZIP_____

(allow six weeks for delivery)